I0213907

INTO THE STORM

ADVANCED READER COPY

This is an uncorrected proof courtesy of Di Angelo Publications. Price and publication dates are subject to change.

Into the Storm is published under Voyage, a sectionalized division under Di Angelo Publications, Inc.

VOYAGE

Voyage is an imprint of Di Angelo Publications.
Copyright 2023.
All rights reserved.
Printed in the United States of America.

Di Angelo Publications
4265 San Felipe #1100
Houston, Texas 77027

Library of Congress
Into the Storm
ISBN: 978-1-955690-48-5
Hardback

Words: Danny Farrar
Cover Design: Savina Deianova
Interior Design: Kimberly James
Editors: Ashley Crantas, Willy Rowberry

Downloadable via Kindle, NOOK, iBooks, and Google Play.

No part of this publication may be reproduced, distributed, or transmitted in any form or by any means without the prior written permission of the publisher, except in the case of brief quotations embodied in critical reviews and certain other noncommercial uses permitted by copyright law. For permission requests, contact info@diangelopublications.com.

For educational, business, and bulk orders, contact sales@diangelopublications.com.

1. Biography & Autobiography --- Military
2. Body, Mind, Spirit --- Inspiration & Personal Growth
3. Self Help --- Personal Growth

INTO THE STORM

DANNY FARRAR

To my daughters, River and Willow. I hope that one day when you are older, this book will help you understand the man that I was—all my wins and all my sins. More importantly, I hope it makes it clear that I'd go through everything that has ever happened to me all over again, because it brought you two into my life.

Never forget the most important thing:
No matter what, Daddy loves you.

Table of Contents

Out of the night that covers me
Black as the pit from pole to pole,
I thank whatever gods may be
For my unconquerable soul.

In the fell clutch of circumstance,
I have not winced nor cried aloud.
Under the bludgeonings of chance
My head is bloody, but unbowed.

Beyond this place of wrath and tears
Looms but the horror of the shade,
And yet the menace of the years
Finds, and shall find, me unafraid.

It matters not how strait the gate,
How charged with punishments the scroll,
I am the master of my fate:
I am the captain of my soul.

—William Ernest Henley

PREFACE

If you have picked up this book, then I am certain that you feel something is off in your life. You are looking for a way forward through the uncertainty and doubt, a way to be in control and live the life that you have always dreamed of, and on your own terms. I am willing to bet that you run the gamut of the negative emotions and thoughts that far too many of us face today. That your life is monotonous. That something is missing. That you are not reaching your potential, or worse yet, something or someone is holding you back.

These thoughts bog you down like quicksand. It seems the more you struggle with them, the faster you sink. You want to be able to turn it around, and you desperately want someone, anyone, to throw you a rope, to help get you out of the mess you are in and that you are sure you'd never find yourself stuck in again. This scenario plays out over and over again, yet it seems you fail to learn the lessons inherent in every struggle. Self-pity has never saved any man, and no one is coming—it's up to you to save yourself.

Just like thrashing around never saved anyone from quicksand, falling to the ground, kicking and screaming about how the world did you wrong isn't going to solve your problems. Matter of fact, it's only going to exasperate them. To paint oneself the victim is to willingly become a slave, to give control of your life over to all external factors that exist in the world.

You were late because of traffic. You are fat because of genetics. You can't stay with your spouse because they don't make you happy. Your kids won't listen. Your boss is a jerk. You don't have time to cook healthy food. There's no time for the gym. You can't afford school. You're too old to start over. This is just a short list of the bullshit excuses you give yourself day in and day out, and what do you trade in their place? The life you want to live.

The problem with negative emotions such as anger, sorrow, resentment, and blame is that they are all warm blankets on our coldest day. Wrapped up in them, dripping with visceral feelings of being wronged, we feel safe and secure because, while we don't like the outcome, these feelings at least let us believe that it's not our fault. They allow us to live in a delusional world where it's not our shortcomings or our lack of commitment and effort that keep us from our goals—no, not us . . . "them."

"They" are the enemy. The ones who foil all our plans. The ones who trip us up near the finish line. They cost us that job. They were a kiss-ass. They didn't teach us how to manage money. They didn't support our vision. They didn't show up when we needed them. They didn't do what they said they would do.

They, they, they. It's all THEIR fault.

And so, convinced it's "them" and not you, you roll over, pull those blankets down tighter, and go back to sleep, where you will dream about the life you want instead of living it.

But today, I am going to challenge you to open your eyes and see the truth for what it is.

It is your fault.

For every single thing that happens in your life, it's either your fault that it happened or it's your fault for how you reacted to it.

Now, before you throw this book against the wall and add me to the long list of people you want to point a finger at, I urge you to read on and see that the advice I give wasn't taught to me in school or picked up on a calendar, and it can't be understood without having experienced true hardship. It's the kind of advice that can only be leveraged after it's been forged in fire. After you've faced down the storms that left your face weathered and lined. A life that hit just as hard emotionally (if not more so) than it did physically. One that leaves your body cracking and popping and your heart with scar tissue that even a blind man can see.

I want to make something abundantly clear before you start the book. Every one of us has trauma. Each of us has a suitcase full of baggage to unpack. The purpose of sharing my story isn't to say my suitcase was heavier or lighter than yours is, but rather, that you can lighten your load, too, if you choose to unpack it as I did. If it hasn't happened for you yet, let me be the first person to tell you: it's okay to heal. It's okay to admit that something has hurt you. It's okay to acknowledge the wounds so that you can let them heal.

We all, inherently, have different levels of resiliency, and each and every one of us can be broken. Yes, you can be broken. If you're reading a book like this, you probably already know that because you've been broken at least once. That's the shitty part of life. But every coin has a flipside, and the flipside of pain isn't pleasure—it's triumph. It's turning that loss into a win. Using rock-bottom as a solid foundation on which to build your empire. To turn heartbreak into knowing your non-negotiables for true love.

I believe that resiliency is just another muscle for us to develop. We can grow and strengthen it if we are willing to do the work. To do this requires hours of beating and pushing ourselves outside our comfort zone, but it can be done. It's why I am such a proponent of working out and martial arts.

In the gym and on the mats, you must face your inner bitch daily. The excuses start to roll in like waves crashing on the ocean. "Just stop, you don't want to hurt yourself." "Why do that last rep? You're tired! You've already done enough!" "Hit snooze, you've worked hard all week. You deserve a break!" "Don't go to practice, your body hurts." "Just give up position; you can get it back." "Don't let the combo go, he may crack you."

It is in those moments that you become stronger or weaker, not just physically but, more importantly, mentally. Every time you quit the work you said you would do, you make it easier to quit other things in life when it gets hard, and believe me, it will get harder. You haven't faced your worst day. I know that sounds horrible to say, but everything you make it through levels you up. That's a good thing, but the flipside of that coin is that you will now face bigger problems that come with that new level.

As you will read in the following pages, my life is like a season of *Jerry Springer*. While I would never claim to have had the worst life (a lesson I will share is: it can always be worse), what I have gone through would have broken the average person. This isn't some form of bravado; statistics show that many people who face even one of the things I have gone through in my life suffer catastrophically for it. Any one of the traumas I have endured in life is enough to leave many folks broken and dissolute, and likely enough to pass their demons on to their children, thus perpetuating the cycle of despair. That's why I wanted to write this book. I wanted to show you proof that if I was able to overcome this Rolodex of almost every bad thing that can happen to a person, then so can you. Not only can you survive with your trauma, you can thrive with it.

But I didn't want to stop at just showing you that a person can overcome their past, their hurt, and their worst days. I wanted to lay out a plan of action that you can use to navigate your own pitfalls in life. I wanted to do more than just inspire you—I wanted to empower you to take that inspiration and do something big with it in your life.

In these sections, I will look back at the lessons I learned. (In truth, I didn't learn much until I actually processed the events later on down the road.) This will save you a lot of collateral in time, money, and psychological damage. More importantly than simply giving you a review of what I've learned, I will take the next step and give you real, actionable steps that you can take to apply those lessons to your life starting the very day you read them.

Success for me in this endeavor will undoubtedly translate into success for you. If you read this book with an open mind and commitment to doing—not "trying"—to apply the lessons that are within, I am positive that you will do what I have done. You will take control of your life, you will chart your own course, and you will become the "captain of your soul."

Chapter One

Childhood—The Coming Storm

"Cows run away from the storm while the buffalo charges toward it—and gets through it quicker. Whenever I'm confronted with a tough challenge, I do not prolong the torment, I become the buffalo."
—Wilma Mankiller

The miracle of life begins violently. There's just no other way to put it. It's violence—beautiful violence, but violence just the same. What's crazier is, that's the case even if everything goes perfectly. You're floating along in the quaint little space you have been renting. It's climate controlled, and you're literally plugged into the fridge. Admittedly, over the past couple months, it's gotten a little cramped in here, but all in all, life is good. Then out of nowhere, the walls start closing and you're getting pushed out a hole you're pretty sure you can't fit through, and someone, somewhere, just turned on the lights without any type of warning!

Now, this would seem like the perfect time to start complaining, but the reality of it is that you got the better end of this deal. Your poor mother—I'm sure she was a nice woman—had to push a watermelon out through a hole the size of a golf ball and more than likely was split open and will require stitches in her nether regions. (Side note: Men, don't complain about shit. Just stand there and do not faint.) If that was not frightening enough, many women have to lie on the bed while the doctor grabs a scalpel, cuts through their bellies, and pulls this little miracle out like a Xenomorph looking for Sigourney Weaver. Both Mom and Dad will wonder if you've been sent here to kill them in about three months' time, but that is another story entirely.

I think the very fact that we forget that this is how life starts is why we are adamant that children's lives should be spared hardship and struggle. Almost universally, we believe that children are innocent and crimes against them should be dealt with swiftly and harshly punished. The sad fact of the matter is that this is not the case.

Children are abused at an alarming rate in this country. According to SafeLives research, just under half (47%) of young people are exposed to domestic violence and are being directly harmed by a family member.[1] Every 9 minutes, child protective services substantiate—find evidence for—a claim of child sexual abuse. Every year, 60,000 children are victims of "substantiated" or "indicated" sexual abuse.[2] Every 1 in 9 girls and 1 in 53 boys under the age of 18 experience sexual abuse or assault at the hands of an adult. Of all victims under 18, 82% are female, and females ages 16–19 are four times more likely than the general population to be victims of rape, attempted rape, or sexual assault.

Sadly, we find that these lives are most likely to be ruined at the hands of someone close to the victim. In fact, only 7% of sexual assaults are performed by strangers. A whopping 93% of attackers are known to the victim.

While those stats are shocking and horrific, the aftermath that follows is where the real nightmare begins. As referenced above, children who suffer from sexual abuse are much more likely to experience the following mental health challenges:

About 4 times more likely to develop symptoms of drug abuse.

About 4 times more likely to experience PTSD as adults.

About 3 times more likely to experience a major depressive episode as adults.

As sobering as statistics are, they are always so abstract. They remove for us the individual whose life has been destroyed or taken. Although many you may be surprised to see me quoting a communist, Joseph Stalin said it best: "A single death is a tragedy, a million deaths is a statistic." Our brains do not really comprehend the enormity of large numbers. We know it is bad, but typically it's not personal for us, and without that personal connection, we can't be moved to action. But behind every large statistic resides the shattered individuals who comprise the number. I know—I am one of them.

I was born out of wedlock to Debbie Knight and Robert Daniel Farrar III on September 28, 1979, in Virginia. The stories that I have been told about how I came to be are numerous and varied. So much so that I do not know what to believe anymore, and to be frank, I no longer bother trying to unravel the mess. I have been told my mother was a "lady of the night," but I can no more substantiate that claim than I can say that she loved me. What I do know is that she was, at the very least, a free spirit and a troubled soul.

She was a petite woman, small in stature and in frame. She had a strong Native American bloodline, and it was evident in her features, with long dark hair and high cheekbones. I remember her as being almost like a flower child from the sixties and often looked as if she would have been at home in Woodstock.

She had (to my knowledge) five boys, only two of which were fathered by the same man. My oldest brother I have not met and have only seen the others a handful of times. She was a talkative, unmoored person, and my father was a lost soul himself. He's a convicted felon (of what, I am not sure; this is only what has been told to me) and spent a lot of time on the road. I was told that he had full custody of me at some point, right up until my mother "stole me from him." I'll delve deeper into my father a little later.

Getting back to Debbie. According to the legends, she had me with her when her favorite aunt, Sadie Robertson, was visiting. Sadie, who already had five children of her own, was looking to take in my oldest brother; however, his father would not let her take him. That is when Sadie saw me and said, "I want that little girl." Turns out that back then, I had long, flowing blond hair, and it was pulled back into a ponytail. I often find myself wondering about the mental state of a mother who was actively looking to see who could take her children.

Well, it has been said that you find what you are looking for, and Debbie found people willing to take her children. What is more, Debbie did this with zero legal application applied to it. I say that I was adopted because it sounds so much better in casual conversation. Adoption sounds respectful. Even in the worst circumstances, it at least implies there was a professional process applied to the passing of a young life between consenting adults and the system. In actuality, I was given away with the same casual indifference someone would have when giving away an old piece of furniture they had no more use or liking for. That casual exchange among friends would lead me to the first house of horrors in my life.

As I came to the age of understanding who my family was, I was too young to remember the fact that I was adopted in the first place. Growing up, I had no cousins, no nieces or nephews. Truth is, I did not even know what those were. I had no way of knowing at the time that this was because my brothers and sister were really my cousins. So, I grew up believing that I was the sixth child in the Robertson clan. I would ask Sadie growing up why my last name was Farrar when theirs was Robertson. My mother would always reply that it was because of her family's reputation that she did not want people to know I was part of it. Let that mindfuck set in for a while. A six-year-old boy getting told that his family was so messed up that they gave the last child a different surname.

To hear my mother speak and tell tall tales of the Abernathys (her maiden name), you'd think that you were listening to a tale of the Hatfields and McCoys, or at the very least a gang that ran moonshine down the backroads away from Johnny Law during prohibition. According to her, all of them had an insane temper—something that was clearly passed down to her. They died in all sorts of horrible ways. A couple of ways that come to mind was one uncle had his lips eaten off by moonshine (I don't even know if this is possible, but for a young boy, it was most definitely frightening) and another was struck by lightning in the tub. I still freak out about showers and thunderstorms to this day.

Sadie was a firecracker of a woman, and while we had a strange and strained relationship, I still love that woman to this day. I have no doubt that, like many boys, my relationship with my mom is the root cause of my poor relationships with women now. I was a momma's boy growing up, and for better or worse, that has profoundly shaped my life ever since. In my childhood, she beat cancer twice, and I'll always view that as undeniable evidence of her immense strength of will. She was everything in my eyes, yet she also committed acts of immense cruelty. While I am not able to say with 100 percent certainty that she was bipolar, she was definitely a complex woman with a tangled web of contradictions.

My youth was dominated by a fact that I didn't understand at the time: the only person who wanted me in that family was Sadie. The story, as told to me by her, was that she brought me home with no input from Bobby (my adoptive father). He simply came home one day and I was there. I don't really fault him for not being thrilled with the situation.

As much as my adoptive mother influenced my worldview of women, my father influenced (more so than anything else) how I perceived a relationship with a woman should be. Bobby, unlike me, was a man of few words. One thing that I absolutely have to credit the man for was that he was a hard worker. He owned a logging company and was out the door before dawn six days per week, and he often didn't come home until after dark. For "fun," he raised cows recreationally. The man lived to work.

Our family never took a vacation. The concept was foreign to me. There were literally no days off. Sunday, the closest thing you'd see to a rest day, would be spent waking up early, doing chores, followed by lunch, and normally Dad would take a nap in the early afternoon. My job during that time was always to wash his truck, a task that I never did up to his standards.

Bobby never told me he loved me. Never said he was proud of me. Never attended a football game or came to a school function. Matter of fact, I can remember vividly the one and only time he did anything remotely fatherlike: much to my surprise, he pitched a softball to me one afternoon. I still remember that thirty-some years later.

In his eyes, I was lazy, trifling, and "scared of the sun." Which stands in stark contrast to what people tell me today. I am often asked how I get so much done or applauded for my drive and work ethic. Such a far cry from the constant belittlement I endured as a child. His disdain kept him from teaching me next-level skills. I was never given the opportunity to try my hand at more complex stuff. I was simply the tool-getter, floor-sweeper, wood-splitter, and car-washer.

Now, let me be clear: I don't think those things are bad at all. I very much agree with the notion that you should earn your rite of passage. Matter of fact, I believe that one of the biggest issues in our country is that we have removed all of them, especially for men. That's why our country is full of beta-ass bitches, but I digress. No, my problem wasn't starting at the bottom of the totem pole. My problem was never being given the tools, teachings, or opportunities to climb up it.

I have always been an "idea guy" that has a vision for some point far down the road. It wouldn't be wrong to say that I am a dreamer. But to Bobby, that represented a fictional world that didn't exist. Anyone who sought a different way was simply trying to skip the hard work, and that just wouldn't do. These conflicting ideologies only led to a widening of the divide between two people who were bound by no more than the affection of a woman they both adored.

And adore my mother Bobby did. She stood above all else. Truth is, the only time I saw them fight was over me. Sadie was always quick to come to my defense and my father was faster to rebuke it. I think my father believed she put me before him, and he probably wasn't too far off. But outside of that, what that woman said was the law.

There was no doubt that Dad was a tough man. One time, he was unloading a hay baler by himself when the jack gave out. The tongue of the baler fell off the hitch and onto his foot. The results were devastating. His foot was absolutely mangled. How he didn't lose it is still beyond me. However, he jacked it up off of his foot, crawled up on the tractor, and drove himself home. He required multiple surgeries and skin grafts to fix his foot, and months of bed rest. Like I said, he was hard as nails.

However, he damn near trembled in the presence of Sadie. I have been told that when Bobby was younger and they were first married, he was quite the drinker and partier. Sadie was his second wife (which came as a shock to me when I found that out years later), and at some point, she basically had a come-to-Jesus talk with him and he turned it around.

While she ran the household, she was also very submissive by today's standards. She made homecooked dishes for almost every meal. She'd wake up early and make his breakfast and have dinner on the table promptly at the time he said he'd be home. Bobby wouldn't sit down to a dinner that didn't have bread, and as such, Mom made fresh homemade biscuits every single night.

Sadie was a stay-at-home mom and kept the house and yard clean and in order, and she completed any other miscellaneous tasks that needed to be done. She was also a de-facto business partner and headed up the admin department for Bobby's logging company. She often ran the errands Bobby needed in support of the business, and I'd help. She'd drop off payroll and make bank runs. That was our typical Saturday schedule, one which he ridiculed me for relentlessly because I'd often spend my day with her doing "woman's work" rather than being in the shop and barn with him.

Which brings me to the "good son." Robbie was the oldest, the baddest, and the favorite by a mile. In my parent's eyes, he could do no wrong. My parents adored him, and Robbie, despite his many faults, returned their admiration. He was what we call back home "cock strong." And he was a powerful dude. His fingers were like sausages. I have seen him lift pieces of equipment by himself that two men couldn't, and it has been said that whenever he hit a man, he moved his jaw around to the side of his face.

He introduced me to Bob Seager (whom I still love) and was the first person to ever get me drunk (off vodka at sixteen), and he absolutely terrified me. I knew that if he wanted to, he could break me as easily as swatting a fly. I remember one day, I talked back to my mom from the bathroom and heard Robbie promptly beat on the door. If I hadn't been on the toilet already, I most assuredly would have shit my pants.

Next in line was Gene. Gene was the playboy of the family. He was also a large man, and although he was known to hold his own, we all knew that Robbie was the real bull of the house. That is why I think that Gene took to the carefree life of a playboy, chasing women and winning every time.

After Gene came Bubba, who was the oddball in the family. He was small in stature (much smaller than the rest of the boys), awkward, and frail. He was extremely introverted and reclusive. His drug of choice, oddly enough, was sniffing paint or gas. He was almost never around the family and I spent very, very little time with him. When I did, it was almost painful. He barely spoke, and oftentimes just stared at the floor. He appeared almost, what we called in those days, "slow," perhaps affected by some learning disorder or social phobia. At the very least, it was clear that he felt (perhaps even more than me) like he didn't belong there.

The last of the boys was Terry. I do not know how to say this in a polite way, but let's just say Terry wasn't very smart. He was very outgoing but was obtrusive. He'd say lewd or racist jokes that only he thought were funny. Terry was of medium stature with a square head, curly hair, and a wide, flat nose. While all the siblings were heavy into drugs, Terry seemed to be the most committed—at least when it came to weed, much to the dismay of parents, who often found handmade bowls all over the house and in the wash. The guy could make pipes out of anything. He had a stereotypical stoner attitude about everything. I would argue that he was the least ambitious of the family, and that is saying something. He was always found lying down on the job, literally. He would be given a task, and invariably, someone would walk in to find him asleep on the tractor. And, without a shadow of doubt, he cost the family the most money in terms of physical damage. He was always wrecking something: tractors, pickup trucks, or four-wheelers. He actually drove a four-wheeler through a barbwire fence and needed countless stitches in his face. He also stabbed himself with a knife and cut his leg all up with a chainsaw.

To round out the Robertsons, there comes perhaps the most devious of the bunch: Michelle. Michelle was big for a woman, but not in an unattractive way. She always had dates and appeared (as far as I could see, as she was in high school when I was in elementary) to be popular. Her personality was big to match her frame and one thing was abundantly clear: she gave absolutely ZERO fucks. She had a temper that was as quick to strike anyone who crossed her, male or female. Matter of fact, I watched her beat the total shit out of her first husband on multiple occasions. She was a woman who you did not fuck with, or else you'd pay the price. This was the family that I was taken into, and they would be the first to teach me that more often than not, those who are supposed to love and protect you are the ones who wound you the deepest.

Growing up, rules were strict in our household. Yet the five who came before me barely had regard for them. Bobby and Sadie's children didn't just bend the rules, they straight up broke them bitches in half. If there was a line not to cross, they were already on the other side before you even finished drawing it.

None of them graduated high school, and most of the time they spent there was for in-school suspension. Universally, it was known as "the Box" because it was in a trailer outside and run by Mr. White, a former Marine D.I. who was easily well over 6'4" and an imposing figure.

Their offenses ran the length of the trivial, such as tardiness or skipping classes, all the way up to fighting and drug possession. All of them had multiple run-ins with the law. Bubba and Michelle ran away from home so much that I was told our parents used to put pots and pans on the steps so they'd hear them trying to sneak out. I remember multiple times being woken up in the middle of the night to go outside and look to see if we could find Michelle. One time in particular, she ran away and made it all the way to Georgia and damn near got herself killed getting tied up with some crazies she'd met on the road.

They didn't stop misbehaving at school. As they grew up, they grew bolder. They sold drugs, and even committed armed robbery.

Michelle even called the local sheriff (a distant family member) and told him to leave her drug ring alone, or else. I mean, these bastards were crazy.

They were arrested on multiple occasions. I spent much of my youth visiting them in halfway houses, detention centers, and jails. Matter of fact, we drove two hours one Sunday to visit Michelle, only to find out when we got there that she couldn't have visitors because she incited a riot and break out attempt just the night before.

We grew up in an old house (which, to this day, I think is haunted, so feel free to make fun of me) that was part of an old plantation. The house sat on quite a bit of land. To the left and the rear were two cow pastures, and the curve out front was notorious for people underestimating the bend in the road and going through our wooden fence.

Over to the right of the house were several large open hay fields in front of the second (and largest) pasture that we had. In the middle of those fields, there was an old barn building and one of our two ponds. One known for big catfish, snapping turtles, and snakes. Bisecting the fields was a gravel road that led back to a double-wide trailer that Gene lived in up to his death and that Robbie later took over after he got out of prison.

Back by the house, we had a dirt road that led down to the shop where they worked on equipment in the afternoon and on Saturdays. Adjacent to that was an old caboose that was used to store spare parts and junk. The shop itself was very similar, with a wood stove and a radio that blared county music whenever Dad was around and classic rock when it was just the boys and the guys who worked for Dad.

The shop was also attached to the feed shed that housed all the cow feed and dog food. My dad was an avid raccoon hunter and had several blueticks and black-and-tans. Another dirt road took you down through the woods, past the dog pens. Just a few steps back through the woods was the first pond (and my favorite) that the family built. The road continued on down past the pond, running parallel to the big pasture and with several trails branching off of it to cut through various sections of the woods.

The property line ended at the Little Nottoway River, which ran through the property at the edge of a fairly steep hill that ended the pasture line. Sundays, the older siblings could venture down to the river for drinks, drugs, and R&R. The property contained a natural spring, and it was the only place my father would drink water from. One of my chores was to go to the spring and fill up a couple of plastic gallon jugs and lug 'em back to the house to serve as drinking water.

The house had no AC and was kept warm in the winter by three wood-burning stoves. One in the kitchen, one in my parents' bedroom, and one in the living room. Mom would get them so hot that you couldn't walk on the floor barefoot. Those things ate wood, and as such, all summer long was spent bustin' up logs for the winter. All winter was spent stacking up rows and rows of wood in the little room next to the kitchen. It was a never-ending job. As fast as you could bring a wheelbarrow load in, Mom would burn it up.

The house itself still holds a special place in my heart. Despite the tortures and heartbreak that I lived through there, I have often found myself wishing I could purchase the house. I'd love to be able to walk back in through those doors, touch the walls, and remember all the things from it that made me who I am today. The good and the bad. Sometimes, I think it's part of the reason I spent so much of my life fucked up. I long to be abused by people I love.

As you walked through the front door, immediately to the left was a room we never used. It had fancy chairs that we never sat in. The only time we went into that room was for Christmas, and even that stopped when I got a little older. Across the hall was the living room, where we spent most of our time. We had an old big box TV, the kind that looked like it was housed in a wooden crate.

The next room over was the dining room, which also served as a makeshift office for my father. During the holidays, the adults always took dinner in there while the younger ones ate at the kids' table in the kitchen. I have graduated from a lot of things in my life, but the kids' table was never one of 'em. In the center of the kitchen was a big black wood-burning stove, from which I still have red blotches on my right hand it when I fell one Sunday afternoon.

My parents' bedroom was at the bottom of the steps, and when it was lights out, you damn sure better not come down those steps (which creaked loud as hell) trying to get a glass of water. If you woke them up, there would be hell to pay. At the top of the stairs, my sister's room was immediately off to the right and my eldest brother's room was off to the left. My room was just down the hall, and we all shared a bathroom. It had a freestanding sink and an old lion's foot standalone tub that was damn near deeper than I was tall.

That house and farm were all there was to my life. I went to school and came home. I spent the summer digging thistles out of the cow pasture, chopping wood, and cutting grass. I wouldn't see another kid until school opened back up again the following year. I had no real friends until I turned sixteen because, prior to that, I didn't spend enough time with anyone to develop a friendship in the first place.

I didn't have sleepovers until I was sixteen and had befriended a Jamaican boy by the name of Kahili. My family was extremely racist, openly and eagerly using the "N" word around anyone and everyone—including the African Americans who worked for my father. Anyone who wants to pretend that wanton racism ended in the '50s is stupid by choice. So, you can imagine that my parents were less than impressed at my choice of best friends.

School itself was another area in which I struggled. Growing up, I was not a great student, and in my defense, I really didn't have anyone showing me the way. Neither Sadie nor Bobby had graduated (though neither were dumb by any stretch of the imagination) and none of their kids completed high school. I would be the first to graduate, and that would be by the skin of my teeth. While I had a teacher tell me one time that I was "the smartest kid she'd ever seen that didn't use his brain," my poor performance in high school led me to feel like I was stupid most of my adult life.

I wasn't worth a damn in math, but I did love reading, creative writing, and history. I enjoyed the debate team, and the first thing I ever won in my life was an extemporaneous speaking contest where I discussed the events of the Waco siege tragedy. While that was a nice internal pick-me-up, let's just say none of it made the fat kid cool, and I wanted more than anything to be cool in someone's eyes.

I thought the answer was sports, but by the time I was finally allowed to play 'em, I was so far behind the other kids that I was anything but cool. On top of that, most of these kids had been playing together in rec leagues since they were old enough to run. I was not allowed to play sports until I was old enough to get my own ride, and by then, I was so out of shape and so without athletic ability that it was embarrassing to even show up.

As much as I am ashamed to admit it now, the verbal and physical beatdowns I experienced did not make me hard or tough—they made me effeminate and weak. I ran to my mom, first, last, and always because no male in my life took any real interest in me other than to stick their dick in me. So, by the time I was trying to show up on the field as a teenager, I was a little bitch in every sense of the word.

Where my siblings acted out, I caved in. During my youth, I couldn't understand the complexity of the situation. I did not think about it back then, but as an adult, I have asked myself, "Why were all Bobby and Sadie's kids so damn bad? What was going on that was leading them down this path of self-destruction? What trauma was ripping them apart?" Years later, I still do not know, but after my mind let me remember what happened to me, I can't help but wonder when, where, and by whom the rape started.

I'm still not sure of where it started with me. My mind, I think, purposely leaves it hazy to protect me from it. I have often heard people talk shit about sexual assault victims when they can't seem to get the details right or they seem unsure of it themselves. On the surface, I can understand this contempt. After all, sexual assault and rape are not things to be taken lightly, and there are plenty of cases of people whose lives have been destroyed by false allegations.

But, I can assure with 100 percent certainty that, as a sexual assault victim, facts get hazy, doubt fills your mind, and no matter who you are, the perpetrators will always hold powerful sway over you. Part of those problems stems from one of the ways PTS (Post-Traumatic Stress) seeks to protect you from the trauma.

Quick aside: I purposely didn't add the "D," as it is not a disorder. Who knows how many more would crumble right on the spot if not for the protective mechanisms of our brains? PTS response is not a disorder. It is the brain doing what it is designed to do to get us through the moment and allow us to function. The disorder comes in not from what the brain did, per se, but from our inability or poor attempts to process the events later. But more on that later.

The first rape that I remember took place in our shared bathroom. I don't remember all of the details. It's almost as if the memory is wrapped up in a dense fog, and images of it happening float in and out of the mist. I know that Terry and I used to take baths together, and in all truth, there is very little strange about that in a typical family. Terry would have been a teenager at the time and I had to be pretty young; I'd place my age somewhere between six to ten years old. I can't say for sure because I don't know how much older Terry is than me, but what I am positive of is that I wasn't even in puberty.

We would often take baths together. He'd sit at the head of the tub by the tap, and I would be against the end of the tub with its porcelain backside sloping up and out towards the dresser that held the towels. Sitting there in front of me, he'd often start comparing the size of our dicks and would start touching his and making it larger for what my little brain assumed was effect.

Then it gets hazy, and the next thing I can remember is being bent over in the tub and him on his knees, lording over me with his hands on my shoulders, pinning me in place. I still don't remember the physical act itself, and when it runs through my mind, I see it as a moment frozen in time. Me, frail and weak, pinned to the back of a tub while he took pleasure in this moment. To be honest, as I sit here writing that for the first time, I contemplate: did he finish? Did he get off on me?

Instantly, I feel dirty with the recollection, and I understand the intense desire women have to shower after being raped. It's a feeling as if you'll never get it off your skin, that somehow, it made its way in and got tangled up in your soul. It gives me chills and I am reminded that even after all of these years, this shit can still hit you in different and unexpected ways.

I can't recall if it happened with him more than one time. I remember feeling like I should tell my mom, and I even remember where I was pondering that: standing in the kitchen. My gut wanted to stand up and say something. To ask, "Hey, was this okay?" Even at that age, I knew it wasn't okay, but fear took over. I am the different one. I am the lazy one, the kid who's "afraid of the sun." I didn't even know I was adopted at the time, but I knew enough to understand that I wasn't one of them.

Who would believe me? More importantly, what would happen when they didn't? So, in another moment of weakness of my youth, I simply kept my mouth shut and moved on. Now, I would love to tell you that I did that because I was a child, unable to defend myself. But many years later, I found out just what type of hold your rapist can have over you. I was out riding with my ex-wife and the Victory Motorcycle Club (VMC) I am part of, The Desert Knights of America, when we pulled up to a little bar here in Maryland, a full four and half hours away from the town we grew up in.

As we got off the bikes and went to head inside, I was pulling up the rear when I looked up, and standing there was the first person to sexually assault me: my older brother, Terry. Dumbfounded, I stammered out, "What's up, brother?" Everyone else continued inside, my ex-wife included. She had heard me greet him and assumed that he was some other biker that I knew.

Terry made some joke about me being grown and how he wanted to "take a look" at me. All of a sudden, I felt two feet tall. All the confidence I had built up over the years crumbled around me like the Trade Center falling on 9/11. Much like that day, my entire world ground to a halt. Time stood still. That was, at least, right up until he asked me to go get him a pack of cigarettes. To which I jumped back on my bike, rode up the street to the store, and picked up the man who stole my innocence a pack of Marlboro Lights.

I have never felt like a bigger bitch in my life. I rode away with the exterior of a tough guy, someone who if you fucked around with, you'd find out. But, inside I was a scared, isolated little boy. In truth, I was a paper dragon. No more threatening than a little boy on a big wheel.

While Terry may have stolen my innocence, Michelle made sure that there was no hope of ever reclaiming it. I had many encounters with Michelle over the years, taking place in the house and at her place after she moved out. There was a feeling of hopelessness with what took place with Terry, whereas with Michelle's abuse, there remains feelings of intense disgust and self-loathing.

With Terry, I can easily chalk it up to me being a little kid and accepting that I was simply taken advantage of. With Michelle, I was older, approaching my teenage years. She would have me come to her bedroom and undress her. The very first bra I ever removed from a woman I took off my own sister. She would instruct me what to do and I would obey.

But again, the memories get hazy. I honestly don't remember if she ever touched me or if we ever had sex. I just remember she told me to come and I went. She told me what to do and I did it. Writing this all out, my eyes well up with tears, and I am revolted. I ask myself, *Did I want this? Did I ask for it?* On more than one occasion, I have looked in the mirror and thought to myself, *Danny, how fucked up are you? What is wrong with you? Why didn't you stand up, fight back, or say no? Why didn't you tell anyone?* One of my biggest heartbreaks in life is that I don't have any answers to those questions.

I have racked my brain multiple times. I have tried to remember more. I have tried to unpack it, and I have failed each and every time. The last time I tried counseling for the sexual assaults in particular, my entire life spiraled so far out of control that I realized it just wasn't worth it for me to unpack. The deepest I have ever dug into that part of my past has been poured out on these pages. Even now, as I write this, I wonder how many of you will judge me . . . and to be frank, for most things, I wouldn't give a shit. But, here, your indictment of me will hurt because I indict myself every day.

What's even crazier about all of this was the fact that I wasn't alone, and they weren't the only molesters. Robbie would be arrested on the farm one day under allegations from his daughter that he had molested her. I still remember how everyone rallied around Robbie, confirming that my fears of ever bringing up what happened to me were to be well-founded. Instantly, Pam (his wife) and his daughter were excommunicated from the family.

Pam's character was instantly attacked. She became a worthless whore. Which, in truth, probably wasn't that hard because my mother already hated her. So much so, in fact, my mother drove to her house one day (with me in tow) and beat her ass in her own yard. I remember going to court for the case and Pam holding up locks of hair in a Ziploc bag that Sadie had ripped out of her head.

But the fact that they pushed the granddaughter away even at that young of an age was telling to me. To see that they were instantly dismissive of their young grandchild demonstrated the pedestal they held Robbie on. It never even occurred to them that their golden boy could do wrong. It has set in my mind that people will always see what they want to see first and foremost. Anything that runs counter to the narrative they have built in their mind will instantly face resistance. No matter who the person saying it—even in this case of a young, innocent granddaughter finding her courage to speak up.

Eventually, all of Sadie and Bobby's kids would move out and have kids of their own. I cannot speak for the sanity or safety of all of them. I know of them only in passing and brief encounters through social media. Others I only know by name and wouldn't be able to point them out on the street if I saw them today. I don't know if Gene's, Terry's, or Bubba's kids were abused. But I do know that Michelle's were.

I can't even remember her son's name, but I do remember her beating him and belittling him. I think part of it was he looked so much like his daddy, and the other part is that (at least according to my childhood memory of him) he was slow. Her daughter, Samantha, I remember well.

For me, Samantha stands out for a couple of reasons. She had a full head of red hair and always reminded me of Lil Miss Strawberry Shortcake. I literally can't think of the girl and not see that cartoon character in my head. She was often over because whenever Michelle was "in" with the family, she was all in. It was always "for real this time" and she'd start being around all the time. So that meant that Samantha would come around a lot.

I can't remember how much older than her I was, but it was

definitely by several years. So, by the time she started having issues play out in school, I was old enough to at least understand what they were. One day, I overheard Mom talking about how she had to be sent home from school because she had pulled her pants down and was touching herself "like Mommy does with the boys." To this day, I still can't understand how that wasn't the final straw for Michelle.

Years later, I saw Samantha on Facebook, and while I do my damnedest to not judge a book by its cover, because it happens to me so often, to say that she didn't look well would be an understatement. We had a brief exchange over Messenger, where she said she and her mom don't speak anymore and that she was sexually abused for years.

I don't know why I found that so shocking. Maybe because she was a girl. Maybe because I have my doubts about what happened growing up. Maybe because I feel, in some ways, I let her down and failed her. Regardless of the reason why, seeing the girl I remembered as Lil' Miss Strawberry Shortcake grow up to look aged beyond her years and beaten down rocked me to my core.

As years have passed, I've sought to prove that I am a brave man. I have volunteered for the scariest jobs and done things that made my knees shake. I wanted to be someone's hero. I wanted to make a difference in the lives of others. I have fought in a war and a cage. I have run toward gunfire and into burning buildings. Yet, for all the brave things I have done, when it comes to the sexual assault I have gone through, I am, and have always been, a coward.

I didn't stand up then. I didn't stand up years later when I saw Terry face to face and had the skills to make him pay. I have been asked by a few folks why don't I press charges. The truth? I am afraid to. Still afraid of being told I am a liar. Afraid of having to try and prove beyond the shadow of a doubt that I was violated years ago. Afraid to go home and relive everything that happened to me. Hell, just writing this chapter produced a flood of memories and emotions I wasn't ready for. I have dropped tears on this keyboard, and to be honest, I am not sure if I am ready to unpack all of this.

Some things are best left in the closet.

Chapter Two

It Doesn't Get Better

"I am done looking for love where it doesn't exist. I am done coughing up dust in attempts to drink from dry wells."
—Maggie Young

The physical abuse, of course, was devastating and left a lasting scar on my psyche, but what had an equally profound effect on me was the emotional and mental abuse. This, coupled with the poor examples of what a healthy relationship looks like, has forever left me bitter and jaded in regard to love. My greatest flaw is my inability to trust others, especially women.

At this point, I can't tell you if I have bad luck when it comes to finding women or if I'm subconsciously drawn to shitty women. More than likely it's the latter; I think broken people find broken people. We have a built-in beacon that serves as a reverse lighthouse. Instead of warning you about the shore, it pulls you in so you can crash and break yourself against her rocks.

I cannot say for sure that my mother was bipolar, but looking back on my youth, it sure as hell seemed like she was. It took just a blink of an eye for me to go from the greatest thing that ever was to a worthless piece of shit in her eyes. You were always on guard waiting for the split-second switch. It's like being in fight or flight every minute of every day. One minute you'd be her pride and joy, and the next minute she'd be in tears, throwing a piece of chicken at your head.

As dramatic as all of this was and as intense as she could be, when my mother loved me, it was the greatest feeling in the world. I knew that although she might be quick to snap at me, she was the only person in the world who gave a shit about me. I often wonder about the complexity of that woman and what made her that way.

When she was sweet, there was no one else that could compare. She used to make mini biscuits for me every night and put smiley faces on them. She would randomly buy me toys for no reason at all. Every morning, she'd let me wake up, come down the stairs, and curl up with her on our favorite green chair in the early morning before school and watch *Gumby* on TV.

She routinely made my favorite meal—chicken and dumplings— and to this day, no one, nowhere can make 'em like Momma did. Each year on my birthday, she'd do a big batch of them and top off the meal with my favorite part: upside-down pineapple cake. There is no doubt that she went out of her way much of the time to make me feel loved.

She was also quick to defend me whenever others attacked. The only times I heard Sadie and Bobby argue were over me. In an odd way, perhaps that hurt me the worst. To know, at such a young age, that you are a primary source of animosity between the patriarch and matriarch of the family. It always ended the same way: my mother crying and Bobby looking at me with disgust, clearly blaming me for the ruined afternoon that lay ahead of him.

But just as easily as she could demonstrate love and compassion, she could make your life a living hell. On more than one occasion, I have caught the backhand from Hell at a perceived slight. She used to have this leather belt that had her name engraved into it, and thus, I have had her name etched into my ass on multiple occasions.

The worst beating I ever recall came from mouthing off one day after school. I can't remember why I was in a bad mood, but I talked out the side of my mouth as I walked through the door that afternoon. I fully expected to catch an asswhooping on the spot, but no one said much of anything and I went about my afternoon chores. As the afternoon wore on, I thought no more about my snide comments from a few hours earlier.

Later that night, I was taking a bath when the door kicked open like the ATF was coming in to take Terry to jail for drug possession again. As I watched my mother storm in with her redneck belt trailing behind her, I wished it had been the police instead. There, sitting in the very same tub Terry had his way with me in, she proceeded to belt me until I had welts.

I jumped up and tried to protect my backside against the lashings that were coming. I was naked and embarrassed. I hadn't even started puberty yet and there I was, stark-naked, little dick shrinking back inside my belly both from fear of being hit by a belt and sheer shame of being undressed in front of my mother. She grabbed one of my wrists to keep me in place and beat me until she was satisfied. The belt snapped against my wet backside as I slipped repeatedly, trying to gain some form of traction on the wet porcelain beneath my feet.

After she was done, she let my wrist go, and I fell back into the tub. There, my tears added to the bath water that had turned slightly yellow from where I had pissed myself out of fright.

Ass-beatings aren't fun, but psychological warfare is a special type of Hell. One of the surest ways to piss my mother off and ensure that my day was going to suck was to not wake up on her time. Notice I said "her time," not "on time." She never once used an alarm clock, and as such, I didn't have one either. However, that made no difference to her. She'd been waking up before the sun for years and had never slept in. So, in her eyes, if you didn't get up, it was a sign of pure laziness.

If you woke up and heard the lawnmower going or saw that light creeping in through your window, you knew you were royally fucked. No amount of extra work was enough. You'd go outside to find her pushing the lawnmower with a scowl on her face, sweating and cussing. Any attempt to take over the lawnmower would be rebuked with, "If you really wanted to help, you'd have gotten your ass up in the morning. Just go sit your ass back inside."

This was the routine, and I'd have to return to her over and over until she finally granted me my wish and allowed me to take over said chore. Back in her good graces, the storm would subside for a brief respite and all would be well in the world again. Just like that, I was her perfect little boy and the baby of the family who could do no wrong.

But of course, eventually, some little squabble or mistake would occur, and that safe and adored feeling would melt away faster than dew in the sunlight. It was emotional whiplash. By far, my least favorite form of punishment was getting locked in the closet. As I mentioned earlier, our house was old. It had to have been built decades earlier. Matter of fact, we had several aerial shots of the house and land that showed how the old home had evolved over the years. These art pieces were a big thing in the South—eagle-eye views that were then painted and placed on your walls with pride. Anyway, Bobby and Sadie's first painting showed the house was white with wooden siding. Eventually, that would be replaced with a brick exterior.

Inside the house, everything was finished except the closets. My mother loved scary movies and so we spent a great deal of time watching them. I still remember the very first movie we watched on our VHS player: *Gremlins*. So, needless to say, with all these monsters locked up in my head, the last place I wanted to be physically locked up in was the closet. Especially these closets.

To me, they looked like a doorway straight to Hell. They had no drywall covering them, just exposed slats with what appeared to be broken plaster of some sort. This "plaster" was falling off the wall or hanging loosely with sinews of connective fiber. And they were extremely narrow. Evidently, back in the day, no one expected you to put much in a closet, least of all little kids.

The closet had an old locking mechanism to it. There was a box around the doorknob that had a lever you would flip to lock or unlock it. Even creepier, it took a skeleton key—no bullshit—to unlock it. But nothing, and I mean nothing, compared to the totality of the experience of being banished to the closet.

It would normally come from the most mundane things. Like I didn't want to eat fried okra. I hate, I mean *hate*, okra. Well, growing up, not eating all the food on your plate was akin to the seventh deadly sin. And saying that something didn't taste good was the equivalent of smacking Momma in the face. Hell, my dad even made you eat the gristle on the steak. I gag just thinking about it.

Being forced to down food that was literally making you retch was enough to produce the courage to speak up, which, in a house where children were taught to "be seen and not heard," wasn't a great idea. That momentary lapse of judgment would find you getting dragged away from the table in the kitchen, past the living room, and into the master bedroom, where you'd be thrown in the closet nearest to the stove.

When that door slammed shut and you heard the lock click over, it was pure, unadulterated horror. I was positive that I would die every time I was locked in there. The walls felt as if they were closing in and I was sure monsters were breathing down my neck. I would beat on the door and scream with tears streaming down my eyes, "Please let me out! Please don't leave me in here! Please, Momma, please! Help me!"

Eventually, after what would seem like hours, I would be let out and expected to return to the table to finish whatever I had objected to in the first place. Dejected, puffy-faced, and soaked with tears, I'd force down whatever was required of me, help do the dishes, and scurry on out of the kitchen.

This childhood definitely caused me to develop a lot of issues that I could only begin to untangle and deal with long after I left my hometown. The first time I contemplated suicide, I was only between eight and eleven years old. Yet again, I was feeling unwanted, unloved, and like I was a burden on everyone else for existing. One of my brothers had just beaten my ass, and instead of helping or consoling me, my father just talked down to me. My mom was in one of her moods where nothing I did was right. I was playing with a big tobacco stick that had been sharpened at one end. I thought that I should run at the barn with the sharp end pointed at my chest and slam the flat end into the wall so that it impaled me. I figured that would show 'em. Once I was gone, that'd teach them they should have loved me while I was here. But the ideation passed, and I carried on playing.

Perhaps the oddest part of growing up in situations like that is you become oddly comfortable with them. As a young kid, you just assume that this is life. Maybe it's the innocence and naivety of youth. Perhaps it's a coping mechanism. Or more likely, your brain just shuts off memories of yesterday so you can get through today and hopefully face tomorrow. But even in a nightmare house, it's still your home, and the ghost and ghouls are still your family. As such, there is at least some sense of normalcy, even if it's a false sense. At eleven years old, I was about to find out that there are levels to the messed up game called life, and it was just about time for me to reach the next stage.

I was called downstairs one night after school. I had been up in my room doing homework when I heard my mother's voice calling up to me, "Danny, come down here, hunny." Without a second thought, I hurried down the steps and followed her voice into the kitchen.

I called out, "Yes, ma'am."

And then I heard her voice crack as she said, "Come in here." There, sitting in the pantry, with the lights off as she was digging through laundry, I heard her say the words that rocked my world: "I am not your mom."

In a moment like that, a young child's mind can't comprehend what it's hearing. Here was the woman who I had called my mom for the entirety of my life (or at the very least, what I could consciously remember) telling me that I wasn't hers. I could vaguely recall my actual mother, but with Sadie being my caretaker, well, it was just an anomaly I never thought to analyze. Now, as I mentioned before, I should have probably seen this coming. Not only had I been given some bullshit story about why my last name was Farrar when they were Robertsons, but I also had my very own Morpheus trying to break me out of the Matrix for years. I just didn't believe him back then.

In the South, or at the very least, in my case in the South, the only time you were sure to see the whole family was at a funeral. So only at funerals would everyone see the flower child (my biological mother) and her long-haired hippy son (my eldest biological brother). At all family functions, adults would be inside, kids out.

So, at one funeral, sitting there on the fence post, long-haired Shawn told me, for the first time, a truth I wouldn't believe until years later when Sadie finally came clean.

Over and over, Shawn tried to convince me, "These folks ain't your family." To which I'd just giggle and fidget uncomfortably. Then he'd follow up with, "I am your brother, and your aunt Debbie is your momma." Now, maybe it was the fact that even at that age, I knew kids made shit up, or perhaps it was the fact that Shawn was such a weird-ass kid, but I didn't believe it. I put literally zero stock in what he said. I didn't even bring it up to Sadie and Bobby. With that said, somewhere deep inside, I knew something was off. After all, I was nothing like any of the family I was living with. Even in sixth grade, that much was evident.

So, when Sadie told me the same fact and started gently crying there in the dark, it still caught me off guard, despite the fact Shawn had tried to tell me the same thing on that fence outside. The only thing I could offer in defense was, "Come on, Momma, stop playing."

To which she snapped back, "I ain't playing."

Think for a moment about how shocking it would be if the woman you thought was your mother for your entire life all of a sudden turned out not to be. What thoughts would race through your mind? How betrayed would you feel, knowing that you've been living a lie your entire life? More importantly, why now? Why in sixth grade, on a Tuesday evening while doing laundry, did she decide it was the perfect time to drop the bomb on me?

No answers were coming my way, and to be honest, once the initial shock wore off, I found myself excited. Here was proof that I wasn't crazy. Proof that I wasn't the oddball of the family after all! I just wasn't part of this family to begin with! These people were nuts, and now, finally, I was going to meet people like me, people who'd love me and accept me just the way I was. I was finally going home.

Boy, was I wrong.

Almost immediately, we transitioned from "I am not your mother" to "Here, let's get your real mother on the phone." You want an odd-ass conversation? Try figuring out what you call your birth giver on the phone when your ma is there with you in the kitchen. Do I call 'em Mom One and Mom Two? If so, who the hell is Mom One? What justifies being Mom One?

What's worse is this was back when phones were stuck to the wall. Even with a long cord, you were still tethered to one room, which meant you never had a private conversation. And if there ever was a time a young man wanted privacy, it was with his newly reunited, long-lost mother who he thought was a hippy. A hundred questions flooded my brain. *Where do you live? Who lives with you? Why'd you give me up? Are you coming to take me back? Do you love me?*

The truth is, I didn't even know if I wanted the answers to all of those questions, or if I'd even believe 'em in the first place. What I do know for an absolute fact, though, was it was abundantly clear she wasn't happy Sadie had told me. How do I know that? She stated it emphatically.

It's funny how life can go from bad to worse when you think it can't be possible. Just when you think you've been given all you can take, cruel fate will find another way to kick the chair out from under you. Or, on the flip side, when things finally fall into place, the whole board can be shattered in an instant. Now, don't think I take a pessimistic view of the world—I don't. I'm an eternal optimist; it's why I have been able to make it through the things I have. With that said, sometimes it can be raining pussy and you'll still get hit with dicks.

My birth mother was awkward on the other end of the line. To this day, I still can't understand how this all went down without her getting a heads-up. I genuinely believe she was in as much shock and disbelief as I was. She fumbled with her answers and addressed me by my full middle name, Daniel. Which was weird because no one else called me that. It's funny how those little things leave such a profound impact on us.

On the call, we agreed that she would come pick me up so I could stay with her for a weekend. Sadie said very little after the call. It's hard to describe her demeanor. She was unusually quiet, with a look of sadness in her eyes I'd never seen. She simply went back to cleaning, and I went back to my room, still trying to figure out what the hell just happened.

Debbie arrived with Shawn in tow and she drove me back to her apartment on the outskirts of Richmond, where she lived. It couldn't have been any more different from the old farmhouse I had grown up in.

Back on the farm, the nearest group of houses was a cluster of them about half a mile down the road. There, a small community of African Americans lived in about twenty houses; oddly enough, that was the only place African Americans lived on the road. But after that little cluster, houses were pretty significantly spaced out. So, to be "up on top of each other," as my folks would have called it, in an apartment was quite the culture shock.

Walking into Debbie's house, it was abundantly apparent that she didn't have her shit together, especially not compared to Sadie. The tiny space was unkempt and cluttered. Clothes were everywhere and the kitchen was in disarray. The fridge didn't have leftovers of homecooked meals; Hell, it didn't even have real food. Maybe some Oscar Myer bologna and old take-out pizza.

Upstairs, my brother's room was small and in equal disarray. Walking in there made me feel sad for him. Despite that, I'd be lying if I said that he didn't have things I wish that I did. First up was a Nintendo (my parents wouldn't get me one). The dude had nunchucks, too—my favorite Teenage Mutant Ninja Turtle had nunchucks! Lastly, and maybe most importantly, he had a guitar. As I should have guessed by Shawn's long hair, he was secretly a rock star. A rock star ninja. We didn't look anything alike, which stands to reason as we have different fathers. Shawn was a lanky, skinny kid, which was a far cry from my "husky" frame. He definitely resembled Debbie, though, with his black hair, high cheekbones, and lean figure.

While they may have looked like each other, Shawn and Debbie fought like cats and dogs. I mean straight fisticuffs, without warning, and without any direct instigation that I could see. I watched her randomly grab Shawn by his hair and just beat the poor kid like he stole something. Despite the abuse I had experienced in the farmhouse, this scared me because it was fundamentally different in my eyes. Yes, I had had my ass beat—brutally, multiple times—but this wasn't a parent punishing a child for some trivial infraction. This was more like attacking the very thing that made your life horrible: your son.

It was clear that she didn't want Shawn, or me, for that matter. A huge difference between Debbie's house and Sadie's was the fact that Debbie was never home. Looking back on it now as a parent myself, I can't help but wonder what the hell was going through her mind. Shawn had to be eleven or twelve, max, and I was barely eleven. Yet this woman left us at home alone all day and late into the night. There was no semblance of discipline, no rules. Which, honestly, makes all the beatings that more vile, in my opinion. Who the fuck are you to beat the kid when you don't even have any fundamentals of parenting?

During the day, we kind of meandered around the neighborhood, looking for shit to get into. This is probably the number-one reason kids from inner cities get in trouble so much. Mom and Dad, or just Mom or just Dad, either make so little they have to work three or four jobs and can't be home, or they are just giant pieces of shit who do nothing to take care of their kids. As far as I could see, Debbie was the latter.

With Debbie gone all the time, Shawn grew up alone and, I am sure, feeling unloved. That is the perfect storm for going off the guardrails. He started getting into drugs. That lack of discipline and clear lack of love ensured that even though I'd only go back to see Debbie a handful of times, that'd be the last time I'd ever see Shawn.

I would leave and go back to Sadie and Bobby's house after that weekend feeling more than a little dejected and out of place in the world. It's bad enough when you don't feel like you fit in with one family, but to have two that don't want you . . . well, fuck. Still, coming back to the house that built me and broke me at the same time wasn't easy. I now had all these people who I didn't actually have any real connection to treating me like shit and looking at me as even more of an outsider. It's almost as if we painted the elephant in the room bright red so no one could miss it. In fact, everyone was pointing it out.

Finding out that I was adopted gave me the courage to act out, and, surprisingly, the leeway to get away with it. I was quick to pop off and say hurtful things like, "You ain't my real mom." Which, despite the things that happened to me, wasn't justified. To my knowledge, Sadie never knew the liberties her children took with me, and I chalk her actions towards me up to a combination of how she was raised and some form of mental illness.

Justified or not, I said hurtful things because I was a confused and hurt kid. I had no sense of self and anytime something didn't feel right, I would say that I wanted to go live with Debbie. I'll never forget the hurt on Sadie's face each time I said that, but soon, she did in fact book me another trip to go see Debbie.

This time, I would go with her to the house of my two younger brothers (the only sons of Debbie who shared the same father). At that time, Debbie, Luke, and Floyd lived with their father in a small one-story house on the outskirts of Richmond. It wasn't much, but it was clearly a home. The boys were avid baseball fans, players, and collectors.

I was instantly welcomed in, and the ambiance of their house felt comfortable. Their father didn't take no shit, but he wasn't malicious in the way that I had grown accustomed to. We may have been allowed to stay up a lot later than I was at the farmhouse, but they still ran a "Yes, sir" and "No, sir" ship. That balanced combination of discipline and freedom had a lasting impact on me and assured me that I wanted to move back in with this family, what

I felt was my *real* family. What happened next would set the tone for the rest of my life.

The next trip was scheduled for me to go stay with Debbie and the boys, and I was looking forward to it immensely. I had my bags packed and stepped out on the porch one sunny summer day at 10:30 a.m. I had been told that I would get picked up at 11:00 a.m. I didn't start to worry until noon. I paced about back and forth on the wooden porch. Where was she? Surely she hadn't forgotten about me! Could she be hurt? Why hadn't she called? Wasn't she gonna pick me up?

I waited outside until dark. She never showed. She never called. Not that day, not the next, nor the end of the week. This woman who had abandoned me once had done it again. I hated her for it. She was gone like trash on a Thursday morning, and from that moment on, that's exactly what she was to me—trash.

This may seem odd to many of you reading this, given what I've already shared (and what I'll share later), but I believe her standing me up may have been the most profound event of my life. It very well may have shaped my life more so than anything before it or that came after. To be abandoned not once, but twice, by your mother is devastating to a child, especially a young boy. Especially when you had just gotten your first glimpse of normalcy, belonging, and even unconditional happiness. After all, how worthless must you be if your own mother doesn't want you?

Chapter Three

A Fatherless Son

"Fathers, you are the head and strength of the family unit. If you are not in place, there is a weakness in the link."
—Anita R. Sneed Carter

It seems that I have an issue with women and the truth, or, it's more along the lines of women in my life having an issue telling me the truth. Debbie was no exception. She told me my father was dead and that was that. So, you can imagine my surprise when I turned sixteen and got a letter in the mail from my aunt that Robert Daniel Farrar, Junior was indeed alive and, in fact, looking for me.

Reading that letter again brought a flood of emotions. How many times is my life going to take some sick, twisted turn that completely up-ends my world? Turns out, the answer to that was "a fucking lot," and that's why I'm writing this book. I opened that letter and read it, mouth open as my mother perused through a local clipper magazine. Truth be told, I don't know who was more surprised, me or her.

The letter opens with: "I am your aunt Karen. I am your father's sister and we have been looking for you since you were two years old. I knew that you had come of age to get your driver's license and so I did a search at the DMV and found you. Your father would very much like to see you."

Reading that letter, I kept waiting for Maury Povich and a few stripper midgets to come bursting through the door with a paternity test, telling me that Bobby was not my father. No shit, Maury, we've known that for some time now.

Included in the letter was a phone number to reach Karen, and so, much like I did when I found out about Debbie, I made my way to the kitchen and picked up the phone. Karen was a kind voice on the other end of the phone, and I must say that she was (and remains) hands down the easiest person in either family to trust. She had a calming tone to her voice as if she were a grandma well before her time, an old soul regardless of years on this earth. It was clear that she cared about her brother, about me, and about what was right and decent. She had taken the time to look for me ever since I was "stolen."

Now, that brings us back to Debbie. Remember, she told me that "Big Danny" had died. Well, turns out, not only was he alive, but the dang fool was living in the next county over from me the entire time. Well, when Debbie got word he was coming to pay a visit all, of a sudden, she wanted to be "Mom" again. Imagine how odd it was for me to be in the following scenario: everyone meeting at the house of my adoptive parents, with Bobby and Sadie meeting my biological father, grandfather, and aunt Karen for the first time . . . nothing to see here, folks, let's just keep it moving along.

My father isn't a handsome man (which I find disturbing because everyone says I look like him). He was much taller than me. I imagine he must have been around 6'2" to 6'3" in height and wide around the waste. He had a bowl mullet and it looked as glorious as it sounds. He stood in stark contradiction to my grandfather, who appeared strait-laced and conservative.

My father is not much of a talker and is very introverted. To this day, I believe he resides in a trailer somewhere in Virginia by himself. So, it was clear that he was uncomfortable in the moment and struggled to be there. In some ways, I felt, and still feel, sorry for him. One of the things I learned that I take for granted is how easily I can converse with people; it's a talent that I clearly didn't get from him. But that's why, of all the stories I have heard about how my life started, I believe his the most. First, because the man didn't like to talk, and second, because anything that made that little sense couldn't have been made up.

According to my father, he met my mother while passing through the area and working in town for a bit. For reasons unknown (and I ain't gonna speculate), they had a brief "thing," and out of that "thing," I came. The only problem with all of this was that my mother was with another man (this would become a theme for most women in my life, so I am gonna blame it all on Debbie), and that caused there to be a huge issue about whose surname was gonna be on my birth certificate.

Now, my father was adamant about my name because (and he repeated this multiple times) he didn't name me after himself, but after my grandfather. So he was going to make damn sure I had his last name. That's how I ended up as, technically, Robert Daniel Farrar III. From there, over the next year and a half, they shared custody of me, but then "something happened" and he ended up with full custody of me. I am assuming that "something" was my mother not wanting me in the first place.

So, he took me in full-time, and when he had to go to work, Aunt Karen was the one who watched me. That is why she had gotten so close to me and had been looking for me for so long. I am not sure how long he had sole custody, but for some reason, he had agreed to allow Debbie to pick me up for a weekend during the holidays. It would be the last time he'd ever see me until he stepped on the porch at Bobby and Sadie's house.

Now, if you're anything like me, you start to wonder, if he loved me so much, why didn't he go looking for me? I mean, it was clear he didn't look hard; after all, he was just one county over. Hell, the local high school teams played each other. His justification was that he had many run-ins with the law and that he didn't think they'd bring me back to a felon.

I still don't know how much of the story I believe. I mean, as I said earlier, it's just redneck-Maury-Povich enough to be real, but I can't help wondering what parts are being left out. When neither party paints themselves in a poor light, you know both parties are lying.

With that said, the one thing I can say I respect about Robert Daniel Farrar, Jr., was that he never bullshitted me like everyone else. He never claimed he was gonna be there for me. Never acted like he was interested in being my father. Never led me on to believe that I'd be his best friend, or even move beyond being strangers. I think, much like Sadie forced Debbie to meet me, Aunt Karen forced him to come see me, too.

For me, he was just another building block in the belief that family wasn't forever. That those who were supposed to protect you wouldn't. That people would come and go as it suited them. That they'd come into your life and leave on a whim. One day, you understand the world as it is, and the next day, a letter would come in the mail and change it. That the worst is yet to come and it's often going to be delivered by the people you thought you could trust.

There was one benefit to all of this, though. When I was younger, I used to have the same reoccurring nightmare. It won't sound scary to you, but every time I had it, I woke up screaming and scared shitless. In this dream, I'd be driving a car, and get stopped at an intersection, where a little munchkin would come up to the car with a flower in his hat and start talking in Munchkinese to me. I told you it didn't sound scary. Somehow, I understood what he was saying and agreed to follow him. He took me down into an underground cave that was dark and glowing with a blue hue.

In this cave were hundreds, perhaps thousands, of munchkins. And all of a sudden, the cave would start to shake. As the shaking grew more intense, the munchkins would start to freak out. I would find myself off-balance as debris started to fall all around me. Finally, I would look up and notice what was going on and why they were so frightened.

Up to the right, against the wall, were a man and a woman dressed all in black leather. They were in these rocket-type capsules. While I was larger than the munchkins, this man and women were much larger than me. As the shaking intensified, I would notice that the capsules in which they were contained started to shudder as well. What is odd is that I couldn't clearly see their faces, but somehow it was obvious to me that their eyes were closed.

The shaking would reach a crescendo and the hysteria would be through the roof. I would try and do my best to calm the fears of the little guys, but it would be to no avail because I was scared shitless myself. Finally, after what seemed like forever, the rockets containing the man and woman would ignite, and they would take off, leaving the munchkins and me all alone. I had that dream at least once a month until the sixth grade. I'm forty-three years old at the moment and I still remember it. As soon as I found out I was adopted, I never had it again.

Chapter Four

Is Your Mother a Whore?

"What a kid I got, I told him about the birds and the bees and he told me about the butcher and my wife."
—Rodney Dangerfield

I imagine you read the title of the chapter and felt a slight twinge in your stomach. I mean, momma jokes have led to ass-beatings for as long as ass-beatings have been a thing. I don't know much, but I do know don't nobody talk about my momma! With that said, I don't think I can talk about what comes later in the book, about my strained relationships with women that I have loved, without delving into the impact the first women who were supposed to love me had on my life. Perhaps more so than anything else in my life, it was the failure of character of these two women that set the stage for what I would tolerate years later.

Now, before you and I go any further, I figure I might as well explain my definition of a whore before every feminist on the planet loses their minds. First and foremost, I don't have an issue with any woman wanting dick. Not a one. I don't have an issue with them wanting lots of 'em or even all of 'em. They can have 'em in every shape, size, color, and taste as far as I am concerned, up until they say, "I am yours."

Once a woman tells a man she is his and when he says the same (provided you ain't swingers—if so, you can skip this next part), then I expect you to put the dick down. All of them but your man's. After all, no one told you that you had to commit to it; you did that all on your own. So, either be true to him or break up with him, but under no circumstances are you allowed to fuck other people after you made that promise. If you do that, you're not an empowered female. You're simply a lying, dishonest whore, no better than the guys you can't stand in the Lifetime movies.

I've already talked about the rumor that Debbie was a lady of the night, and as I stated before, I can no more confirm that than I can say aliens exist. However, there's a lot of evidence to support both assertions. Regardless of whether she turned tricks or not, one fact remains above all others: the woman could not figure out the simple concept of contraceptives. Five different boys, by four different fathers, proves that beyond the shadow of a doubt.

As I have aged, I have done my best to seek to be understanding of the plights of my fellow man. I understand that every single one of us has had traumatic events. I understand (all too well) that the sins of our fathers (and mothers) can lead us to making some stupid decisions. With that said, I have no respect for people who continue to mess up. To err is to be human, but to make the same error over and over is a decision, not a mistake.

So, for Debbie to continue to fuck men and continue to produce boys (who all grew up into messed up men) remains one of the most detestable things I think a human could do. It is vile in every sense of the word. Nothing is more selfish than to purposely mess up a miracle. That's what every single one of her boys was—a miracle. There is about a 1-in-400 trillion chance that you will be born. This woman wasted five separate 1-in-400 trillion chances because she couldn't get her shit together.

I mean, bearing a child is no small feat. It takes nine months to bring a child into this world, and then who knows how long the labor will be. After that, you've got a little "you" twenty-four hours a day to take care of, so it should be abundantly clear after "thing one" that you ain't cut out for this, and so there should never be a "thing two," much less "thing three through five." I mean, can we please have some respect for our "things"?

Cause that's exactly what it feels like we were to that woman. Not humans. Not babies. Not kids who would grow up to have our own one day. No, we were just things. Things that could easily and carelessly be tossed aside anytime the moment suited her.

As a young boy, you expect to look to your mother as a beacon of virtue. Of course, no one can live up to that. With that side, we at least expect you to hide your worst traits. To have some decorum and taste. To be discreet about it, and for fuck's sake, if you give away your first boy, don't have four more.

So, Mommy Dearest got around quite a bit, and the infidelity she flaunted before her children is an unforgivable sin in my eyes. Nothing will justify it, especially given the fact that she did it repeatedly with the boys that followed. What I can't help but wonder, though, was while Debbie did it in spite of her children, Sadie might just have done it *because* of her children.

While I can only speak about Debbie's transgressions from the outside looking in, I had a front-row seat to Sadie's. Mom was the stereotypical housewife of the '80s. She did far more work than she was ever given credit for and never once billed for hours. However, Bobby did adore her, and he worked insane hours to give her what she wanted.

Our family was not poor growing up. Bobby had a thriving logging business most of my young life. It afforded him the ability to have a very nice house and lots of property, and to spoil Sadie.

She was into collecting antiques and concrete statues. We had lions, angels, and gnomes all over the place. Bobby didn't love me, but he sure as hell loved her, and I do feel for him that he gave all he had to her. And she had an affair with the county prosecutor.

I couldn't tell you exactly when the affair started, but what made it even more torrid, in my opinion, was that she didn't hide it from me. I knew full well that it was going on and I was old enough to understand that it shouldn't be happening. I watched every indiscretion—short of the actual deed—from the back seat of the Jeep Cherokee she drove.

While I can't remember his name, I do remember how he looked. He had the classic 1980's professor look to him. He was tall and lean with dark brown hair and a thick *Magnum P.I.* mustache (Mom always did have a thing for Tom Sellick). He also wore a distinct look every time I saw him: guilty. Which is odd, given he was a prosecutor by trade. He may have been able to face the jury every day in court, but he never so much as acknowledged me in the back seat.

Sadie and him played the game all over town. Every time they'd see each other, they'd tap their brakes. They would meet up during the day for lunch and even went to the motel one time in Blackstone. Which is just insane to me, because it was such a small town. What's worse is that not only did she not hide the affair from me, her friends knew about it, too, and so did Michelle. I would say that she was brutally forthright to protect her children, but it was clear she enjoyed it too much for it to have been a selfless act.

The fact remains that their affair shows that justice isn't blind if you're banging the person dispensing it. All of Sadie's kids wound up standing in front of the county prosecutor on multiple occasions for everything from drug possession to armed robbery, and in the case of the armed robbery, the getaway driver got a longer and harsher sentence than Michelle did, and she held the fucking place up!

Time and time again, the kids received probation, fines, work releases, and shorter sentences than they should have gotten, given their records. It is absurd that they got away with as much as they did, and it was 100 percent all due to the fact that Mom's affair played in their favor.

Chapter Five

Self-discovery

"Like I said, things never turn out exactly the way you planned. Growing up happens in a heartbeat. One day, you're in diapers; next day, you're gone. But the memories of childhood stay with you for the long haul."
—Kevin Arnold, The Wonder Years

While all of this was going on, I was growing up. Middle school was when I'd start to grasp just how far behind most of my peers I was in terms social and physical development. I was a "husky" kid (that's momspeak for politely telling you that you're fat) and didn't have an ounce of athleticism in my body. But the desire to be part of something or fit into something led me to go out for the football team.

I was a young boy trying to play a "man's sport." I was slow, uncoordinated, out of shape, and soft in every definition of the word. When I ran laps, my titties jiggled around, along with my belly, which would soon be joined by the rest of my body as I collapsed from exhaustion. I was fat, weak, and slow. I knew it, and so did everyone else.

I think what surprises me most about that time was that, despite my softness, I stayed. I never asked to quit, even though I was outclassed in every way. I was the poor fucker who only went in if the game was out of reach. I rode the pine every year but one, my sophomore year (it was my second year of JV, so they started me), and then didn't play football again.

Looking back, I am not quite sure why I played or stayed on the team. I wasn't doing it for love of the game. I can tolerate football, and even enjoy a game here or there, but I am in no way, shape, or form passionate about it, and we already pointed out how I wasn't skilled. But, I think it had a lot to do with being on a team. Even the bad players are on the team. Which was something I felt I had been missing. This was also the first time in my life I had a positive male role model. Coach Mumford was really the first man to take an interest in me that was positive and constructive.

Couch Mumford was a big man. He had to be every bit of 300 lbs. He coached the line and defense. When he wasn't on the football field, he was in the classroom, and he taught one of my favorite subjects: social studies. He treated me like I was smart and challenged me in class. He'd give me rides from practice and always had something motivating to say. He was the very first teacher that I ever liked, and it's obvious the impact he had on me because I still remember his name—yet I don't remember any of the head coaches' names.

Middle school was also where I would start to learn that you better have a quick wit or be able to throw them fists if you're gonna be a chunky boy. To make matters worse, I had two major embarrassments in middle school that happened on the "world stage" in front of my peers. Those defining moments would ensure that no one was going to use the word "cool" in any sentence about me for the foreseeable future.

Let's just say I was a late bloomer, and students started having to take showers together in the eighth-grade locker room. I was already nervous enough about sharing a shower with other folks based on what had happened to me at home, but now, there was another level to my shame. Not only was I fat with jiggly titties, I also hadn't started puberty yet, and all it took was one trip to the shower to realize that I was alone in that regard, and one really is the loneliest number that you've ever seen.

So there I was with these other boys who had hair in places I didn't, and, well, they were hung and I hadn't even sprung yet. So, I had a simple solution to this. I'd just wear my underwear in the shower. Now, it's absolutely pointless to wear underwear in the shower. It's just like when overweight folks wear a t-shirt to the pool or beach. You might as well just take that shit off because all of us know why you're wearing it. What's worse is that as soon you get in the water, it defeats the purpose anyway. We can see you're overweight and now you're just wearing clinging clothes that highlight the fact.

So, with my tighty-whities on, I strolled into the shower and quickly faced the wall. Some of the other boys started talking shit to me and making fun of how fat I was and how little my dick must be. Now, it gave me no consolation that it wasn't my fault and I just hadn't started puberty. All that mattered was that I, once again, was on the short end of the stick—literally and figuratively in this case.

I would wait till they left before I would come out myself, which proved to be a grave error in judgment. One afternoon, those bastards took my clothes as I showered. I had to walk out to the gym floor to get someone to help me find them. Sheepishly, I covered myself with one hand and walked out of the locker room. That turned out to be another mistake, because everyone was quick to point out how I could cover myself with just one hand, and this time it wasn't just the boys. Girls were there too, and let me tell you, not much is more demoralizing than women pointing and laughing while you stand there in the buff. I thought that would be the highlight of my lowlights, but I have been an overachiever my entire life, so I guess I figured, why not top being Little-Dick Dan by letting a woman beat my ass?

I met Christiana Edwards at a middle school dance, and I fell in love. She was a stunningly beautiful young lady. Long, straight, dirty-blonde hair, and always in her glasses. She had moved here with her family from Alaska and that only made her more exotic. I am pretty sure that "Kiss from a Rose" by Seal was the song playing that night, and who doesn't fall in love with the first person they see after hearing it? That shit is like Cupid's arrow.

You could say we got serious pretty quickly. We exchanged numbers and I spent the next few weeks attached to the phone that was attached to the wall. We held hands. Wrote notes. Shared our most intimate secrets (which ain't that impressive in middle school). Hell, I even went over to her house once! Can you imagine, chubby, unathletic, late-bloomer Farrar was at a girl's house! I mean, this is it. This is the moment we've all been waiting for! I made it!

Except, I hadn't. Young love can be so fleeting, and as George Straight once said, "Easy come, easy go." She broke up with me. Sadly, I didn't let it go gracefully. I was sad and embarrassed. The problem is, I didn't know how to process that loneliness and embarrassment alone, so I figured I should let the entire school see it on full display in the lunchroom.

Now, I can't remember what caused us to be standing in the middle of the cafeteria. I also don't know why I called her a whore. She was actually one of a handful of girls who didn't cheat on me. But, when you're in your teens and you want to make a girl feel as bad as you do, you say stupid shit. So, in front of the entire cafeteria, I called her a whore.

I instantly regretted that decision as she smacked the shit out of me. I'd have said that she knocked some sense into me, but with that smack, she said, "Say it again." And I did, and she smacked me again, and said, "Say it again." And I did. We must have repeated that process at least four or five times before the teachers broke it up.

And there I stood with red cheeks. One side red from her handprints and the other side red from the humiliation of having a girl smack the shit out of me in front of the whole school. Oh, and trust me, the kids were ruthless. Quickly, the only thing I heard in the hallways was: "You got your ass beat by a girl."

I'd shoot back, "I didn't get my ass beat by a girl. I didn't even fight back!" But, in hindsight, even if I had fought back, she'd have probably beat my ass. She had a mean right hook.

So, dejected, I was sent to the office to meet with the principle, and we both got suspended from school. Which, if I am honest, never really felt like a punishment. So I spent the next three days nursing my face and my bruised ego. I worked around the house and dreaded the thought of returning to school. At least I had a major benefit of being born when I did: no one caught it on video. I couldn't be bullied online, and children's memories are pretty fleeting. It'd be no time at all before the only one who remembered that day was me.

As I went into high school, I found my first opportunity to be good at something when I enrolled in the Navy JROTC program at my high school. I could hardly believe that such a thing existed, and I thought the fact that I got to wear a uniform was amazing. On top of all of this, the cadets took a big trip every year, and to me, that was the most amazing thing on the planet. Last year, it was San Diego, and this upcoming trip would be to Puerto Rico.

Like I said earlier, we didn't take vacations and we didn't travel. The most you got out was to go to Bug's Island for the day on Sundays in the summer, about an hour drive down the road. So, the idea of going to Puerto Rico was like a dream come true. But the truth is, I would have done it just to wear the uniform.

It was there that I fell in love with the idea of being in the service, and it was in no small part to the men leading the program. Nottoway County had one of the biggest programs in the area, and as such, we had three great men leading it. The overall head honcho was Commander Rawls. He was a tall man, both intimidating and endearing at the same time. He was like everyone's favorite grandpa from the movies.

He had a gruff voice and a sense of humor that was funny, but only in an old man way. His door was always open, yet he seemed unapproachable, not because he was short with you—in fact, it was the opposite. He was quick to take the time to chat with all of his cadets. But there was something about his stature and the ribbons stacked high on his chest that made a young seaman apprentice nervous about approaching him.

His Number Two was every bit his polar opposite. Whereas Commander Rawls was all business, Lieutenant Commander Telion was every bit the cocky fighter pilot that you saw on *Top Gun*. Whereas commander Rawls was long, tall, and lean, Lt. Commander Telion was short and barrel-chested. Whereas Commander Rawls was like a seasoned grandpa, Lt. Commander Telion was like the crazy uncle who never really grew up, and I loved him.

While I respected and revered Commander Rawls, Lt. Commander Telion was the type of man I wanted to be: quick, witty, and handsome. He also appealed to me because he was intellectual, but I still bet serious money he could whoop your ass in a heartbeat. I imagined him to be just like Maverick. Fun, flirty, and fearless. What teenage boy doesn't want to be that?

Rounding off the cadre was what every military unit needs: a stellar NCO. Enter Master Gunnery Sergeant Elliot. Similar to Lt. Commander Telion in build, he was short and thick. Every bit the image of the classic Marine bulldog. His voice had a bit of impediment to it . . . I don't know quite how to explain it. It wasn't a stutter as much as it was just a unique voice inflection. He had a close-shaved fade, a thick neck, and wide shoulders and back. If Rawls was the grandpa and Telion the uncle, Master Gunnery Elliot was the badass big brother with whom you did not fuck around.

In classic military function, the NCO served as the backbone of the program. Master Gunnery Sergeant Elliot did it all. He handled uniform issue and wear, the drill team, and any other teams we fielded for competition. He was also active in other areas of the school by helping to coach various sports teams. I didn't appreciate it as much as I should have at the time; that man gave his all, especially to a rural southern town that could be less than accommodating to an African American.

I really dove in deep with JROTC. I was active on the drill team, and even became the drill team commander. I participated in every event and worked in after-school programs. It was hands down the first place I felt like I belonged. I loved the uniform and lived for Wednesdays when we wore them to school. I also thought that the classes were interesting and fun. I loved studying the history of battles. Most importantly, for a young man of my limited confidence, it gave me the chance to build some. It afforded me leadership opportunities such as drill team commander, color guard captain, and ultimately, a senior leadership position within the organization. It also gave me my first taste of humility after I started thinking I was the shit.

I had my goal set on one thing for my senior year: to become the commander of the Nottoway High School's JROTC program. I knew I had my hands full, as there were two other students who were in the running as well. Our first test would be the first real one of my young life. We'd have to attend the coveted Leadership Academy, a week-long boot camp course that was run by the infamous Marine DIs. It would be, in my young eyes, a baptism by fire.

The biggest hurdle I had in my life at that time, in regard to advancement in NROTC, was what had haunted me my entire life, and still does to a certain extent: I was fat. I could blame it all on genetics (Lord knows I didn't get the pick of the litter), but most of it came from how poorly we ate at the house. My mother kept a can of grease and fat that she used to cook everything in. I mean, we fried everything. That, coupled with not having what one could call a strong workout routine, meant that I had titties, and no one in the early '90s was respecting any man with titties. Especially not Marine DIs.

We stepped off the bus and into my first experience ever in a "sleepaway camp." Let me tell you, it wasn't s'mores and kumbaya around the campfire. It was asses and elbows moving down the line as they hustled us off the busses with duffel bags in tow.

But looming large on the horizon was one thing that left me afraid: the physical training (PT) test. I knew headed in that it would be a huge mountain for me to climb, and sitting at the base of it, I damn near shook with fear. Now, I would learn later on that it was customary for you to start all military schools with a physical fitness test, a rite of passage to ensure that you have what it takes to even be there in the first place. It's pretty straightforward. You pass, you move on to the next evolution. You fail, and you go home. Luckily for me, NJROTC isn't quite that strict.

Because let me tell you, back then, my fat ass couldn't run. I came in next-to-last place, right behind my titties and just in front of my wounded pride. There I was, day one, a fat fucking failure. Not the way I had hoped to start off my week; and what's worse was that I now had to go talk to the camp commander, and everyone knows in the military (or even in the pretend military) you don't want 'em to know your name, especially not for failure.

Standing there, I felt three inches tall. The good news was that they wouldn't be sending me home. The bad news was I would get one more chance to pass the test, and that would be the day of graduation. I would either pass it or my folks would be picking up their loser son who didn't make the cut again. That amount of pressure would make Leadership Academy one of the longest weeks of my life.

While it was long and the stress was real for me, it was a shaping experience—as all stressors are and should be. It's a fundamental reason we must challenge our youth and stop sugarcoating shit for them. It in no way prepares them for the real world. During that week, I got a piece of advice and coaching that has stuck with me for the rest of my life, and it didn't come from any DI or class instructor. It came from a young man who lived in the inner city.

We were working to get our uniforms completed and ready for inspection when it became clear that I didn't know how to iron. This young man (his name eludes me now) asked me matter-of-factly why I didn't know how to iron. Dumbfounded, I looked at him and said, "My mother does it for me."

His reply wasn't meant harshly, but it still cut through to my soul. He looked me in the eyes and asked, "What happens when she's gone?"

This is part of the reason I don't claim to have the hardest life out there. This young man clearly carried pain from the fact he didn't have a mother at all, and here I was with two. His pain was different from mine because it was a different perspective on the same issue: problems with mothers and the lack of love you get from them. In his case, she was gone, and in my case, they might as well have been. However, it also shows that there remains truth to the old saying, "It could always be worse."

In his case, he had no mother to iron his clothes, and in my case, I had no one to protect me from my siblings. Those issues may seem worlds apart, but they are not. They both revolve around young men failing to have their needs met in regard to a family dynamic, and they both have lasting ramifications, good and bad. In order to paint that picture, I often share with folks a story that, ironically, was shared with me by Lt. CDR Telion.

I want you to imagine you are walking through the park when you come upon two women sitting on benches and crying. You're obviously concerned (you're not a dick, after all), so you ask the first woman, "Why are you crying?" She responds back to you with puffy eyes and swollen cheeks, "My husband lost his job. We used to send our son to football camp and our daughter to band camp. Now that we have no income, we can only afford to send one. How do I choose and how do I tell the other we can't afford to send them to camp?"

You then turn and walk to the other woman and ask her, "Why are you crying?" She looks up, withered and broken. It's clear from the lines in her face this isn't her first time crying. No, she has had miles of tears. As she looks up to you, her voice cracks and she says, "I am homeless and I can't afford to feed my children."

Now, I ask you, who has more of a right to cry in your eyes? The first or the second? Almost universally, everyone says it's the second. Why? Because we imagine that as the worst case scenario. Because we often use the mindset that "it could always be worse" to justify the toughen-it-up mentality. And, in truth, I ascribe to that notion as well. But with that said, it could always be better, too. It's with that understanding we improve our lives.

So, the answer is neither and both. Neither one has more of a right to cry, and both are entitled to crying. Because here's the reality of it: they both arrived at this moment in time based on the decisions they made (either poor choices or poor reactions to circumstances) and they both have to process the pain they feel, which, at that moment, is the worst thing they've ever faced. So, both have a right to cry.

That story and that young man telling me I needed to learn to iron my own shit were my first lessons in stoicism. Life is about perspective and how you apply it to your situation. As humans, we all fail this test from time to time. We lose sight of the fact that the thing is just the thing. What makes the thing hard on us is how we view it.

I would get my first chance to put this newfound worldview to the test that week at Leadership Academy. I had to remain focused on all the tasks that were assigned to us while knowing full well I could run that entire week and still not be allowed to graduate. The fear was very real that my parents would come to get me only to find out I hadn't made it. I could only imagine the loathing look Bobby would give me for wasting a Sunday of his with my failure.

Admittedly, for the most part, it wasn't that hard. They kept us busy from sunup to sundown. We were always in class, running "field training," doing drill and ceremony, or pulling guard duty at night. An occupied mind doesn't have much time to be upset—another lesson that I'd apply many times over later in life. But, as the week came to a close, even a busy mind wasn't enough to calm my anxiety.

The problem was that I was continuing to come up short on my mile time. We ran it a couple more times that week and I failed to hit the standard each time. I just kept thinking to myself, *How in the hell am I gonna do this?* But the final lesson that week would teach me is to never underestimate how much change you can make in a day, a week, and, later on down the road life would show me, a year.

The final day came, and I was one of only a handful of cadets looking to prove I deserved to graduate. Walking to the track, I realized I was at the biggest moment of my life so far. It seems silly when you think about it practically, the desire to have this silver chord to hang on your shoulder. It probably only cost a few dollars to make, but in my eyes, it was priceless. It represented doing something hard, something only a handful were selected to do. In my high school NJROTC world, it made you elite. And I had never been elite in my life.

So the very notion that I may fail at this was terrifying. Proof that I was what Bobby and his children had told me for years. That I was worthless. That I was lazy and trifling. That I didn't matter. All of it would be true, and a million "I told you so's" would be coming if I failed to cross that finish line in time.

As I stood at the starting blocks and waited to be released, my heart was already beating at sprint pace. I'm surprised I didn't pass out right then and there . . . and then it was time. On your mark, get set, go! And the last of the last, the slow kids, were off to the races. Now, I didn't know much, but I knew I couldn't be last in the slow group. Which actually gave me the advantage that I needed: a pacer.

Knowing that I needed to stay ahead of them never allowed me to slow down. It didn't give me a chance to catch my breath or take it easy. I knew I had to go, go, go or die trying. I ran as fast as my fat ass and bouncing titties could go. I was positive I would have an asthma attack on the spot and die. As I rounded the corner, I saw the finish line up ahead. There, screaming for me, was the command staff from our school. These men showed up early to cheer me on. It was the first time anyone ever showed up for me, and I am grateful that I was sweating so that they couldn't tell it was tears streaming down my face as I crossed the finish line and passed the mile test for the first time in my life.

With this hurdle out of the way, I was sure that I was destined to be the next commander of our unit back home. But, little did I know that my junior year would see me throw it all away and teach me I had a lot to learn about leadership and modesty.

Rolling into my junior year, I was given command of a full company. There was no doubt about it: the command position would come down to who was the best of the three individual leaders of our junior year. We had a full year to interview for the position and I was positive that I could make a strong enough case for me to come out on top, but I had some stiff competition.

Up first was Eric, who was basically the most perfect human on earth. The guy was captain of every academic team at the school. He played in the band (now that I think of it, I am pretty sure he was drum major). He was ripped to shreds and he was a black belt in karate. He was literally everything I was not, but I knew he was involved in too many things, and that would hinder his ability to take the reins of the unit.

Next up was Tameeka. She was a little badass. She was co-captain of the drill team with me, was on the girls' basketball team, and was Master Gunnery Sergeant's stepdaughter (I think at the time, he was just dating her mom). However, I thought that worked against her as it would have implied favoritism if she were selected. So, just like everything, we all had pros and we all had cons. Then I decided I'd just fuck it all up on my own.

It would happen, ironically enough, doing the very thing that caused me to join NJROTC in the first place: the trip to Puerto Rico. Everything up until the moment I screwed up had gone swimmingly, and then, in a moment where my mouth wrote a check my ass couldn't cash, I ensured I'd never be given the command my senior year because I clearly hadn't learned about respecting my superiors.

We had been asked to have a formation and a head count. I reported that all my people were accounted for when, in fact, two were still upstairs. Now, I didn't knowingly lie. I thought everyone was there. But I failed to double-check my triple-check. For people who don't believe that everything is your fault (which I didn't at the time), it's easy to pass that off on the knuckleheads who rolled out of formation without letting anyone know. But I was in charge, and I didn't have full accountability of my people, and losing track of high school kids outside of the continental United States is actually a pretty big deal.

Standing there in formation in front of the entire unit, Master

Gunnery Sergeant Elliot let me know how big of a deal that is. As a grown man now looking back, he was 100 percent in the right to do so. But my fragile little ego couldn't handle it and I shot off at my mouth to him. I was both loud and disrespectful. My mouth moved before my brain, and right there, on the spot, I was relieved of command.

I was beyond humiliated. I looked so stupid in front of everyone. I had just ruined the dream trip of my lifetime and was now on the verge of losing all the hard work I had put in for the past two years. I was sent back to the barracks to contemplate my actions. Sitting there alone, I knew I had messed up. If there was one respectable trait I already had at the time, it was an ability to admit that I was wrong after I cooled down. I didn't make any excuses and I apologized to Master Gunnery Sergeant Elliot.

I was reinstated as company commander and actually finished out the year in solid fashion, even winning some awards. However, when the list came out for the chain of command (COC) the next year, I came up short and was given the battalion XO position. Tameeka would serve as the Battalion Commander. After the positions were assigned, I was to stay in the office. There, Master Gunnery Sergeant Elliot told me what I had assumed all along: that my actions on our trip had effectively cost me the Battalion Commander slot; they couldn't give me that honor after I had made a mistake that bad. It was the first time that I really understood that actions have consequences and "sorry" doesn't always cut it.

As I was starting to gain traction with NJROTC, I happened to meet my first long-term girlfriend. Robin attended a private school in the next county over, but lived within a relatively short drive from me. My biological father had actually set up some type of fund that paid me a few thousand dollars when I turned sixteen. I took that money and did what any self-respecting fifteen-year-old boy would do: I bought a car.

My first car was a used Ford Thunderbird. It was white with red interior. And it was my ticket to freedom. During my short journeys along the ROAD, I met Robin, and in what would become the story of my life with women, I would fall hard and fast. Little did I know at the time, but Robin would actually end up charting the course my life would follow.

Robin's family was everything my family wasn't. Namely, an actual family. Her mother and father were extremely loving and generous people. I will always have a strong love for "Momma Bolick." She was a heavyset woman with curly black hair and a belly laugh that you felt in your soul. Her body often looked as if it were in constant physical discomfort and she had a bit of a waddle to her walk, but man, that woman loved her friends and family.

She was extremely involved in her kids' lives, which was a stark contrast to my parents. She worked at the private school her kids attended, and whether she was there or at home, she was certainly doing what she did best of all: being a mom.

Robin's father was a man of shorter stature, with a bald head and a full beard. He was not quite a quiet man, but he wasn't boisterous either. He simply had fits where he'd seem to come alive and make himself and everyone else laugh. Then, almost as fast, he'd retreat back into himself and go silent again, surveying the room. Every day, he drove an hour-plus up the road to work at the Phillip Morris, where he repaired equipment on the factory floor. Despite his short stature, something about the man was intimidating to me, and I was always respectful around him.

Rounding out the family was Robin's little brother, Luke, and as far as little brothers go, he was amazing. He was his father's boy through and through, and it was clear that he wanted to impress him. He was a little redneck and he had acquired his father's love for tinkering on things. He had a dry, quick wit and was always ready to deliver another joke. Unlike the rest of his family, he was long, lean, and lanky with a square jaw line and thick brown hair.

Robin was the way I like my women: thick as fuck. I am sorry, but I am just not a fan of little skinny-ass girls. It makes me a bit of a hypocrite because I have no ass at all, but I cannot date an assless woman. I need all the junk in the trunk, and I need the trunk too. She had long brown hair and thin lips. We fell in friendship and then in love. Robin and I did everything together, spent every waking moment together, and much to my surprise, her parents didn't really try to stop it. Matter of fact, I all but moved in with them.

Their world was foreign to me. One where parents not only loved their children, they did everything they could to be an active part of their lives. This wasn't just at their house, but it permeated the entire school that they attended. All of the kids at the Fuqua School had it made in the shade as far I could see. While my family wasn't poor, per se, the kids at Fuqua were on another level from me by far.

The best way to describe it is, I felt like Jed Clampett going to Beverly Hills when I was up there. All the kids had new cars and nice clothes. They all seemed to be beautiful people, completely happy with their existence. Now, at the time, it never occurred to me that they might have troubles of their own at home, and I am sure some did, but the fact remains that these kids had the life I wish I'd had.

Longing for that life was both an intoxicating lure and an isolating force field at the same time. It made me want to be around them, and at the same time, it reminded me that I would never be "one of them." They were a different class of people, and just like a lowly peasant, I had to show up and see what the royalty would do next. I stopped hanging around my school almost entirely and would spend my afternoons driving the half hour to forty-five minutes north to be a fly on the wall of the beautiful people.

While I never told the Bolicks my life story—not the adoption, molestation, or the fact that my family was a redneck crime cartel—I think they must have sensed something was off with me. In response, instead of being wary or mistrustful, they were always welcoming and accommodating to me. I was always allowed to spend the night and come to family functions, which meant the world to me.

Robin and I continued to date in high school. While Robin was a straight-A student, I was far from the same. Matter of fact, I was barely getting by. I often tried to get better at studying, but I had zero understanding of *how* to study. I had no one to mentor me. No one in my family had graduated or even come close to doing well in school themselves, so they were in no shape to be the ones to help, and that was even if they wanted to . . . which they didn't.

It would always go the same way: I would say I was committed to getting better grades, and then as soon as I'd hit a concept I didn't understand, I'd fold like a lawn chair. I would turn assignments in late or not at all. I wanted to improve but lacked the confidence to believe that I actually could on my own merits. So, class after class, I failed. I struggled most in math, science, and foreign languages, but I would do pretty well in things like history, social studies, and English.

It wasn't that I was dumb; I just had absolutely zero confidence in myself. In fact, that would haunt me for years to come. That negative mindset dominated my life until my mid-thirties and if I am honest, still affects me to this day.

My eyes were finally opened about halfway through the first semester of my senior year. The counselor pulled me into her office and told me that it was very likely that I wouldn't graduate that year, and would need to, at best, go to summer school, and at worst, fail and need to repeat the twelfth grade. The thought of being stuck in school one more full year, of being stuck at my parents' house one more year, was more than I could stand.

With that wake-up call, I did everything I could to muster enough to pass the classes that I needed to graduate. I didn't kill it. I wasn't even sure I'd pull it off till literally the last minute. But, with everything on the line, it was the first time I proved to myself that if I could put my mind to something, I could get it done. I'll never forget my counselor telling me that I had pulled off the impossible, and scored high enough to graduate. So, with that diploma in hand, it was time to make my move and get the fuck out of Dodge.

Looking back on my childhood, I can't help but wonder what bad things took place in that farmhouse that I don't know about. What evil resided there, and who was the keeper of the secrets and the pain? You cannot tell me that all those kids went bad for no reason. That half of 'em ran away routinely just for shits and giggles. That three out of five (that I know for fact) were molesters. That all of them used and sold drugs. That all of them would spend time in jail, albeit less than they should have. None of that happened "just because."

I didn't think about all of this till much later in life. I've tried to unravel this mystery and I still have no answers. Who could have been the one to start it? We never had folks over to the house—like, ever. No uncles or aunts. No friends came over and hung out. We rarely entertained guests. Why was that? Was it because Bobby and Sadie had a dark secret?

But that idea is challenged in my mind because, if they were the perpetrators against their kids, then why didn't they do that to me? They did a lot of things, but sexually assaulting me wasn't one of them. But somebody, somewhere, had to start the cycle. A cycle that ruined their lives. A cycle that still has lasting effects today.

Furthermore, Debbie's and Sadie's actions have caused me to tolerate things from women that I shouldn't have. The molestation I experienced still affects me. I hate to give my kids baths. I don't want my kids to see me naked; which, as a single dad, becomes next to impossible because I had to shower or go to the bathroom when my kids were young and didn't recognize boundaries well.

All of those things together during my upbringing caused me to eat like shit, get fat, and feel stupid, which led me to have zero self-confidence. I was a young man getting ready to step out on my own, and in no way, shape, or form was I prepared to face it. I didn't have strong social skills, I knew nothing of finance, and I was weak, overweight, and out of shape. The only thing that prepared me at all for the storms to come was all the storms I had faced already. The sad part about it is, I don't know if they actually prepared me, or ensured I'd eventually crumble in the face of one down the road.

Chapter Six

A Military Man

"No man is a man until he has been a soldier."
—Louis de Bernières

I literally said this sentence verbatim: "I ain't joining the Army, I ain't joining the infantry, and I ain't jumping out of no fucking plane." Damn if I didn't do all three for a woman. I would repeat the "for a woman" mistake over and over throughout my life. But hey, we already established that I was a slow learner.

High school was coming to an end and I still had no plan on what I was going to do afterward. The only thing I was positive of was that my options were extremely limited. As you can easily have guessed by now, I wanted nothing to do with the family logging business, which Bobby chalked up to me just being a lazy piece of shit. The only other two worthwhile jobs in the town were to get on with either the railroad or power company, both of which were competitive as hell and required some level of basic mechanic skills that I didn't possess. So, that only left gas station attendant, farmhand, or Walmart, none of which sounded appealing to me.

The other major drawback was that college wasn't an option

either. Bobby and Sadie weren't going to pay for it—not even community college—and with the grades I had, community college was the only option. Hell, it was even doubtful if they would take me. With no colleges beating down my door in search of a fat dumbass, no jobs to do in town, and with my girlfriend leaving me to go to college in the Shenandoah Valley, I was fresh out of ideas, save one: the military.

Enter SSG. Festman Pullatosi. In the interest of fairness, I have zero clue if that's how you spell his name, but let me tell you, that guy gave me my first taste of how the Army will sodomize you with its big green weenie and lie about it. He came into my life and sold me more bullshit than a 3:00 a.m. infomercial. I mean, the OxiClean guy didn't have shit on Pullatosi.

I can't say I necessarily blame him, though. When a chunky little fucker walks into your office and says that his list of priorities begins with, "I need to be close to my girlfriend who's going to college," you know you got a sucker on the line. So, he sat me down and started telling me all about my amazing future in this man's army. Which, oddly enough, none were the job he had chosen for himself.

Now, I never went to recruiter school, but I am assuming they have quotas for each military occupational specialty (MOS), and I must have come in on infantry day, 'cause that son of a bitch sold the shit out of infantry. The only thing he compared it to was fueling specialist, and who wants to be a gas station attendant in the army? Sorry if that offends you fueling specialists out there, but for real, why do you want to do that?

With the options of only glorified gas pumper or steely-eyed death-dealer laid out before me, death-dealer was an easy choice. Now, with infantry selected, Pullatosi decided that it was time to sell me the upgraded vibrator but leave off the lube. I mean, who wants it to slide in easy? Am I right, or am I right?

Now, remember how I said my list of priorities began with "be next to my girlfriend," who was going to Shenandoah University? Well, according to him, the only base close to that college was Ft. Bragg. Which meant I just *had* to be Airborne to be close to her. Besides, I was "gonna look soooooo good in a maroon beret." In hindsight, that was probably the only truthful thing he said to me. Everything after that was a crock of shit, because the second base I'd get stationed at was forty-eight minutes away, compared to Bragg's five hours and eighteen minutes.

But wait, there's more! Remember how I told you my "requirement" was that I had to be close to my girlfriend? Well, he hit me with that 11X option, which, unbeknownst to me at the time, meant I was "needs of the fucking army." I could have literally been selected to be anything. I could have been chosen to be 11B (Eleven Bravo, main land combat force), 11C (Eleven Charlie, indirect fire infantry), or 11M (Eleven Mike, fighting vehicle infantry, which has since been absorbed into another group). I could have gone to Ft. Bragg, Alaska, or Italy. I wouldn't find out until I arrived at Hell on earth: 30th AG (where you go to wait to be processed into basic training).

So, I bought his sales pitch hook, line, and sinker. I even got a cool little black-and-yellow shirt with paratroopers jumping out of a plane to hopefully attract more suckers. I mean, after all, birds of a feather flock together. Of course, I didn't see it that way. I thought I was legit gonna be a badass—Hell, I thought I already was one, right? I hadn't done shit, but clearly I had already gotten the t-shirt, and if I remember correctly, that was one-third of the "been there, done that" requirement. I enlisted in my senior year of high school and selected to leave at the end of summer.

Now that I had secured my future in this man's army, I was poised to make my next move: secure my bride. I had been dating Robin for well over a year by this point, and to me it only made sense that we would be wed. I mean, I was gonna have Basic Allowance for

Housing, after all. Which was big-money balling in my eyes. So, with that in mind, I decided I would ask for her hand in marriage.

Well, that went over about as well as a wet fart. Her dad didn't tell me so much as to fuck off, but it was clear (in a very fatherly way) that he wasn't going to give me his blessing. It's like he was a smart, middle-aged man who knew a thing or two because he'd seen a thing or two. I am sure that he knew what I know now: getting married is hard as shit to begin with. No need to make forever even longer and more difficult to attain by getting married before your brain is even fully developed. That, and let's just say you are a fundamentally different person at thirty-five than you were at eighteen, or at least you better damn well hope you are.

So, after being effectively shot down in her backyard, we decided that we'd just continue to date while she was in college, and then, of course, get married afterwards. I would spend the rest of the school year and that summer just trying to have as much fun as I could. Having fun as a teenager in a small town meant driving in circles up and down the main street, waving at the same folks over and over, until you found a parking lot with those same folks to post up. For us, we always stopped in the McDonald's parking lot, 'cause food. Or, we headed over to True Value because it was big and wide open.

I am sure that doesn't sound all that exciting, but when you're growing up in Small Town, USA, you live for it. It's intoxicating because it feels like freedom. High school parking lot hangouts are a point in life where you have some of the benefits of adulthood with very few of the drawbacks. That summer didn't do anything to prepare me for what lay ahead, but it did finally give me freedom from the hell of growing up. And, for a brief moment in time, all was right in the world and the future seemed bright.

As the summer wound down to a close before my ship date, a familiar adversary was rearing its ugly head again: my weight. I was too heavy to send off, but I came up with a good idea on how to get past it. I wasn't to be allowed to eat any food at MEPS (Military Entry Processing Station), and the night before weigh-in, I downed an entire bottle of laxative. I shit my ever-lovin' brains out, but I made weight and was "clear to close," as they say in the real estate business. I was gonna become a soldier.

I had one last thing to do before I shipped off: say goodbye to Bobby and Sadie. Weirdly, I don't really remember my goodbye with Sadie. Writing this, I sat here looking at the cursor blink for what felt like eons, and not one single memory of goodbye came up. In contrast, my final goodbye to Bobby is etched in my brain.

He was down at the shop, working underneath a piece of equipment. It was a hot August day and the sun beat down on us. I'd like to pretend that was the reason he didn't come out from under the truck as I stood there, nervously kicking the dirt. My hands were in my pockets as I squinted in the dog-day heat and prepared to tell him I was leaving.

Bobby had said no kind words to me. Never told me he loved me, and in truth, he probably didn't. Or maybe he did. Maybe he was just the strong, silent type. I don't know. All I can tell you is I never felt loved or wanted, and what I desired was for him to come out from underneath the truck and talk to his youngest son—his last son, the only one who didn't fuck up and break the law—and say, "Good luck, son," or, "I am proud of you."

But, as I stood there and told him I was leaving, I heard him grunt out an, "Okay," and that was it. I stood there for a few moments longer to see if perhaps he'd just gotten confounded by a problem under the truck, but it was to no avail. After a few moments of listening to the silence being broken only by the occasional wrenching, hammering, or mumbling under his breath, I turned and made the quarter-mile walk from the barn back to the house, got in my car, and headed off to my new future in the Army.

I spent that night in a hotel for the first time in my young life.

We were instructed not to drink at all and to not stay up late, as we had an early day the next day. I realized then that I was one of the few people going into the military who followed the rules (I did exactly what I was told, meanwhile everyone else was drinking and partying), which seemed odd to me because, well, in the military you're expected to follow the rules to a tee.

The next morning, I was grateful that I did, as we were up at the asscrack of dawn and headed off to MEPS to get our orders. They did some final checks, gave us our packets, and took us to the airport. I'd be flying into Atlanta—you know, where the playas play—as my first stop on my way to good ol' Sand Hill, the home of the infantry.

We waited around for hours for everyone's flight to get in, and by midnight, we were ready to head out and leave the airport. From Atlanta to Fort Benning took roughly an hour and a half. With the reality starting to take hold that we were almost at basic training, the ride was relatively quiet. I am sure most, if not all, young men that have ridden in those seats, or seats like them, took the time to contemplate if they'd made the right choice with their lives. After all, you are about to turn over all sovereignty in your life to a machine that is designed to do one thing: use you to kill (or support the killing of other people your age from adversary countries). It's the ultimate team game.

We pulled through the gates up Ft. Benning, passing the "Home of the Infantry" sign, and made our way to 30th AG. It was between 0200 and 0300 in the morning and I was looking forward to getting some sleep. I fully expected us to be loaded off the bus and shown to our bunks for some rack and start fresh the next day. Clearly, at that stage in my life, I was a dumb shit, 'cause absolutely none of that happened.

Matter of fact, we were instantly told that sleep was not on the schedule. We were hurried off the bus sternly, but not shark-attack style. They were saving that for the real day one. We were ushered inside and promptly taken to get chow. I remember my very first meal in the Army plain as day: cold steak and fried shrimp.

After we powered that down, we were moved into a room where we were required to ditch any contraband we had brought with us, and from there, we began the process that the military fucks up more than any other entity on the planet: paperwork. Now, I lead with me talking shit about the Army's ability to do paperwork correctly, but in truth, I was the first person to screw up my own.

Sitting in that seat after being up for well over twenty hours with a belly full of rubbery steak and cold fried shrimp, I began to get sleepy. So it should come as no surprise that I missed some part of the formal instruction on how to fill out the paperwork. To this day, I could have sworn that drill told us we should fill out every single block when putting our names down. However, right after I had finished doing just that, some unlucky-ass private started getting his ass absolutely reamed for doing the same thing. As I listened to them lay into him, I realized my fate was sealed and feebly began raising my hand to alert them to my incompetence as a human being.

I am assuming they felt a disturbance in the force because my hand wasn't even above shoulder level when they picked up on it and eagerly asked, "What the fuck now, Private?"

I sheepishly replied, "I filled out every block without skipping a space, Drill Sergeant." Welp, fuck me, 'cause that was all they needed to hear to know without a doubt that Private Farrar was indeed a dumb fatass in need of their constant attention and supervision. In a world where most recommend you stay under the radar, popping up like a star cluster is a sure way to guarantee it's gonna be a long thirteen weeks. Failing the PT and fat test the next day ensured it was gonna be much longer.

Now, forty-one-year-old Danny looking back on nineteen-year-old Danny fills me with disgust, 'cause I see the world now the way my drill sergeants saw it back then. "What the fuck did you do all summer, Private?! You're fat as fuck and you're out of shape. It wasn't like boot camp snuck up on you! You signed up for this shit a year ago and you did absolutely nothing to un-fuck yourself before you got here, Private. Not only does that show a complete disregard for the seriousness of this profession of arms, it fucks the American taxpayer, who now has to feed and clothe your worthless ass while we try and get you in some semblance of shape to be able to ship you down range. You, Private, are worthless as fuck!"

Before I get any further, for those of you who were never in the military, "down range" is some mythical place you never make it to. I have been trying to get down range from day one, and every time you get to where you thought down range was, they tell you, "Just wait till you get down range."

The only thing I knew at the time, however, was that I wasn't going any-fucking-where after I failed the PT test. I was moved to the fat-boy platoon and instantly put on remedial PT and a reduced diet. The army back then wasn't all that concerned with asking the question, "What is the best way to get a private to lose weight?" so much as they were "What's the fastest way to get a private to lose weight?" The answer to that is, unequivocally, "PT his dick in the dirt and hardly feed him shit while doing it." On top of that, back then, the army had this insane anger against starches. You could get as much dessert as you wanted (well, not me, I was fat) but Lord have mercy, you better never stack rice and mashed potatoes on the same plate.

I have yet to meet anyone who was ever there that enjoyed 30th AG. As far as I am concerned, it is Hell on earth. Time stands still. There is literally nothing to do and no forward action. There is no benefit of being there. Matter of fact, the only purpose of 30th is to get the hell out of there. You could most aptly compare it to purgatory—a temporary purification of your most superficial civilian qualities before you head down range to be shaped into a soldier.

What made it worse is that, for fat kids, you seemed stuck in limbo as you watched others leave one way or the other. Either shipping off down range or getting chaptered out for medical or mental reasons. One guy I'll never forget is "Bubbles." Back then, the military didn't give a shit about the mental health of soldiers—oh, who am I kidding? That's still the case now.

Well, they found this one private unconscious in the bathroom and covered with laundry detergent. Sitting in a puddle on his chest was his suicide note. Evidently, this private had decided that the Army was not for him and he was ready to go back home. His answer? Drink his laundry detergent in a desperate attempt to get the hell out, one way or the other. How they revived him and got the chemicals out of his stomach, I have no idea, but he survived. He was an odd kid, and looking back now, it's sad that no one took him seriously. Who knows if he was for real or simply trying to outsmart the system.

What I can tell you is how that system handled this indiscretion. They publicly shamed him and made everyone in his peer group hate him. They gave him the nickname Bubbles. Took his belt and shoelaces and created a "suicide watch" guard duty. This would be a recurring theme throughout the process anytime someone attempted to take their own life. It was another full guard shift (no clue why it needed to be) that someone had to be up for. There was fire guard, suicide guard, someone-left-their-footlocker-unlocked guard, and any other guard they could come up with.

The end result was you stayed up all night, and so, as you can imagine, no one in the platoon cared for anyone who added another hour of guard duty. The kid was mocked relentlessly. I can't help but have mixed emotions about it. On one hand, I do understand the mentality as it existed: the need to make sure that only the hardest could make it through. But on the other hand, I am challenged by the belief that if our job was to be the protector of the weak, we failed that guy pretty bad.

Bubbles got off lucky, all in all. He got his chapter and was headed home. We heard of another soldier who didn't fare so well. One of the things they didn't let you do back in my day was get on the phone. You got a phone call when you got there to let someone back home know you had made it safely, and from there, you got one call per week, and only for a handful of minutes. The more rebellious of the recruits would sneak out and call home. Which seemed silly to me because the phones were in the open and they always got caught.

At the time, I didn't understand why they didn't let us call home more often. I thought it was to toughen us up at first, but later on, I figured out the real reason: Jody. That motherfucker became the representation of any guy that rides in and lets your girl ride him while you're gone. Story goes that, evidently, when this one private called home, Jody picked up the phone. This was back before everyone had cell phones, so folks still answered other people's phones. Welp, that was all it took for that poor fellow. The love of his life broke his heart and he went to the top of the building and jumped off the roof. And so, no one got to call home.

I believe far more young men and women than we realize enter service with a lot of baggage and trauma that never gets addressed. In many cases (such as mine), service just adds on to it.

I finally passed the PT test and body measurement, and my trip down range was set. Finally, it was time to get this show on the road. They lined us all up in formation inside one of our bays. We had two duffel bags packed full of shit, and on the end of one we were instructed to secure our detergent by running our lanyard through it. We were then told to "take seats" and wait for our escorts to arrive.

We waited there for what seemed like forever when in walked

in an almost-comical display of disparity: two drill sergeants, one a large hulking figure and another more akin to Napoleon Bonaparte—stubby would be the best way to describe him. They didn't explode on us like I expected; they simply told us to gather our belongings and head over to the "cattle trucks."

These things were actual cattle trailers that had been retrofitted to carry privates anywhere they needed to go. Inside them were benches to stand on and metal piping to hold on to. They were graffitied with the names of those who came before us and sayings like "thirty-two days and a wake-up." A "wake-up" refers to the last day you will be a certain location (generally while deployed). So, if a service member is getting ready for bed on a Sunday, and flying out on a Friday, he'll say "four days and a wake-up." This enlightening bit of graffiti was warning us how long we'd be there, minimum. Taking all that in caused us to load the trailers much slower than was desired, and it was at that moment that we were reminded to get our asses in gear so that we could get on the road.

Crammed in there like sardines in a can, we shifted uncomfortably under the weight while the truck bumped us down the road. We drove around for at least half an hour to get to our final destination. I say drove around 'cause a week later when we went on a run, our training barracks were only a mile away from 30th AG. To this day, I don't know if they drove around to kill time, up the nerve factor, of if they just weren't totally ready for us when we got scooped up.

Either way, that truck finally came to a stop, and based on all the moving and grunting you could hear, you would have thought we were making a porno back there. Everyone struggled under the weight of their gear and limited ability to move and shift in such crammed corners. Then, as if God himself said, "Let there be light," the doors to the cattle truck opened up and all hell broke loose.

The first Drill Sergeant stuck his head inside and screamed, "GET THE FUCK OFF MY TRUCK RIGHT NOW!!" Scared absolutely shitless, everyone tried to hit the door at the exact same time. It was like watching a monkey fuck a football. We were just trying to fit something through a hole much smaller than what its original parameters were.

As we fell out the side of that damn thing like Ace Ventura falling out a rhino's ass, the rest of the hungry Drill Sergeant pack was waiting for us in what was referred to as a "shark attack." The truth is, I don't know if the military does 'em anymore, 'cause, well, we're pussies, but I digress. Anyway, as I finally stepped outside the truck, I met a man whose hate for me would eclipse all who had come before him, and I do believe all those who came after.

Drill Sergeant Eskamia was the meanest dickhead son of bitch I ever met in my life. The only thing that surpassed his hatred for me was my hatred for him. I still hate that bastard. When his eyes locked on me, I musta reminded him of someone who fucked his wife, because from that moment on, I was his special project. "Oh my God! What have we got here?! A fat body! One, tubby, tubby . . . two, tubby, tubby." He glued himself to my hips and didn't leave my side for the rest of basic training.

The shark attack commenced and we began to get our assess smoked—which means PT'd half to death. As it was broiling with the sun and humidity and they didn't want us to become heat casualties, they would make us drink all the water in our canteens and then hold them over our heads. If one dripped, you had to fill it up and run it all over again. That led to a lot of folks puking. Kinda defeats the goal of hydration, if you ask me.

On top of this, everyone then had to put their duffle bags over their heads and hold 'em there. Well, it took next to no time for everyone's detergent to rupture, which meant everyone was covered with water, sand, puke, and detergent. Looks like old Bubbles was ahead of the game after all.

Hands down, my favorite part of basic was all the guys I met from across the U.S. and beyond. The very first non-Southern accent I ever heard was from this short but insanely muscular "Southie" kid from Boston. He was telling a story and it sounded like, "So we grabbed our cah-kees jumped in the cah and drove to the bah."

I was like, "What the fuck did you just say?"

Which he, in turn, interpreted as sounding like the dueling banjos from *Deliverance*.

But he wasn't alone; we had every stereotype you see in the movies and then some. We had the big Texan, the street-smart New York kid, an old guy, and this one big, mean-ass redneck from the Midwest. One of the most fascinating guys we had was a Native American kid who, at first sight, didn't look like much, but he may have been the most badass dude in the bunch.

He was a heavyset guy and flabby. He had thick scars on his forearms that he said came from a ritual he did back home where they had to pick up a steaming hot pot of water and hold it between their forearms while it seared the flesh. I typically would have called bullshit, but he didn't flinch when he told us about it, and the scars were located on the exact same spot of both arms.

The dude didn't talk much. He was kind of like Billy from the movie *Predator*. He didn't say much, but when he spoke, you listened. And the guy could run like the wind. Seeing him go was kind of like a bee in flight: neither looks like they have the tools required to get their fat little body going, and yet bees fly and that dude lapped everyone.

We soon fell into a routine, which ran pretty much the same every day: wake up, PT, chow, train, chow, train, chow, clean, bedtime/guard rotation. Of course, sprinkled throughout was lots of getting smoked and reciting out loud any number of required weapons nomenclature or unit manifesto that we'd be instructed to learn. For me, our chow hall chant, which must be said perfectly in order to be permitted to enter the chow hall, is still seared into my brain.

> *Delta Dragons,*
> *Men are we.*
> *Airborne Ranger.*
> *Infantry.*
> *We breathe fire.*
> *We breathe gas.*
> *Delta Dragons, we kick that ass.*

Then, when the nice lunch lady who called you "Suga'" and "Baby" was satisfied with your demonstrated manhood, your platoon was permitted to begin the process of moving through the chow hall for your few minutes of food.

Now, as I had already mentioned before, I was fat, and Drill Sergeant Eskamia knew I was fat. And that, my friends, just didn't set well with him. Which I did find hypocritical 'cause his two little rugrats were husky, fat little bastards themselves. Well, I made the mistake of thinking that I could get potato salad, which turned out to be the most offensive thing I could have done to him.

"What the fuck do we have here, Private Ferrari?" The dickhead always called me that.

"Nothing, Drill Sergeant, just getting something to eat," I replied.

"Don't you know you're too fat for mayonnaise, Private?"

Now, I am not sure when or where it happened, but somewhere along the line, my nuts dropped and I started thinking I should start talking up for myself. So I fired back, "No, Drill Sergeant, I thought I was just pleasantly plump." That resulted in me putting my potato salad on someone else's plate and proceeding to get my ass smoked to death right there in the chow hall, but it was well worth the pools of sweat on the floor and a missed meal to have stood up for myself for a change.

As much as I hated that motherfucker, I must admit that he had some pretty damn good lines while we were in basic training. Some of his best ones I'll remember on my death bed:

"Private, you better go to church on Sunday because I am gonna smoke the Jesus out of you."

"Men, there are three types of -ea in the world. Diarrhea, which most of you have had, gonorrhea, which some of you will get, and Korea, where all of you will go!"

"That's all you think about, Ferrari: eating and sleeping."

Ferrari was his little petname for me, as it was both mocking and sounded similar enough to my actual last name. If the hero of every story needs a level boss to beat, Drill Sergeant Eskamia was mine. He zeroed in on me like a heat-seeking missile and stayed locked on me all the way to the end. He never wasted a good chance to fuck with me or dick me over. Whenever and wherever he could, he applied max punishments or restrictions to me.

For instance, this one private and I had gotten into it and came to blows. Now, fighting in an infantry unit isn't all that unusual. I mean, after all, these are the guys who signed up to shoot motherfuckers in the face. You'd think it would not only be expected, but actively encouraged. It's not like you sign up the least-aggressive folks on the planet to do that.

Well, this kid wouldn't stop fucking with me and so we got into it. What started off as jaw-jacking back and forth got heated pretty quickly. Before you knew, it we were being separated by the rest of the platoon and the ruckus caught the attention of good ol' Eskamia. Then this guy acted like I was some major crime boss who manipulated the platoon into siding with me in pointing out that this fucker started it. Now, as you have probably gathered by this point in the book, if I screw up, I'll tell you. I didn't start it with this kid.

Regardless of the facts, Eskamia decided to fuck us both over.

We had mid-cycle family break coming up. During this time, your family can come in, and if you don't have family, you got to go to the PX and get some pogey bait or some shit. Nope, not me. I got tasked with KP duty for the entire weekend. Zero break, all because I got tired of taking someone's shit. So much for standing up for the little guy.

At the end of basic, you have final FTX (Field Training Exercise), which culminates with your warrior breakfast and the issuing of your crossed rifles, signifying you are now part of the infantry. It's meant to be the most badass moment of your young life. I would remember it for the rest of my life, but at that moment, I didn't feel like a badass at all.

The final evolution is "a movement to daylight." Now, according to legend among privates, it's anywhere from a 25–50-mile road march with standard equipment load through the night. If I had to take an honest stab at it, I'd say it's probably more along the lines of 12–15 miles, max. Either way you look at it, it sucks because it's probably the longest you have walked up to that moment.

Well, we get loaded up and began the process of heading out. We were all nervous about the march but excited that, come sunrise, we would finally be infantrymen. The march was going all well and good until around midnight—that's when the first break happened.

Now, I don't mean that was the first time we took a break, but rather, when the first bone broke in my foot. I would break three metatarsals in total. It shouldn't have come as much a surprise to me because I had dealt with stress fractures around the mid-point of basic training and had to walk around in what was referred to back then as a "Japanese jump boot." I have no clue why they called it that, but I am sure it wasn't for flattering reasons.

So, as that first bone broke, I knew I was in for a long night. I was lucky that I had one Drill Sergeant (whose name escapes me now) who was motivating and encouraging to me. I was starting to limp and having difficulty keeping up, but I was determined to keep pace. Then the second bone broke. It was about that time that Dickhead of the Year popped up to add insult to injury.

"What the fuck is wrong with you, Private?"

"Well," I said in labored breaths as I limped along, "something is wrong with my foot, Drill Sergeant."

With a grunt of his own, he bellowed back, "Only thing wrong with you is you have a little heart disease, Ferrari." And with that, he took his grumpy, unmotivating ass on up the formation.

Luckily for me, I had the good drill with me too. I was in misery and was limping pretty bad, but I was able to keep up close enough to the formation to not be considered a dropout, which meant I was still in the running to complete the prerequisite to graduate.

I saw the sun coming up over the trees and did what no one should ever do: I thought I had made it. It was at that very moment, where I had started to feel some sense of relief knowing that the worst was behind me, then my left ruck sack strap broke. So there I was, with broken bones in my right foot and a broken rucksack strap on my left side. I was the most pathetic steely-eyed killer you'd ever seen.

My limp made the one-strapped ruck slap against my back awkwardly and violently. Every time I stepped, it would swing out and the snap back, crashing into my shoulder blades. All of this made me lurch forward in an awkward and gangly manner. With old camo paint and dirt on my face streaked by sweat, and shuffling with a forward gangster lean, I am sure that I looked like I was a "walker" from The Walking Dead.

I may have been a sad sight to see as I came hobbling across the finish line, but I was filled with pride because I hadn't quit on myself, and no one could take that from me. I had pushed through pain and self-doubt to make it through to the other side. I am reminded that basic was where I first learned the lesson of "quit tomorrow," and more importantly, where I learned to apply it.

As the sun rose and our final march came to an end, a great sense of relief, pride, and accomplishment came over all the young men there. As we stood in formation and were awarded those prized crossed riffles, we realized we were part of a unique warrior brotherhood. So many people (even some in the military) seek to poke fun at me and my fellow ground pounders. They have classic names like "bullet catchers" and "dumb grunts." Be that as it may, as we stood around eating our "warriors' breakfast" of steak and eggs (because we were fucking *men*, and that's what men eat), we realized that we had one leg up on all our fellow service members. We'd never say, "I was basically infantry," when trying to impress someone else, because we were infantry, the queen of battle, the tip of the spear. I am the infantry, follow me!

I once read the following from a blogger named Knottie, who was the mother of a son KIA in Iraq. I think it sums up how we feel as infantrymen quite succinctly.

Infantrymen have a pride and arrogance that most Americans don't understand and don't like. Even soldiers who aren't infantrymen don't understand. The pride doesn't exist because we have a job that's physically impressive. It certainly doesn't exist because it takes a higher level of intelligence to perform our duties. It's sad and I hate to admit it, but any college student or high school grad can physically do what we do. It's not THAT demanding and doesn't take a physical anomaly. Nobody will ever be able to compare us to professional athletes or fitness models. And it doesn't take a very high IQ to read off serial numbers, pack bags according to a packing list, or know that incoming bullets have the right of way.

The pride of the infantryman comes not from knowing that he's doing a job that others can't, but that he's doing a job that others simply won't. Many infantrymen haven't seen a lot of combat. While that may sound ideal to the civilian or non-infantry soldier, it pains the grunt. We signed up to spit in the face of danger. To walk the line between life and death and live to do it again—or not. To come to terms with our own mortality and let others try to take our life instead of yours. We have raised our hands and said, "Take me, America. I am willing to kill for you. I am willing to sacrifice my limbs for you. I will come back to America scarred and disfigured for you. I will be the first to die for you."

That's why the infantryman carries himself with pride and arrogance. He's aware that America has lost respect for him. To many he's a bloodthirsty animal. To others he's too uneducated and stupid to get a regular job or go to college. Only he knows the truth. While there are few in America who claim to have respect for him, the infantryman returns from war with less fanfare than a first-down in a high school football game. Yes, people hang up their "Support Our Troops" ribbons and on occasion thank us for our service. But in their eyes the infantryman can detect pity and shame; not respect. Consider this: How excited would you be to meet the average infantryman? Now compare that with how excited you'd be to meet a famous actor or professional sports player and you will find that you, too, are guilty of placing the wrong people on a pedestal. You wouldn't be able to tell me how many soldiers died in the war last month, but you'd damn sure be able to tell me if one of the actors from Twilight died.

Yet the infantryman doesn't complain about that. He continues to do his job; to volunteer his life for you, all while being paid less in four years than Tom Brady makes in one game.

It's a job most Americans don't understand, don't envy, and don't respect. That is why we have pride for the infantry.

As we concluded breakfast, we were once again reminded of a most valuable military lesson: you are not done until everything is clean as a whistle, inventory is accounted for, and police calls are finished. But as for me, I had more pressing matters to attend to: my broken foot.

I was taken to the hospital on base, where they confirmed I did in fact break the bones in my foot, and put me in a plaster cast. I'd be lying if I didn't feel some sort of relief that my foot was actually broken. To me, it was a subtle told-you-so to Drill Sergeant Eskamia, who had doubted me this entire time. Who had mocked me when I was actually displaying the grit that they said they wanted from us. I had walked half the night with a 35 lb. ruck, K-Pot, and weapon system, so fuck you and your "little heart disease."

While it did feel good to look at him and say, "See, I told you, motherfucker," that good feeling was short-lived. You see, since my foot was in a cast and I was on crutches, I wouldn't be allowed to "walk" with my class. There would be no formation for me on the parade deck. I wouldn't stand there at attention during the ceremony while proud family members looked on (none of mine were coming anyway). I wouldn't get to participate in the "turning blue" ceremony, which is where they give you one of your proudest possessions as an infantryman: your blue chord. Not only would I not walk, I would be stuck in those barracks as a holdover until my foot healed. Nothing, I thought, was worse than that, and I'd have given anything to be able to participate. Little did I know at the time that the universe gives you what you ask for, so you better be careful how you ask.

I was sitting in the bay doing cleanup work with my broke-ass foot when Drill Sergeant Eskamia called me into the office. "Private, sit down; we need to talk with you." Standing behind him was a tall man with a cross on his lapel. Eskamia said, "This is the chaplain, and he needs to speak with you."

The chaplain stepped forward and said, "Son, we've been notified that your mother is going to lose her fight with cancer. A request has been made for you to go home to see her and pay your final respects."

I just sat there kinda stunned. Sadie had beaten cancer twice before, and sadly, it looked like the third time wouldn't be a charm after all. Even though my mother and I had a strained relationship, even more so by the end of my time there growing up, I still had a huge place in my heart reserved just for her. Realizing she wouldn't be making it through cancer again struck me, for once in my life, speechless.

I was told that they would be getting me on a plane ASAP and I would be using emergency leave to go home to pay my respects. Drill Sergeant Eskamia would take me to the booking agency on base to secure my travel. I remember quietly walking to the vehicle and riding with him to go book my flights. Not one time did that dickhead say, "Hey, sorry for your loss, Private." Not one time did he show one single ounce of concern for his soldier, and that, more than anything else, is why in my eyes, he will always be a giant piece of shit.

The welfare of your men comes second only to mission accomplishment when you're in the military. And he didn't care about how I was doing. Matter of fact, the only thing he said to me the entire trip was, "Stand the fuck up, Private," when I leaned on the desk while talking to the attendant. Mind you, I wasn't even in basic training anymore and I was still processing that my mother was dying, and I was headed to see her for the last time. Coincidently, it would be the last time I would see Eskamia as well, and that was no sweat off my back.

I would leave Ft. Benning, GA, and fly back home. I had been granted a block of leave to see my mother and get a break from training. I was out of the cast by now and was awaiting an assignment date for a slot in Airborne School. I arrived back home with no fanfare, no family waiting to meet me at the gate. Just a plane touching down and me walking through the airport in my greens. I had Robin pick me up and take me home. It was good to see a friendly face, especially after boot camp and headed home to see my ailing mother. I made a beeline right back to that ol' farmhouse to add a new batch of horrible imagery to my nightmare deck.

At the house, they had built a parking lot, so to speak, that cut into the adjacent hayfield. It had been cut out in a rectangular shape that was rounded on the corners. It was designed to hold four or five vehicles at a time, and when I got there, it was overflowing into the field.

I walked into the front door expecting to find her sitting in her favorite chair in the living room. Instead, as I rounded the corner, I could see that the living room was empty with just a single lamp on. My eyes immediately darted to the left into the dining room, where I saw my family gathered around Sadie.

As he had been for over three decades, Bobby was there by her side. I think we all long for that kind of love. I know I still do; the kind that would stay by you even in your worst moments, right up to the end. No matter how poorly I viewed his parenting skills, by all accounts that I could see, he was everything a woman should want in a husband.

After looking at Bobby, my eyes finally moved to her for the first time since I left . . . and I stopped dead in my tracks. She had always been a short little thing; maybe you could say a little chubby later in life, but by all measurable means, she'd been a beautiful woman. Cancer had reduced her to a shell of her former self. She was clearly on her last legs as she was in hospice care at home. The hospital bed seemed cold and sterile, standing next to the old rolltop desk Bobby used to store all his business paperwork.

The treatment had robbed her of her hair, which she loved so much. In its place was a short and patchworked section of white strands that appeared to barely cling to the top of her skull. The skin was taught against her high cheekbones, leaving her eyes looking sunken. Her frame was devoid of musculature and looked as if her skin were simply draped across her bones.

I felt myself gasp in shock and instantly felt bad for doing so, as if I had just insulted her by not being able to feign a smile and pretend that this was life as normal. Just a typical welcome-home party for the baby of the family who just returned after completing basic training. But this was far from typical and there would be no fairytale ending.

I walked up next to her bed and said a feeble hello. All my words rang hollowly, given how our last few years had gone. We had grown distant as much from my longing for teenage independence as from all the bullshit I had to endure growing up. Furthermore, throughout high school, she had become even more temperamental, and that had placed even more of a strain on our relationship.

But all of that faded from memory as I looked down on her in that state with the sands of time slowly but unstoppably falling through the glass. She looked up at me and weakly said, "Hello, Daniel."

Incredulously, I asked, "How are you feeling?" I instantly felt stupid, as it was obvious to everyone that she was feeling like shit. But in moments like this, the social norms we live our lives by seem to take over, as we move through uncomfortable conversations on the same autopilot that we use to navigate small talk.

If she felt I was an idiot in that moment, she didn't let on. She said she was doing as well as could be expected and to let her take a look at me. I stood there in my dress greens, trying to look like a squared-away soldier. I hoped and prayed that I could give her some sense of pride, some sense of accomplishment that one of her kids didn't totally fuck his life up.

She smiled and gently nodded. "Good boy," she said. Then she closed her eyes and drifted back off to sleep. I made small talk with everyone else around the room, but as always, I felt out of place. In fact, I felt even more so now. With the matriarch on her deathbed, there would be no one else in the family who felt the need to entertain the addition that only she wanted.

I'd have rather been anywhere else on earth than in that room with my dying mother and a family I'd grown dead to long ago. I lingered a few more painful moments, kissed my mother's forehead, and walked out the door.

Now, there are many things I am not proud of in my life, but this was the first that would cause me to look back years later with the sting of regret. I was home only for a few days, but I only went back once more to see her. I spent the bulk of time doing something I would learn later in life never works: running from the pain and my problems. For the next few days, I blew the money I'd been forced to save in basic training (you can only by tennis shoes and haircuts there) and spent my time running up and down the road with folks I'd grown up with.

I stopped by the house once more to see her in that fragile state before I left. This time there were less folks in the room and that made it a bit easier, but words escaped me and her. I am sure for her it was due to sheer exhaustion, but for me, it was just one of the handful of times I was speechless. Looking at her, I could only think of the words from the Reba McEntire song, "What do you say in a moment like this when you can't find the words to tell it like it is?"

How do I look at this woman whom I loved and feared and find some closure on all that she'd done for me and to me? How do I say, "I still love you, despite all the unholy liberties your children took with me under your roof?" How can I make her understand that, with her passing, there'd be a hole in my heart for the rest of my life, as much from her absence as from the feeling that even in her presence, I was never enough?

I didn't know the answers then, and sitting here writing about it twenty-two years later, I still don't. All I can say is, I wish I'd tried harder when I was there. Instead, I sat in silence until it was deafening. I counted down the minutes until I could honestly say I had to leave. I gently kissed her forehead and walked away. It was the last time I'd ever see her alive.

I'd return to Ft. Benning and continue to wait for orders to Airborne School. My days would consist of more hurry-up-and-wait menial tasks, and for the most part, trying to stay out of sight and out of mind. Later, I would learn this is both an art and science perfected by the sham shield and "E-4 Mafia."

I would hang out for a few weeks and finally get my orders. I would also get another Red Cross message: Sadie had passed away. Now, this came at an odd time as far as the Army was concerned, because I was in the middle of transitioning between units, which meant the departing unit wasn't going to approve my emergency leave and the receiving unit couldn't do it until they in-processed me.

Standing there in the bay, a discussion was had regarding exactly how I would get placed on leave. Ultimately, the decision was made that since I was going to Airborne School, they should be the ones to grant me leave. I was assured that when I got there, I would be a top priority to be in-processed and set up for emergency leave.

So, with faith in the system, I loaded up my duffle bag, hopped on the cattle truck, and took a little ride to arrive at the United States Army Airborne School. We offloaded the trucks, set up a formation in the fields next to the barracks, and were told to pop a squat.

There I began the game I'd grown accustomed to: hurry up and wait. Only problem was that, this time, every minute I waited jeopardized my ability to get on a plane and be home in time to make my mother's funeral. At the time, however, fresh out of boot camp, I had been conditioned to keep my mouth shut. Clearly, those in charge would take care of me.

With that mindset, I sat down on my bag and waited, and waited, and waited. After a few hours of not moving, I started to ask up the COC what was going on and about the status of my in-processing. I was routinely told, "It's getting done" and "You'll be out of here in no time." No time to them must have meant, "We have no time to help you out, Private," because many more hours would lapse before I finally got fed up and walked inside.

I wandered the halls of the barracks, and much to my surprise, no one asked, "What the fuck are you doing, Private?" While there was still a level of seriousness to Airborne School, it was much more relaxed than the basic. I continued down the halls until I came upon the 1SG's office and summoned the courage to knock.

Up until that point, I'd barely had any interaction with anyone above a E-7, and that was limited to, "Roger, Platoon Sergeant." So to knock on his door took all the balls I had.

"Excuse me, First Sergeant, I need some help." I was halfway expecting him to jump across the desk, rip off my head, and piss down my neck for having he audacity to speak to him.

Instead, he looked up from his desk and said, "What is it, Private?"

I explained my situation, how they had promised me to in-process me quickly and had not only failed to do so, but hadn't even started after losing hours of precious time. Instead of getting angry at me, he got up from his desk and said, "Let's go, Private." He led me down the hallway, where I was introduced to the company commander and given the backstory of my situation. From there, both of the men quickly got me assigned a room in the barracks, made phone calls, and signed required paperwork to get my leave approved within a matter of hours. I was checked in and on the road back home to lay my mother to rest.

I arrived back home shortly before the funeral. As is customary for a funeral in the South, everyone and anyone who knew her came out. I think they do so as much to pay their final respects as to get some homemade fried chicken. All of which means that the room was filled with people I didn't know or didn't like, neither of which made a shitty situation better.

I think the thing that surprised me most was how well Bobby was taking it. In truth, we all expected him to fall apart with Sadie gone; after all, he did nothing around the house. Didn't cook or clean. I wasn't even sure the man could boil water. On top of that, he worshiped the ground she walked on, so I couldn't help but wonder what he'd do when she was no longer walking around. Despite how he must have been feeling, he remained steadfast and stoic. He seemed to be concentrating on the task at hand: burying his wife.

When I say everyone shows up to a funeral in the South, I mean *everyone*. I looked up from the pew I was sitting on to see Sadie and Bobby's eldest, Robbie, getting escorted in, restrained by handcuffs and shackles. He kept his head down and didn't look at anyone else in the room. The deputies escorted him up to Sadie's coffin and stepped back to give him a moment to pay his respects.

One of the reasons Robbie was so intimidating was the size of his hands. They were like bear paws. His fingers looked more like hotdogs than they did digits. Matter of fact, it looked like he was having a major allergic reaction to a bee sting. They were so big that the cuffs looked almost comical in comparison, as if he could easily break free like Superman in the old cartoons.

His weathered, calloused hands were known to break every jaw he ever hit. And yet, those same hands looked weak and almost childlike as he raised them, chains and all, one final time to touch Sadie's. There was no doubt that, despite his troubled past and vile acts, he, too, had a complicated relationship with the woman he called "Momma." Standing there shackled in front of friends and family, the words escaped him as they did me the last time I stood by her side.

I couldn't help but wonder how sad that day must have been for him. There, standing beside the body of the matriarch, in front of the judging eyes of all in attendance, including the deputies, who disturbed the sacredness of the moment. To want to have a private moment to say goodbye, and knowing that you forfeited that with your actions, must have hurt worse than actually being locked up. They gave him his few moments to make peace and then, clinging and jangling, they escorted him back out the door and back off to prison.

We buried Sadie and, as is customary, everyone went back to the house for food and fellowship. I remained surprised at how well Bobby was processing it. I hadn't even seen him cry once. That part didn't shock me that much, as I hadn't ever seen him really display any emotion before, but I still expected him to show more emotions with her gone. I had my dinner, said my goodbyes, and headed off to become a paratrooper.

Chapter Seven

Airborne!

"After the demise of the best Airborne plan, a most terrifying effect occurs on the battlefield. This effect is known as the Rule of LGOPs. This is, in its purest form, small groups of 19-year old American Paratroopers. They are well-trained, armed to the teeth, and lack serious adult supervision. They collectively remember the Commander's intent as 'March to the sound of the guns and kill anyone who is not dressed like you...' ...or something like that. Happily, they go about the day's work..."
—The Rule of LGOPs

I arrived back in Benning to find I had a new bunkmate: Pvt. Hammock. We became fast friends. He had a mischievous streak in him a mile long. He was a little taller than me, not really lanky, but not "skinny fat" either. He just had long, lean arms and legs and a wider-than-normal torso. Kid was also damn fast, an attribute I longed to have myself.

Both of us were on hold for the next class and still had a few days to go. With this newfound free time, we poked around Ft. Benning, finding things to do to kill time and doing our best to stay out of trouble. For us, that consisted mostly of going to the PX to buy pogey bait (BXes and PXes are tax-free retail outlets on bases) and hitting the bowling alley. The rest of the time, we hung around the barracks and shot the shit. Just a whole lot of nothing to do until it was time to learn how to throw our asses out of a perfectly good airplane.

"All right, listen up! Over the next three weeks, we are going to turn you into an airborne-qualified soldier. At the end of those next three weeks, you will make five jumps from a high-performance aircraft. If, at the end of your four thousand count, your T-10 Charlie doesn't deploy, you have the rest of your airborne life to figure it out." Now, I don't know if that has always been the standard speech, but I know they gave one real similar in *Band of Brothers*.

The paratrooper unit is a shock troop. They arrive to field and do so violently, knowing that they will be surrounded. Their primary mission is airfield seizure, and the famed 82nd Airborne can be anywhere in the world within eighteen hours. Paratroopers earned their reputation as "devils in baggy pants" during World War II. It was a long, proud, and storied history we were seeking to add to, and everyone who was there had volunteered at least twice to get there: once in the army, and again for airborne.

Now, as much as I take pride in being a paratrooper, the truth is that the school isn't all that hard, especially if you are following up infantry basic training or are doing it from another service branch in the middle of more advanced training. The biggest hurdle most had to overcome was shin splints, because you did a slow-ass "airborne shuffle" everywhere you went in boots. You also did a dick-ton of pull-ups so that you'd have the strength to "reach up high on that set of risers, pull deep down into your chest, and prepare to land."

Now, let's talk about that preparing-to-land bullshit. Being a paratrooper is not like skydiving. Skydiving is done for fun and enjoying the view. Paratrooping is about getting your ass to the ground as fast as possible without it killing you. Which it rarely does. "Preparing to land," as they say, is akin to that episode where Homer Simpson gets dumped out the back of the ambulance and falls down this giant cliff, busting every part of his ass on the way down. Let's break down the breakdown, shall we?

"The final item I will cover is PARACHUTE LANDING FALLS. We will now move to the PLF platform and conduct one satisfactory PLF in each of the four directions. Jumpers, be prepared to conduct a PLF, because you will hit the ground approximately five-to-ten seconds before

you think you will. When jumping under instrument meteorological conditions, do not lower your equipment until you have passed through the clouds. Do not turn unless you have to avoid a collision. If you have any malfunction, or any reason to believe you are falling faster than fellow jumpers, immediately activate your reserve parachute, because you cannot compare your rate of descent with your fellow jumpers. Ensure you recheck your canopy once you pass through the clouds. The fifth point of performance is LAND. You will make a proper parachute landing fall by hitting all five points of contact. Touch them and repeat them after me. One, BALLS OF YOUR FEET; two, CALF; three, THIGH; four, BUTTOCKS; and five, PULL-UP MUSCLE."

Let me tell you, I have NEVER in my life done a real PLF in anything other than training. PLFs are real-life unicorns. They do not fucking exist, and anyone who says they have done one is either a liar or delusional. And nothing ensures you do a worse PLF more than doing a rear one at night. Almost every time I did one, I landed ass, neck, head. I don't give a shit how much you weigh, 120 lbs. or 280, you still hit the ground like a bag of rocks. And that's why none of us can walk by thirty. For years after, the military gave me fairly strong pain meds for my back.

The school, as I said, isn't difficult, and it culminates with "jump week." You have to make five jumps out of a high-performance aircraft to earn your wings. For the first jump, you're on a static line, so everyone clips in their fixed line from the top of your pack to this rope that runs the length of the plane to the door, and once you hurl yourself out, the tension in the line opens the chute opens automatically. Well, I have no shame in telling you: I am petrified of heights. I get a weird feeling in my balls when I get close to the edge up high in the air, and let's not forget I said I would never jump out of one, and yet here I was, chute on my back, standing in a chalk line to head to a waiting C-130 (that worked and had no issues, by the way) to jump out of it around 1,250 ft. above ground level.

The truth of the matter is that, if it hadn't been for this little-ass female ahead of me, I may have chickened out. But, as proud infantryman, there was no way on God's beautiful green earth that I was going to be showed up by a non-infantryman, so I stood up like a man and walked my punk ass up the ramp and got settled in to do the damn thing. Now, C-130s always look like they still need more work to 'em to be finished, and I swear each one of them sounds different while flying. I am always waiting for the damn thing to crash, which you'd think I wouldn't be that worried about since I had on a chute, but still, I hate to fly.

Once up in the air, it's a quick rip. You start getting ready for the jump damn near as soon as you get in the sky. The Jumpmaster stands up and starts giving the required time warnings.

(1) "20 Minutes." As the Jumpmaster issues the verbal command, "TWENTY MINUTES," extend hands and arms forward while spreading the fingers and thumbs, then return to shoulder level in closed fists. This motion will be repeated twice.

(2) "10 Minutes." As the Jumpmaster issues the verbal command, "TEN MINUTES," extend hands and arms forward while spreading the fingers and thumbs, then return to shoulder level in closed fists.

(3) "1 Minute." The Jumpmaster will issue the one-minute time warning by extending the lead arm toward the jumpers and raising the index finger or raising the lead arm to the elbow-locked position and extending the index finger, sounding off with, "ONE MINUTE."

(4) "30 Seconds." The Jumpmaster will issue the 30-second

time warning by extending his lead arm toward his jumpers, with the index finger and thumb approximately 1 inch apart, and sound off with, "30 SECONDS." Jumpmaster students may also execute this command by raising their lead arm and conducting the actions previously described.

This is then followed by the nine jump commands.

1. "Get Ready"
2. "Outboard Personnel, Stand Up"
3. "Inboard Personnel, Stand Up"
4. "Hook Up"
5. "Check Static Lines"
6. "Check Equipment"
7. "Sound Off for Equipment Check"
8. "STAND BY"
9. "GO"

At that point, the lead jumper gets a light little tap on the ass and out the door you go. From there, you are to "walk, not run" to the door. You keep your eyes on the Jumpmaster. With your static line extended, you shuffle towards the Jumpmaster and the door. Once there, you hand your static line off, both hands go to your reserve, you tuck your chin, and step out into the wind.

Once you exit the bird, maintain a tight body position, keep your eyes open, chin on your chest, elbows tight into your sides, hands on the end of the reserve, and your fingers spread. Bend forward at the waist, keeping your feet and knees together, knees locked to the rear, and count to four. "ONE ONE THOUSAND, TWO ONE THOUSAND, THREE ONE THOUSAND, FOUR ONE THOUSAND!!" At which point, you look up to check your canopy and gain canopy control.

Now, that is how it's supposed to go. Let me tell you how the shit really goes, especially after Airborne School and wearing a real combat load.

You somehow manage to stand up wearing the weight of an entire second person on your back and hanging between your legs. Under the strain of the load, you then hook up to the static line and go through your final checks. I, no bullshit, hooked up to a static line that fell down. You want to talk about a limp-dick moment, that was it. Good ol' Jumpmaster said, "Unhook from that one and hook up to the other one," and away we went.

You then full-out run towards the door because your adrenaline is pumping a mile a minute, you're sweating your balls off, and your back is breaking. *Dear Lord, please get me the fuck off this plane.* The poor Jumpmaster is trying to catch three flailing static lines at one time in order to save the poor soul behind you from getting tangled up in yours and getting all fucked up as he tries to exit the door.

Speaking of exiting the door, that static line looks more like a ping-pong ball than it does some high-speed, killer death-dealer from above. You throw your static line at the Jumpmaster, try to pivot towards the door, hit the door on your way out, and start to spin like a top while you try to count to four. Then your nuts get ripped to your nose as the parachute catches (which you're actually happy about because this experiment in human flight actually worked), and then you check your canopy.

Only problem is, because you banged the door on the way out, your risers are twisted all the way to the top. That means you have to untwist yourself, which means you are once again spinning like a top. This can't make for a very intimidating sight: you sitting there looking like you're running in air, twirling in circles.

Now, you would think the sky would give you plenty of room to stretch out in—absolutely not. Because mass exists, the sky is filled with other spinning bastards that are trying to move their nuts out of the harness as well. That means no one is looking out for no one until they are on top of each other. At which point you scream to the dumb fuck across from you, "Move out the way!"

Now, there are rules of the air. "Lower jumper always has the right of way." Well, thanks, Dad, have you tried to move these fucking chutes that haven't been updated since World War II? I honestly think they tell you to "pull up high on that set of risers" just to give you something to do to occupy your mind before you bust your ass so you can't think about how bad this shit is gonna hurt.

Once you get below the clouds, or as soon as you can see that it's safe, you lower combat load by pulling a tab and letting it fall about 10–15 feet below you. From there, you survey the ground below, which in many cases consists of "What shitty thing do you want to land on?" Trees, tarmac, rock, your battle buddy, etc. From there, you just pull a set of risers in and wait to absolutely bust your ass. The benefit of having a combat load is you hear it hit and you know, since you are falling at a rate of 22–24 feet per second, you're about to bust your ass.

While all of those things happen in Airborne School, you do at least get some coaching. Soon as you gain canopy control, you start hearing the voice of God; at least, that's what it sounds like 'cause you're up in the sky and someone is talking to you, telling you to "slip away." Turns out it was just a Black Hat on the ground with a bullhorn reminding you that now would be the perfect time to un-fuck yourself.

Five of those jumps later and you are certified as one bad mother—shut your mouth! You are AIRBORNE! Now, this is frowned upon in today's super-pussified world, but back in my day, you got your "blood wings." That was when you placed your pin-on wings on your uniform without the clutch on the back, leaving the sharp points exposed. Then, everyone lines up and punches them into your chest, producing blood and leaving a gnarly bruise as proof that you ain't no bitch. Sadly, in light of recent years and crying, we have learned that the world is, indeed, full of bitches.

With Airborne School complete, it was time for me to move on to greener pastures. Hammock and I were both assigned to the famed 82nd airborne, but we needed a ride to get there. Well, I was just a dumb fucking private, so I went to buy a truck. I didn't know shit about financing or purchasing things, and the bases are surrounded by predatory business that will finance you anything on planet earth because they know for a fact Uncle Sam will set your ass up with a monthly allotment that comes out of your paycheck before you ever see it. Not only will they sell you some shit, they are gonna do it at an insane interest rate.

I purchased a used purple (what was I thinking?) Ford Ranger. Also, it happened to be stick shift and I didn't know how to drive stick. But I felt like a fuckin' king. So, we loaded up the truck with our duffel bags, pointed the truck north, and lurched out of the parking lot, headed to our next adventure in life.

Chapter Eight

Blue Falcons

There was blood upon the risers, there were brains upon the chute;
Intestines were a-dangling from this paratrooper's boots;
They picked him up, still in his chute, and poured him from his boots.
He ain't gonna jump no more.
Gory, Gory, What a helluva way to die.
He ain't gonna jump no more.
—"Blood on the Risers," paratrooper song from World War II

Welcome to the 82nd AIRBORNE, home of the paratrooper. We pulled into Fayetteville, which we came to refer to as Fayette-nam, eager and excited to be assigned to our new unit. As is customary with everything in the army, you first arrive to reception to begin your in-process. Much to our surprise, Hammock and I got assigned to the same unit, same company, and even the same platoon.

We were assigned to 3/325, the Falcon Brigade. We were part of Charlie Company, the Blue Falcons. Now, most folks made fun of that because "blue falcon" was slang for "buddy fucker," and no one wanted to be a buddy fucker. Ironically, the 325th hadn't been paratroopers in World War II; they had been glider men. Now, for those who are unfamiliar with history, this is what one might refer to as a shit assignment.

These guys would get towed behind a plane in a lightweight glider that they decided to make heavy by adding a bunch of grunts to. They would tow these things behind a plane and then release them so they could glide in stealthy without enemy detection, or at least that was how it was supposed to work. As is always the case, real life proved to be a lot more difficult.

If everything went right, success! However, the list of things that can jack up a glider up is numerous and likely to happen. They were easily susceptible to ground fire if detected. They had no engine and couldn't maneuver worth a shit so they were sitting ducks (along with the plane towing them) if they came across enemy aircraft. They needed a clear and soft landing zone, which the enemy always said, "Fuck that" to. Lastly, and most importantly, it should come as no surprise that these fragile things fell apart during crash landings, which every landing was. So, more often than should have been acceptable, the men aboard got fucked up or dead as a result. Oh, and no extra hazardous duty pay for the job.

Once we completed reception, we were sent down the street to meet up with our unit. That's when I met my first soldier that was getting ready to ETS (End Terms of Service): SPC. Erickson. He was a glorious creature. No fucks to give about anything. He was unlike anything I had seen so far in this man's army. He was literally counting down the clock until it was time to bid the army adieu.

He was slightly taller than me, with a square and pronounced jawline. He had a quick wit and a sly smile. He scooped us and said, "Come on, cherries, follow me." He led us back to our new home, the barracks. As we strolled up to 'em, he looked back and grinned, "Welcome home, cherries."

The barracks were long, rectangular, and in dire need of repair. Clearly we wouldn't be living in the lap of luxury. Out front was the area where'd we hold what seemed like an endless amount of accountability formations. There were two sets of steps that took you into the building and the stoop was a favorite hangout place for smokers and jokers. It's also where almost every photo was taken while doing your best to look like a stone-cold killer.

Erickson walked us up inside, where they had us wait by the HQ office. There, we were assigned to 3rd Platoon and told to follow him again upstairs. We walked up to the top floor where 3rd Platoon was housed and I instantly felt like I was getting a frat house tour.

The very first thing you learn about the real army is who really runs the place, and that title belongs to the "Spec-4 Mafia." The sham shield rules 'em all. Yeah, the NCOs and the officers may be in charge on paper, but when everyone goes home, the mafia takes over. They get out of most of the shit work because, well, they have the privates do it.

How can you tell who's in the Spec Four Mafia? Well, of course, there is an easy tell—their rank—but you don't even need to see it. They have an earned arrogance about them. All of them are "fucking getting out." They don't have time for your shit, and the only thing they are more positive of than the fact they are getting out of the Army is that you, Private, are doing the shit work.

They may sound horrible on the surface, but by God, they make the Army great. More times than not they are solid-ass soldiers. They are more focused on having fun than staying clean, and while they might not pass inspection, you can bet your ass they can fight. More importantly, they are what makes the army bearable and the ones whose stories you tell for the rest of your life.

As I walked upstairs, I felt as if I had just entered a frat house. Loud music was blaring out of a speaker from one of the rooms and guys kept going in and of rooms like Scooby and the gang running from a ghost. Every door you walked past gave you a glimpse into another dimension, it seemed. In a world where conformity is enforced, one of the few ways to be an individual is how you set up your room. No two rooms were the same and every soldier took a great deal of pride in setting theirs up.

As I was led down the hall, I could feel everyone's eyes upon me.

I was the new fresh meat and it was clear now that everyone had moved one rung up the totem pole, because I had just taken my place at the bottom of it. As we walked down the narrow hallway, I heard voices yelling out, "What the fuck are you doing in our hallway, cherry?" or "Don't you dare fucking look at me, cherry." It was then I realized that completing basic didn't mean shit.

We walked down the hallway until we came to the next-to-last door on the left. Turned out I would be rooming with SPC Erickson since he was next to leave the unit. His room reflected his reality. He didn't care. There were posters of hot chicks and pictures of him and the old heads, the guys who'd been in the unit for a while, scattered all over the wall. Back then, we printed 'em out.

There were magazines piled high on a coffee table and nasty-ass-looking futon in the corner that you wouldn't want to hit with a blacklight. What made it worse was that SPC Erickson informed me that I would not be sleeping on the bunk above him—that was an absolute fucking no-go. Instead, I would sleep on that nasty-ass futon that I am 100 percent sure that had more cum stains on it than the local strip club down in Fayetteville, and that's saying something.

I stuffed my gear in one of the lockers Erickson so "graciously" allowed me to use. From there, I decided it was time to meet the cast of characters that made up 3rd Platoon.

By "decided to meet," I mean I walked down the hallway and everyone began to introduce themselves to me. Which, in truth, was simply them doing what high-testosterone men do: busting my balls. Every door I walked past, they shouted, "Fuckin' stop, cherry. Where the fuck you think you're going?" In response to which, I'd open my mouth, and the jokes would really start.

"Listen to this country motherfucker! You sure got a pretty mouth, boy! Just where the fuck you from?"

I'd respond, "Virginia," but no one would believe me.

"That's the North. Everyone up there is Yankees!"

I tried to educate them on where exactly the Mason-Dixon Line started, but that was to no avail. Matter of fact, it pissed them off that I had the audacity to speak back, so that resulted in me getting smoked in the hallway in my flip-flops and underwear. Lesson learned.

The cast of characters in "Dirty Third" couldn't have been scripted better if they were in a movie. In every platoon you have the same cast of characters, they just all go by different names and from different places. I have found a million memes that talk about various versions of this roster, but because this is my book, then I'll use my own.

1. The Leader. Dathan Hurt was the first really squared-away SPC that I met. The guy took the fucking job seriously, and while he may have busted your balls a little bit, he did so more to make you better than to haze you. I was in awe of him when we first meet. He was my first team leader and he knew everything there was to know about weapons and tactics. The only sad thing was I didn't get him long before he switched services and went to the Coast Guard.

2. The Jacked Dude. Fucking Sergeant Veith was the first man who scared the absolute living shit out of me. He was everything you wish God had made you. He was tall, blond, and well-muscled. Looked like he was carved from a Greek statue. His pecs were like boulders and he could even run. I remember on battalion runs he carried the battalion colors. You know how many streamers are on those things. The dude was a freak of nature.

3. The Ladies' Man. Joe Delauro, I don't know what it

was about this guy, but he always seemed to have the in to parties, especially college ones. He wasn't handsome like Sergeant Veith, but his give-a-damn was most assuredly busted. That led him to having the nuts to approach anyone, and I never saw him with an ugly woman, which is saying something in Ft. Bragg, because most all of us dated ugly women.

4. The Dirty Bird. Private Jaron. The nastiest fuckin' guy I ever met in my life, and that's saying something. He had one goal, and that was to become a Ranger. As Sgt. Veith once joked, "he'd failed PRC, not once, not twice, but three times." This desire to become a Ranger precluded him from doing anything even remotely close to cleaning his body or his room, because "that's garrison shit" and Rangers only care about fieldwork. To this day, he's the only case of poison ivy acting as an STD.

5. The Virgin. Dan Henneberger. He came to our platoon as one of the most innocent souls I'd ever seen. He was a committed Mormon and proud that he had abstained from sex. He had an endearing quality to him and that, coupled with his virginity, made everyone in the platoon committed to corrupting him. It was like some unsaid rule that we had to be the ones who were responsible for the loss of his virginity. I'm pretty sure some of the guys would have fucked him themselves to have gotten the title.

6. The Klepto. Mathew Clinker. Now, don't get me wrong, he never stole anything in a malicious way, but my man was forever borrowing your shit. If you had lost something, you could damn well bet you could find it in Clinker's room.

He was another one of the good-looking kids, though, and had a pretty infectious personality, one that got him in with the ladies but also got us into a lot of fights. Clinker was a magnet for pissed-off boyfriends' punches.

7. The Salty Sergeant. Justin Evans. The only man in the platoon who had seen combat. He was Ranger-qualified and could drink your ass under the table. Gave absolutely ZERO fucks about anyone's feelings, up or down—the COC was rumored to collect Article 15s for speaking his mind—and was an absolute animal in the field.

8. The Country Boy. Billy Craft. The only one there with a worse twang than me. Billy was the other side of the squared-away coin from Hurt. He would become my second team leader, and just like Hurt, he knew his job forward and back. He always struck me as the Lee Greenwood kind of soldier: he did it 'cause he loved his county and his home.

9. Hates the Morning Guy. Adam Bishop. Solid-ass guy. From upstate New York and everything seemed to come easy to him except waking up early. The guy hated it. I remember walking through the hallway to find his alarm clock shattered against the wall. He had just done twenty-four hours of CQ and couldn't figure out how to turn it off, so he just threw it out of his room.

10. The Dick. Tine Sledd. Tine was the first guy who I met that wasn't a NCO that just really didn't' give a shit what anyone thought. The dude was a tank, a natural athlete. He was strong, fast. He could lift as well as run. He'd tell you to fuck off as fast as he'd say good morning. In truth,

in many ways, he was what you wanted to find in a soldier: aggressive, athletic, and ruthless when needed.

11. The Cowboy. Joshua Smith. Dude always had his trusted cowboy hat and rope. Could drink beer like a fish and always had a wad of dip in his mouth. Till the day I die, I'll never forget getting a knock on my door as a cherry only to find him standing outside butt-naked in his cowboy boots, hat, beer, and rope. For a few moments, I was legit worried I'd be hogtied and raped in my room. Sadly, that didn't happen; Smith was a handsome fellow.

12. Southie. Michael Darrah. Now, I ain't sure if he was from Southie, but I always seemed to have someone from Boston in my platoon, and since being a Southie is all I know about Boston besides the Red Sox, that's what I call 'em. He was the consummate practical joker and a proud member of the Spec Four Mafia. He was squared away, and ended up being the RTO at the platoon and the battalion level, which meant he knew more about what was going on than the officers did. As a result, he became our lifeline to the pipeline of the information, 'cause Lord knows no one else told us shit!

13. The Socially Awkward Kid. Paul Polis. Polis was the guy who had no understanding of how to act around women. Solid dude with zero game. Matter of fact, more often than not, he'd make it extremely uncomfortable to be around him with a woman. He wasn't just borderline rude to them; he was blatantly so.

Together, those thirteen guys, coupled with a few whose names

I can't remember, made up (in our minds, anyway) the greatest fighting force ever assembled—3/325 Blue Falcons, the "Dirty Third." And the stories I'll share next will stay with me fondly as I think back to the time "we were soldiers once, and young."

All proceeded as normal until the weekend. Little did I know at that time that I was due to begin my initiation into the greatest fighting force ever assembled by surviving a hellish weekend of killing my liver. It all began Friday night when a knock came on my door and I was instructed that it was time to "defend the falcon." I was told to get out in the hallway and was given a trash can lid, a hockey stick, and mask, and placed in front of a falcon painted on the wall.

My job was simple: protect the falcon. Against what, you ask? Beer cans and bottles that were hurled down the hallway at my head. At random times of the Spec Four Mafia's choosing, someone would step out from their room and discard an empty by hurling it down the hallway at my head. They all claimed they were aiming at the falcon, but either their aim was shit or, along with those bottles, they were slinging bullshit too.

This was just the first thing in a long line of "fuck with the new guy" games. I had to go feed the falcon up at Battalion HQ. They sent me up with a loaf of bread and concertina wire gloves to feed this thing. You get there and it's just a wooden falcon and you stand there looking dumb as fuck. You also had to go find a long list of shit that didn't exist.

- Keys for Area J: Area J is a training area in the woods. Clearly you can't lock up the woods.
- Batteries for a chem light: See the name—chem lights don't use batteries.
- Bore brush for a 203: No such thing exists. It shoots a fucking grenade. You can clean it with anything.

- A Prick E7: Made to sound like a piece of radio equipment they always sent you to ask the PSG (Platton Sergeant), who was an E-7.
- A role of flight line: You don't roll up a runway.
- A box of grid squares: The shit's on the map—you can't find a box of 'em.

All of this was done in good fun and helped pass the time, all while making the new guy understand that he should use his hat for something other than a hat rack.

The crowning moment of your initial acceptance is your "cherry party."

Cherry Parties took place back when men were men. Nowadays, pansy ass people call them hazing. Fuck that. It was just another glorious rite of passage into the brotherhood. You were smoked all while drinking copious amounts of liquor and getting into drunken wrestling (or full-on fighting) matches with your fellow cherries. In my case, I was so drunk I literally fought a dumpster.

Now that that's out of the way, let's talk about what the 82nd Airborne does best: throw your ass out of an airplane in the worst conditions humanly possible. Fuckin' hurricane? No problem; time to do a mass tactical jump. I have seen conditions and times I was absolutely positive there was no way in hell that the jump was gonna be a go, only to hear 'em say, "Load up," and head off to the Pope Army Airfield.

List of shitty things the 82nd will throw you out in and onto includes, but not limited to: thunderstorms, gale-force winds, heavy drop equipment not moved, swampland, trees, hard-ass tarmac, other planes, helicopters—oh, and last but not least—when the sky's already full of as many paratroopers as it can hold.

I have seen a lot of crazy shit happen in the bird. I've seen the plane bank and the jumper fall out the wrong door. I've seen 'em throw a guy who had heart attack in the plane out the door so that they could get medical treatment faster on the ground than landing. I've seen a guy who didn't speak great English think "NO" was "GO" and jumped out the plane a full two miles before the drop zone. Took us all night to find him.

But, by far the worst jump experience I ever had was a daylight jump for an airshow. I can't remember which event it was at—part of me believes it was at Andrews Air Force Base—but regardless, the entire battalion got absolutely fucked up on that jump. It started off bad from the get-go. At takeoff we got too close to the prop from the plane in front of us. The plane did a sudden drop, which, of course, scared the shit out of everyone on it, including the pilot. He came back shaking and the loadmaster said they were two seconds away from telling us to bail out.

Then we got to the drop zone and we were told the wind was just a few knots. Those motherfuckers lied. We came out the plane and it felt like we were hooked up to a slingshot. Guys were crashing into each other, getting tangled up, and stealing each other's air left and right. I watched chutes collapse and guys having to pull reserves, and others having to run off the top of someone else's parachute.

All of that was bad, but the moment I knew I was fucked was when I looked down. Typically during a daylight jump (because you can't see shit at night), you see everyone collecting their chute, packing it up, and humping over to the rally point. But when I looked down, everyone looked like they were waiting to be outlined in chalk.

It was insane; almost no one looked to be moving. All over the drop zone, folks were splayed out, just lying there like they were dead. The wind was whipping us all across the place and I kept floating over the tarmac and over the grass. It was like a shitty game of Eenie Meenie Miney Mo. I just knew I was going to land on the tarmac, but at the last minute I was blown over the grass.

Forget five points of performance, I was ass, head, ass, head. I got wrapped up in my risers and they wrapped around my neck. The wind caught my chute and started dragging me across the DZ. I thought to myself, *Ain't this about a bitch? I am gonna die on the drop zone of a fucking airshow with little Timmy clapping in the stands.* Luckily for me, the wind died down for a second and I was able to get some slack, catch my breath, and get up and Charlie Mike (Continue Mission) to the link up point.

At the rally point, dudes were coming in jacked the fuck up. We had several guys with broken tailbones, shattered elbows, and broken arms. By the end of the airshow, our attempt to demonstrate our combat readiness had, in fact, reduced our capabilities by 30-50 percent. At least half our guys were on profile afterward. Just another example of how you can cross that fine line very easily in an attempt to prove how hard you are.

In between jumping out of airplanes, doing stupid-ass details like post police call (while all the "dependapotomases" sit on their asses, chain smoking Marlboro Lights), we actually found time to go out and have fun. Oh, and by fun, I mean fuck shit up.

There are just some things that don't mix: oil and water, fire and ice, orange juice and toothpaste, Apple and Microsoft, infantry soldiers and frat boys. We absolutely couldn't stand them prima-donnas. Wherever we went on college campuses, we stuck out like sore thumbs. The close-crop haircuts and military demeanor gave us away every time. Frat boys might have been there for the party, but they were also there for the education. Not us; we were there for two reasons only: the women and to fight.

One of the guys was dating a girl who we went to school with up at Chapel Hill (I believe it was Delaro, but I can't be sure) and so it seemed like a great idea for us all to go up there and party with them. We loaded up the car and headed to the land of milk and honey. Now, by and large, most (not everyone, mind you) people who went to that school came from well-to-do families. They got good grades, had loving parents with good jobs, and in our eyes, were generally spoiled brats.

On our side, a lot of us came from shit families, with little in the way of education or advantages to get ahead. For most of us, the military was not only a way to be part of something bigger than ourselves and to make a positive difference, it was also a way out of the life we were born into. So, as you can imagine, when kids from the wrong side of the tracks, who've been trained to be aggressive and take pride in fighting, mix alcohol with what we deemed as "rich-ass momma's boys," shit is gonna hit the fan.

We made our way onto campus and started looking everywhere we could for parties. Now, let me lead with the following: what I did next was assholish and I was wrong. Point blank, end of discussion. I refuse to paint myself only in an honorable light when I spent a lot of my life fucking up. Like I have always said, the only reason I am not in jail is I either didn't get caught or someone took pity on my dumb, angry ass.

At some point in the night, we found ourselves seriously torn up and walking through the frat house causing problems. Now, I won't say the names of the folks who were with me, as I'll only throw myself under the bus, but several of us descended upon this frat house. We walked in through the front door and as if we were doing CQB split-up and started "clearing" the house. Me and my battle buddy went upstairs and started going room to room. Let me tell you, you walk into a lot of shit going through those places. You could find anything from dudes playing video games, to doing coke, or banging out some chick. We'd kick open the doors, scare the shit out of whoever was in the room, talk some trash, and move on. Word started spreading through the house that there were unwanted guests at the party pretty quickly.

By the time that had started to happen, one of my NCOs who was with me at the time was admiring a big picture on the wall. This picture was of everyone who had been a member of the fraternity, past and present, and was clearly a big deal to the house. My NCO looked at me and said, "I bet you don't have the balls to take that off the wall and walk out the door with it."

Now, I don't know much in life, but I did know this: if my NCO was doubting that I had the balls to do anything then I was going to prove to him that I had the biggest balls in the room. So, I walked right to the wall, took the picture off the wall, and started walking out the door with it. Now, mind you, this wasn't some small picture. The thing was longer than I was tall. I could barely get my arms around it. Imagine me carrying a chunk of drywall out the door.

No sooner than I got out the door and down the front steps, someone yells, "Hey, where the fuck you going with that?" Now, I don't know why my mind went here, but I all of a sudden had an urge to pee. I sat the painting down, unzipped my pants, and started pissing on it. Now, as you can imagine, that rightfully pissed all the frat boys off. And much to their credit, they decided to do something about it.

What followed next was an all-out battle royale. I got clocked out the gate and as soon as I could put my dick back in my pants, we started fighting out in front of the frat house. This quickly caused the frat house to empty, both frat boys and soldiers. There on the front lawn, we went to work. It was an epic battle and I'll give them frat boys a lot of credit. They showed up and showed out. We went toe to toe and battled. When it all ended, however, we came out the other side bruised, but victorious, and then we did what you after every successful mission: pop smoke.

Now, whatever happened the rest of the night, I cannot tell you. What I can let you know is I woke up the next morning getting nudged by a baton. I was half in and half out the window of the pickup truck. Clink was passed out behind the steering wheel—

luckily, there were no keys in the ignition—and Adam stood up in the truck bed wrapped up in a woobie. I followed that baton up to the hand that held it and ultimately on up to the arm and body it was attached to.

There, standing over me, were a couple of Raleigh's finest. I wiped the drool from my mouth, which was a quite long and disgusting string, mind you, and mustered up, "How can I help you, officer?"

He looked me up and down and said something that filled me pride and worry at the same time. "You boys must be from the 82nd Airborne."

Not knowing much, I at least knew enough not to smile back at the question. Acting as if I were ignorant to the possible reason to he could have deduced that fact, I simply responded, "Why yes, sir, we are."

He shook his head and said, "We got a couple of your boys in lock-up downtown. You may wanna come down and get 'em." So, we drove down to the precinct, picked a couple of our boys up, and headed back to the barracks. We knew that when we got there, there would be hell to pay. You see, when you are in the military and you get in trouble, they treat you like an underaged kid and call your parents. In the case of the military, that's your company commander and 1SG.

We all did basically the same dirt, but not everyone got caught. So, the guys who did stood before the man, took an ass-chewing and an Article 15, and the rest of us got an evil eye in the hallway. It wouldn't be the last time we'd get those, that's for sure.

We didn't go back to Chapel Hill after that; however, that wasn't the end of our college shenanigans. On a trip to the beach one summer, we met these girls from High Point University. I ain't saying I was in love, but hot damn, boy, we were in lust at least. High Point was a little over an hour and half away, but when your options were drive for a couple hours to see some hot chicks or stay in your barracks in Ft. Bragg, trust me, driving won out every time.

We used to run up there on the regular and part of the fun was sneaking into the girls' rooms and dodging this really unhappy female security guard who walked the dorms. We always figured it was because she was less than attractive and was jealous that the young girls got us sexy stud paratroopers and she couldn't have us. Looking back, she probably didn't give a single fuck about us, or them; she just didn't want to get fired.

She'd make her rounds and we'd climb out of the windows and hang out on the ledge. We were paratroopers, after all, so why not show of our stupidity . . . er, I mean, our bravery. We'd hang out on the ledge until she was gone and then go back into the rooms, where we'd crash for the night. Everything was great until it wasn't.

Like I said, infantry and frat boys don't mix and it never takes long before there's a strong enough disturbance in the force to make sure that our paths cross once we've shown up on campus. We had been coming up to the college for a few weekends at this point, but one of the guys stopped talking to one of the girls. On the surface, that's not that big of deal; however, in a world fueled by peacocking testosterone-fueled young men, eager to prove they are big shit, it's a monumental problem.

We had just arrived at a party when one of the girls came up to me and said, "Hey, you may want to get out of here. Some guys are looking for y'all." In the time it took me to turn around and say, "It's all good" and then turn back towards everyone else, both frat houses emptied. I mean they absolutely fucking emptied.

There were so many people outside that I wasn't even counting individuals. It looked like seating in a stadium. I mean, outnumbered grossly underestimates our predicament. We were there, maybe ten guys deep, and they had what appeared to be the entire school. They 100 percent at least had the football team's offensive line, and in that moment, you realize that the average infantry soldier is around

5'7" and 174 lbs. Large men we are not, and large men they were.

Of course, standing there in the middle talking shit was this little runt-looking motherfucker who had more mouth than he had ass, but when you got an entire O-line behind you, and the rest of the school to boot, well, it's easy to have big balls. Now, one of the rules they teach you in the army is to engage with no less than three-to-one. We are in the business of killing the enemy, not fighting fair. In this particular case, we jacked his all up and were staring down at least ten-to-one. It was time to perform retrograde operations.

Now, this meant it was time to work on deescalating the situation while we continued to look for an avenue out of the kill zone. The schools were to our left and right, crowd to our front. That meant we only had one way to go: back down the path and onto the road. As we worked to work our way out of this shitty situation, the crowd actually followed us. We were a pack of dudes getting pursued by a bigger pack of dudes. My "oh-fuck meter" was all the way in the red.

Somehow—I am not quite sure how it happened—Clinker got enveloped by some of the group. Out of nowhere, a fist darted out from the crowd and tagged him. We ran back in, grabbed Clink, and pulled him out of the group. From there, sensing it was about to go to shit, we officially broke contact and double-timed our asses back to safety.

Now, lesser men may have decided to cut their losses and head home, but we weren't lesser men. No sir, we were paratroopers, so you can bet your sweet ass we were getting revenge. We decided that we would simply stay up that night and conduct an early morning raid on their compound. We waited out until 0330 and kept eyes on the objective the entire time. We used cover and concealment to make our approach, clearing one phase line at a time. Once were within striking distance, two of us deployed to LPOP position on the front porch, observing the window and looking out for motion.

Next, we sent in the heavy-hitters to secure the PHI BETA

GAMMA sign (or whatever the fucking Greek letters were) off the front of the house. At the same time, we kicked a secondary tactical team to acquire one of the kegs that were out back. In a targeted and coordinated attack, we ripped the sign off the wall and yanked a keg out of the ice bucket.

The sign proved both difficult to break off and loud as fuck in doing so. The lights clicked on and we had movement in the house, but by that time it was far too late. With both the sign and the keg in hand, we ran off into the night and tore off back to the barracks, never to be seen at High Point University again. The keg and the sign ended up becoming a badge of honor that was passed down from room to room as guys ETS'd and PCS'd out of the platoon. I often wonder who has 'em now.

While living the frat life without the ability to sleep through class was fun, we also spent a lot of time growing up there. The 82nd started to teach me that basic training was just that—basic. I didn't really know shit about being a soldier and I was far from the combat killer we all claimed to be. We were just young boys, really, still wet behind the ears and naïve to all the aspects of life. We didn't grasp just how serious and dangerous soldiering was. But a little trip to the desert was going to change all of that.

We were set up for a rotation to Oman. The Sultanate of Oman is a country on the southeastern coast of the Arabian Peninsula in Western Asia and the oldest independent state in the Arab world. Located in a strategically important position at the mouth of Persian Gulf, Oman is a friend to the West. As such, that meant we spent time cross-training with them, both in Oman and hosting them here stateside.

We were all excited about doing the training. For us, living in the world prior to the War on Terror, this was as close to a deployment as we were getting. Besides, anything that got us out of the shitty-ass woods of Ft. Bragg was a blessing from on high in our eyes. The orders came down and the ADVON party went out to get things set up while we packed up all our gear, got issued desert camo (we thought we were the coolest), and prepared for the month under the sun.

Now, I'd like to say they set us up in the most luxurious accommodations, but that would be a lie. We were put in a tent compound with a raised bin that held water for our showers. Let me tell you, that water was cold as fuck in the morning. Almost no one took a shower then unless it was life or death; we waited until it was late in the afternoon and the sun had the time to warm it up. We'd spend our days training and then our nights up on the ridgeline pulling security. It was the first time that we'd ever pulled security with live rounds, and while none of us really believed there was a need for it, one can't help but wonder, was this the next international incident waiting to happen? So, even with doubt, we took security seriously.

The trip was mostly training and playing soccer with the Omani soldiers. Everything seemed to be just like training back home, and we had settled into a rhythm and routine, and to be honest, we were enjoying ourselves. Most of the training that we were focused on was clearing the waddies, these natural trench lines that ran through the desert floor. Back home, we were still practicing World War II tactics, so Battle Drill 7AP Enter/Clear a Trench was our specialty.

Inside the waddies, we had placed targets to simulate enemies that needed to be terminated as we maneuvered through while clearing the area. We were doing this in bounding overwatch formation when a moment of carelessness almost turned fatal. As Henneberger was bounding forward, Jaron was moving up the waddie behind him. Jaron had placed his SAW up on a rock and was attempting to engage targets on his tiptoes due to his relatively short height.

As Jaron engaged his target, his weapon's bipod legs slipped off the rocks. This caused his barrel to drop to the left. All of this occurred in a flash and Jaron's finger was still on the trigger. As the weapon slipped, Jaron slipped, and the rounds entered the back of Henneberger' s right arm. Their team leader, Sgt. Robb, was pretty shaken by the scene and needed the heroic, debonair SSG Veith to calm him down and get control of the situation. I do not recall how many rounds hit Dan, but he was able to make a full recovery.

Our whole purpose of flying halfway around the world to the Sultanate of Oman was to train with their soldiers and earn Omani jump wings. Having the coveted silver wings on your chest is cool and all . . . but having a pair of foreign wings on your chest is otherworldly.

Well, thanks to this friendly fire clusterfuck, we never got a chance to make the jump. All training was shut down and an investigator from Bragg was sent out to figure out what the hell happened. So, yeah . . . we flew 7,533 miles there and never got a chance to jump. Paratroopers don't like to fly that far and not jump.

The platoon as a whole was pretty shaken up by everything, and in truth, we were happy to get back stateside and put it all behind us. We were already looking forward to the block leave we had coming up. I was slated to leave in two days when I got a call from my ex, Robin.

Ex, you say? Yeah, I forgot to mention that I got "Jodied" while I was gone. There had been several friends who told me she was cheating on me with this guy named Colin back home. Every time I asked her, she denied it, but always added another detail to the story.

"Oh, no, I didn't do anything with him."

"Oh, well, yeah, he stayed with us at the lake, but nothing happened."

"I kissed him, but I didn't want to tell you because I thought you'd freak out."

"Okay, I sucked his dick."

She was the first girl to cheat on me, but Lord knows she wouldn't be the last. For some reason, I tend to attract un-loyal-ass hoes—err, I mean "women who value different dick opportunities." Anyway, as you can imagine, I was surprised to get a call from her, but it turns out, much like the phone call saying she sucked his dick, it was more bad news. My brother had killed himself.

Gene had continued to have problems with drugs and run-ins with the law since I had been gone. I am sure that Sadie's death had done nothing to help him face down his demons or get control over his reckless impulses; no doubt it only exasperated the problem. He had already had several close calls. He'd gotten his arm broken in a drug deal gone wrong, and he was actually locked up at the time. He had been cleared for work release, and if my memory serves me correctly, he was working for Bobby at the time.

There remains some conspiracy surrounding the night that he died. Apparently, the night that it went down, two cars were seen headed down to the bars. Some don't believe that he actually killed himself. Others do. To this day, it remains an unsolved mystery. The only thing that is known is, the next morning when the electric company came to read the meter, the meterman found Gene hanging in the barn, dead.

Now, this would be the second Red Cross message that I had gotten in the military, and for the second time in a row, they would fuck this up. Keep in mind, I was supposed to head out for block leave in two days anyway, and they still couldn't get me out earlier. What made it even worse was the uncomfortable exchange I had with the unit chaplain.

After I got off the call, I found myself sitting in a room trying to process what exactly had gone down. This was the second family death in a really tight time frame. To their credit, the army did try their best to console me and provide some help with dealing with the loss. The chaplain stepped up to the plate, swung hard, and struck right the fuck out.

Now, I can't tell you what the correct thing is to say to someone who is reeling from the recent news of a friend or family member killing themselves. I don't know if there is such a thing as the "right thing" to say. With that said, what I can tell you is, do not open with, "Your brother might not have gone to Hell."

Sitting there in my room in the barracks, the chaplain asked if I was Christian, to which I replied yes. He then went on to say, "I know the Bible says that those who commit suicide will go to Hell, but we don't know his mindset at the time. We don't know if he asked for forgiveness before he did it, or soon after he jumped. That is between him and God."

Now, before everyone Bible-thumper gets pissed and throws a temper tantrum screaming, "Goddamn right he's burning in eternal damnation and hellfire for his sin!! How dare you say otherwise?!" just pump your brakes. 'Cause none of us know, and we won't know until we get to the other side. What we do know is that mental health issues are a very real thing and that the chemical makeup in someone's brain is dramatically affected by depression, and I personally believe God accounts for that.

With all of that said, I didn't ask the chaplain about Hell and my brother, and in my opinion, it was in very poor taste to bring it up, especially to lead with it. All that did was make me tune out the rest of his conversation. In my eyes, this conversation was more about his judgment of a man he never met and less about consoling me and my loss. I stayed in the room until I was cleared to walk out and never spoke to that man again.

The Army took its absolute sweet fucking time approving my emergency leave which, once again, almost made me miss a family member's funeral. They finally approved me the night before his service and I was cleared to leave the next morning. I arrived home just a few hours before the service and walked into the kitchen to see a sight I hadn't seen in my entire life: Bobby crying.

I have often heard it said that nothing is worse than experiencing the loss of your child, and Bobby exemplified that. As close as he was with Sadie, I never saw him shed a tear for her. Matter of fact, even though we all thought he would die soon after her, he actually blossomed in a weird way. The man started dating and even settled down (I can't remember if they got married or not) with Mom's best friend, who had become a widow herself.

But, sitting there in the kitchen, it was clear the death of his second-oldest son broke his heart, and he was reeling from it. Despite the estrangement that we had in our relationship and all the years I felt less than a son to him, I felt sorry for him. It was clear he loved his boy, and now he was gone.

Despite that fact, I knew that my time going home was done. Sadie had been the glue that held the family together, and with her gone, it was falling apart. Some of them were upset Bobby had moved on. Which, in his defense, was a selfish opinion. What was he supposed to do, be lonely for the rest of his life? But with Gene's death, it was abundantly clear that the splintering family had officially broken. I watched them put my brother into the ground, said my goodbyes, and walked away, never to go home again.

Back in Fort Bragg, life resumed as normal, and I spent the next year learning the ins and outs of soldiering. I took part in numerous FTXs, did a dick-ton more jumps, and worked my way up to lead gunner in the weapons squad. I had gotten a new computer right as AOL was kicking off, so I decided that it was time to connect with the world through chat rooms. Around this same time, I had gotten a new roommate, a young and impressionable kid who seemed innocent and was a natural athlete. It never occurred to me at the time that those attributes would work in unison to set up the next chapter of my life—and ruin it, too.

I met Emily in a chat room and we hit it off right away. Up until that point, she was easily the prettiest girl I had ever talked to. She was short and petite with a big bubble butt, blonde hair, and blue eyes. That alone would have been enough to make me drive my bitch ass to D.C., but the fact that her daddy was an officer sealed the deal. After all, there is nothing us enlisted guys like more than getting with an officer's daughter. It's like payback for all the fucking they did to us.

We "dated" online and even had a couple of visits. She was hot and we were sleeping together. That alone is enough to make a man do stupid-ass shit, but when you couple that with what I saw when I visited her, I was ready to sign my life away for a second time.

On one of my trips up, she took me on base at Fort Myer, in Arlington, VA. For a young grunt "growing up" in Fort Bragg, it looked like a slice of heaven. The land of milk and honey. As we drove around the base, it was pristine, but more importantly to me, there were no details of "joes" out doing post police calls or cutting the grass with scissors. Nope, they actually had contractors doing this shit. I was floored.

I then had an epiphany. I didn't have plans for after the military. I didn't really like jumping out of planes, especially the way that the 82nd just threw your ass out in anything and everything, and I could use that bonus enlistment cash. Not only that, but getting into the Old Guard actually had height and weight requirements that precluded many soldiers from getting in. At 5'11", I made the cutoff, but most soldiers were shorter than that, as I already alluded to.

I added all of that to the fact that I was in love and said, "Fuck it, why not re-enlist?" So that's just what I did. Now, let me give you young cats a little bit of advice: if you are making life choices that include someone else's life, you'd be wise to talk to them before you make 'em. I was not wise and didn't have a conversation with her. I was in love with her and thought she was in love with me. So, instead, I went the surprise route and, in turn, got a surprise of my own: she was fucking my roommate.

Now, this was starting to become a theme, and if I am honest, I have looked in the mirror and thought to myself, *What the hell is wrong with me?* on more than one occasion. I still don't know, and so here we are, years later, still asking the same question. What wasn't in question anymore, though, was that I was headed north and my time in the 82nd had come to a close.

This would be my first time leaving a unit, and when you do you get a sense akin to graduating high school. You look back at the time spent and the lessons learned. You reflect on how you have grown and you hope for promise of the future. For me looking back, I knew I had grown immensely, not only as a soldier, but as a man. I had found my footing and started to believe that not only could I do this soldier thing, but that I could actually be pretty damn good at it.

I had gone from a kid who couldn't climb the rope to a pretty solid PT stud (thanks to Drill Sergeant Escamilla never letting me fucking eat). I was crushing my PT tests and had started to find a love for working out that would stay with me for the rest of my life and shape my future in ways I couldn't have even dreamed of back then.

I had learned that leadership meant you take care of your guys, even if it meant sacrificing your ass. I learned that your boys better have your back, even when it means that all of you are about to catch an asswhooping. Most importantly, I learned how to be tough, arguably for the first time in my life. I learned that I wasn't glass. That taking a punch wasn't gonna kill me, and that getting yelled at when I messed up didn't mean I was a horrible human; it just meant I fucked up.

It's a lesson I wish we could teach to society today. Now, I am not advocating for yelling at your people. It's a shitty way to lead. Anytime this happens, You need to do this to remind yourself that you lost control of your emotions and the respect of your team.

As I loaded up the truck and pulled out the gates of Ft. Bragg one final time, I realized that I was saying goodbye not only to my time there, but my time as kid. I was an E-4 and getting ready to be promotable. I knew that arriving at Ft. Myer, especially coming from a "line unit," I would be expected to lead right away. I could no longer fall back on being "just a kid." It was time for me to grow up and start acting like a man. I drove out those gates with a smile on my face and excitement for the future. Little did I know that what lay ahead of me would change not only my life, but the world as we know it.

Chapter Nine

Gardens of Stone

"I walked a mile with Pleasure;
She chatted all the way;
But left me none the wiser
For all she had to say.

I walked a mile with Sorrow;
And ne'er a word said she;
But, oh! The things I learned from her,
When Sorrow walked with me."
—Robert Browning Hamilton

Pulling into Fort Myer felt like a totally different world. It was a small base; I think the entire thing was maybe two miles long. It sat just outside of D.C. and backed up to Arlington National Cemetery. The base was home to the 3rd U.S. Infantry, "The Old Guard." This unit had the distinction of being the oldest active infantry regiment in the U.S. Army, and had been tasked with the most important ceremonial duties in the Army, such as the Tomb of the Unknown Soldier, The Army Drill Team, Army Band, and Caisson Platoon.

Reception was rather quick this time and I found myself assigned to "Cell-Block C," or Charlie Guard. Arriving there, it really felt more like a frat house than military barracks. At Ft. Bragg, we had nothing to do and almost zero good-looking women within a sixty-mile radius. Ft. Myer was the exact opposite.

Sitting on a hilltop overlooking D.C., it was literally the epicenter of entertainment. I know of no other base that sits that close to that many things to do. I mean, everything was within walking distance (at least for a grunt) and the mass transit available there ensured that nothing was out of reach. In the 82nd, we may have mastered making the most of what we had, but at Ft. Myer, they mastered making the most of having the most.

The Spec Four Mafia was in full effect at Myer as well. I instantly fell in lockstep with Andrew Johnson, a guy we called "Rockbiter" because of his teeth, but the dude could pull ladies like it was going out of style. He was a laid-back roughneck and one of my favorite people I met in the Army. The road dog was Wayne Myers, a pretty boy with a sad past that put everyone else to shame. His girlfriend was so hot that everyone else used to just stare at her when she walked by. Then there was PFC Price. He was a young African American kid who could dance his ass off and had a thing for the larger ladies.

My first night in the barracks was surreal. Now, keep in mind, at the 82nd, I never saw women in the barracks. Hell, unless you were in another fucking town, you never saw any women at all. My first night at Ft. Myer, there were more women in the barracks than I saw in clubs in Fayetteville. And not just any women, I mean really, really good-looking women. I even saw one woman go room to room and get a "DIB" (dick infantry badge) by sleeping with dudes from several different rooms. I was stunned.

What was crazy about Ft. Myer is that it seemed like it was a respectable way for rich girls to go "slummin'." These girls were going to prestigious colleges and had pedigrees that were far above the raising of the young grunts in the Old Guard. But, because D.C. was such a populated place, they didn't get overrun by the young military males like at Ft. Bragg.

In Fayetteville, Ft. Bragg made the town. Without it, the economy would collapse. Despite that fact, the locals loathed the military. So, that meant that you always felt unwelcome most anywhere you went; that, or you knew the goal was to take advantage of you, which in turn made you feel unwelcomed.

Not at Ft. Myer. There you were actually cool. Most of the college kids thought you must be a steely-eyed killer and the fact that you were always in dress blues made you seem a lot more badass than you were. Plus, as it wasn't a hike to get back to the barracks, it was actually fun for the females to come on post with you. It felt like they were getting access to some top-secret world, and that made it even easier to convince 'em to come back.

On top of that, there were so many schools in and around the area that there was never any big drought in dating. What's more, because the nightlife in D.C. was so prominent, you didn't really ever have to deal with college boys 'cause no one was going back to frat houses; they were going out clubbing instead. I didn't know much about much, but I knew that I had made the absolute right choice to move up here. It may have happened for a bad reason, but as I learned in life, it's all about making the fuck-up fabulous, and that's just what I did.

We lived in D.C. and Baltimore Clubs. From foam parties to late night after-parties, all we did was, well, party. Women were always in the barracks and you didn't need to ask if anyone wanted to go out, cause they were literally already out. I had gone from large chain-smoking "dependas" (overweight Army spouses) being the only women around to smoking hot college girls with Daddy's money and futures. It was a glorious rebellion against the women who broke my heart to get me here.

Besides the crowds of women, one of the first things you have to go through upon your arrival at Ft. Myer is ROP. Regimental Orientation Program is designed to teach you all you need to know in order to do your duties. This covers everything from how to press your uniform (each barracks had its own set of presses and it was up to you to press your uniform every day) to the different form of drills and ceremonies they used in the Old Guard compared to the rest of the Army. You also learned how to stand at attention, for like, a long-ass time.

You see, besides performing funerals in Arlington, you also spent a dick-ton of time doing things like cordons, GOs, and DAs (both forms of retirement ceremonies), all of which included you standing at attention for hours at a time, in the freezing snow, pouring rain, and blistering heat. This is to simulate any number of the ceremonies you may be required to participate in. All of which you did wearing a thick wool uniform. Which somehow couldn't keep you warm in the winter but absolutely baked your ass in the summer.

The worst sin you could do in the Old Guard was pass out or break military bearing. That's why the last thing you did in ROP was a stress test. For that, you get in full uniform, go though inspection of said uniform, demonstrate proficiency in following drill and ceremony commands, and stand at attention for an hour. I know it doesn't sound bad on the surface. I mean, how hard is to stand for an hour? Well, let me tell you, it's hard as hell.

You can't move. You can't wipe the sweat from your eyes. You can't swat the fly off your nose. You just stand there and let that fucker crawl all over your face. If someone farts, you can't laugh. You can't scratch an itch and you can't get a drink when you're thirsty. You simply sit there, cocooned in that wool jacket, like a pig in a blanket, and bake in the hot summer sun or have your nose freeze off in the winter

Oh, and just for fun, they bring a rubber chicken around and make it squawk in your ear. It is damn near impossible not to laugh with a rubber chicken and a shit-eating-grin-wearing specialist agitating you in front of your face. But when you pull it off, you're welcomed into a pretty unique brotherhood. Lot of folks look at the Old Guard as toy soldiers, and I understand why. The limited field time. The pomp and flair of the drill and ceremony and spit and polish give credence to the idea that you're more show than soldier. Little did we know that in due time, we'd show just how much of soldiers we actually were.

Upon completion of ROP, you are then cleared to go represent the Army to the world. I was lucky enough to be assigned to an eight-man casket team, and to this day, it remains one of my most loved jobs I've ever done. To me, not only was eight-man the coolest, but it was one of the most respected jobs you could get. I looked at eight-man as the show. There was only one squad in each company that could do it. You had to be decently strong because the caskets were heavy, so not everyone could fit the bill. You were always the focal point of each funeral and you only did "full honors."

On top of all of this, you are there at a very personal and intimate time in strangers' lives. A point of both great grief, and great pride for the family. Knowing how much that means to them, and the importance of getting it right, made every day hell, and every funeral matter.

Full honors funerals are for commissioned officers, warrant officers, and senior non-commissioned officers (pay grade E-9). Full honors includes an escort platoon (size varies according to the rank of the deceased) and a military band. Normally, the deceased service member's branch of service is responsible for carrying out the military honors at the funeral. Those eligible for full military honors may also use the caisson if it is available. Also, it became effective in January 2009 that all service members who die from wounds received as a result of enemy action and are being interred, inurned, or memorialized at Arlington National Cemetery are eligible to receive full military honors, regardless of rank.

I worked in Charlie Guard for two full years and I had an absolute blast doing so. I was quickly promoted to sergeant, about six months after arriving to the unit. From there I performed well in PLDC, and was in the running for honor grad until I messed up and missed an alarm one day. I am still pissed my failure to plan cost me that accolade.

The worst part of getting promoted was getting pushed out of caskets and moved to a firing party. Now, don't get me wrong, giving the commands for the 21-gun salute was an honor in and of itself, and I took the job extremely seriously. But in my eyes, it still lacked the seriousness of the eight-man casket teams. Regardless, I still loved being in Charlie Company and was really falling in love with being a soldier. For the first time, I felt like I had found a place that I belonged and a job that I loved. Little did I know that I was about to get a firsthand lesson that everything rises and falls on leadership, and why people don't quit jobs, they quit leaders.

I had become so enamored with soldiering that I was looking to make it a career. I knew that if I wanted to make it to the top in the infantry, I needed to secure one feather in my cap above all. I need to become Ranger-qualified. With that notion in mind, I began to train to do just that.

Chad Pickering became one of my battle buddies and best friends. He was an absolute wildman. It could be argued that out of everyone I've met in life who didn't give a fuck, he gave the least. He was a smartass who was as quick to bust a private's balls as he was any senior NCOs or officers who crossed his path. Chad loved Brazilian Jiu-Jitsu and I credit him 100 percent with getting me started in the art.

Because he could beat almost everyone's ass in the company along with being a Ranger (actually served in Battalion), he carried a level of respect among the men that was second to none. And with good reason; most of the NCOs there weren't worth a whole lot, so when good ones like Pick came around, they really stood out in the crowd.

Both of us were E-5s and in SSG Muller's squad. SSG Muller was a good guy in his own right but he had a kinda Eeyore personality. I wouldn't call him negative, exactly, but he really wasn't that excited of a guy. He cared about his guys but he also wasn't inspiring, and to be fair, with Pick and me, he had two solid knuckleheads to deal with.

Rounding out the squad were the first two privates that I got as babies during my first years as an NCO: PFC Daniel Holmes and PFC Eric Church. It would be hard for me to express the love I had for those guys, even though they made it difficult all the time. Looking back on my time with them through the eyes of the father I am today, I see similarities in how Pick and I "raised 'em" and how I raise my kids.

In the Army, when you are NCO, you are responsible for everything your men do and fail to do. I mean every single thing. They get in a fight, your fault. They bounce a check, your fault. They fail to show up for formation, again, your fault. No matter what happens, no matter if you were aware of it or not, no matter if you were even in the same state as the transgression that happened when it happened, it still remains your fault.

It goes without saying that leads to a lot of micromanaging. When you are a young leader and you are doing your best not to get yelled at for some dumb shit your guys have done, it tends to make you get on their ass 24/7. All of this was, of course, conflicted by the fact that some NCOs live in the barracks with the guys and most NCOs are barely "grown" themselves.

I mean, think about it. The average age of the NCO chain is as follows:

Sergeant (E-5) – 22 (join + 4.2 years)
Staff Sergeant (E-6) – 27 (join + 8.5 years)
Sergeant First Class (E-7) – 32 (join + 13.6 years)
Master Sergeant/First Sergeant (E-8) – 35 (join + 17 years)

At twenty-two years of age, your brain hasn't even finished

developing, and we got these guys in charge of eighteen-year-olds fresh off their momma's tit. It doesn't always make for the smartest decisions. But, as Terry Prachett said, "Wisdom comes from experience. Experience is often a result of lack of wisdom."

It was from those early years of learning how to lead that I begin to lay the foundation for leadership style. I learned that yelling will get you an immediate response, but coaching will get you lasting results. I learned that leadership isn't a popularity contest and it's not about being friends or the most-liked guy in the room. It's about accomplishing the mission, and more importantly, getting your men to want to accomplish it as well.

As life progressed, I continued to excel in my new home. I was one of the "go-to" sergeants when things needed to get done. I was respected by the men in the platoon and those up and down the COC. I absolutely loved our 1SG, EJ "Skullcrusher" Snyder. He was a maverick and I'll never forget him forming us up after the company had gotten shit on. He was out in front wearing a World War II helmet and a short stubby little baton thing just like in the *Patton* movie. He formed us up and turned around and screamed, "We're not gonna take it anymore!"

EJ was a massive guy. Tall and block-thick. He had a way that resonated with his men. You had zero doubt he'd skull-fuck you and smile, but at the same time, he wasn't brutish and was actually very approachable. I'll never forget how he came up on me on the EIB (Expert Infantryman's Badge) lanes and talked me through my nerves at the hand grenade lane I had double "no-go"ed the year prior and had failed my first attempt again that year.

When you throw the grenade, it must land and "explode" within a fifteen-meter radius of the target. Year after year, mine either rolled out of the kill zone or, in an effort to not overthrow it, landed several feet short of the target. I was 100 percent in my head and it looked like I was headed down that same path again this year. EJ came in and told me to "aim small, miss small." He even made a bit of a jig to go with the chant.

Relieving the tension made all the difference, and he was the first person I looked for when I completed the twelve-mile road march in under three hours to earn my EIB. He was one of the best NCOs I have ever known, then and now. I was so happy when I saw that he continued to dominate after he retired by becoming a celebrity in the survival world. He has competed multiple times on *Naked and Afraid* and made his own badass survival knife. I love seeing great things happen to good people.

While the command climate was great when I first got there, the subsequent commanders I would face in the Old Guard would be the reason I would decide to get out of the Army. The change wasn't overnight and I was still very much committed to being a soldier for life. As I mentioned before, if you are going to rise in the ranks in the infantry, you must get Ranger-tabbed (i.e., deemed qualified). Pick, my fellow E-5, had been helping me with the preparations. I was starting to study the Ranger Handbook and working to ensure I was in tip-top shape for when my time came (no more saggy titties for this guy, I actually had pecs!). The first step would be for me to pass the company's Pre-Ranger course.

The Pre-Ranger course is a mini Ranger School conducted at the unit level. It is run by individuals who are, at minimum, Ranger-qualified, or, at best, from BAT. I applied for the next iteration of the course along with one of my privates (Holmes) and we both got in. Pick had also been slotted to be an instructor, so we knew we had a special beatdown coming.

We packed up and headed down to Fort A.P. Hill, which is where the Old Guard did all of its field training. No one liked the place, and it also had a particularly difficult land nav course. The course was rumored to have been created by Navy SEALs, but then, anytime something is hard, people make up shit, so who knows. Heading up the program was one of the toughest men I have ever met in my life: 1SG Reha.

He was the first African American redneck I had ever met. Now that I think of it, he's the only one I have ever met. He was short and had a bald head. He would come to work in bib overalls, no shirt, and always had a wad of chew in his mouth or dip in his lip. He took no shit, and he absolutely broke us off.

Pre-Ranger course was the hardest thing I have ever done physically. They smoked us nonstop. All we did was patrol, PT, and classroom setting instruction. Truth of the matter is that, in many ways, I found the classroom to be harder than the field. Sitting there cold, wet, sleep-deprived, and hungry as fuck made it impossible to pay attention to what you were doing.

One minute you'd be writing notes, only to wake up and look down at your paper to see straight lines that were produced because you fell asleep while writing and the pen just continued to drift across the paperwork. Not only were you sleep-deprived, you were also starving because food restriction was the norm, so your brain is in the worst possible state.

Ranger School, and by default Pre-Ranger, is a leadership school first and foremost. The goal is to break you down and simulate a combat environment as best as possible in a peacetime situation in order to see how you lead under the stress with little sleep and food. As a result, you spend the bulk of the course learning how to plan and conduct squad- and platoon-level operations.

Every man (and woman, nowadays) gets an opportunity to lead at some point and you are judged by the cadre. There has been said to be politics involved in this, and in my case that's exactly what happened, but more on that in a few. Pre-Ranger taught me that when I thought I was done, I had more to give. There were numerous times during the course I felt like saying, "Fuck this." I am sure it enters the mind of almost everyone who goes through that type of training at least once. The key is to push it out of your mind as soon as it enters.

I was never the biggest, fastest, or strongest in anything I have ever done. I'll never forget, we had one night where you couldn't get released until you won a shuttle race. I tried over and over and over, but I was just never fast enough. On top of that, I gave it my all every time, but other guys would hedge their bets and go easier in the races they knew they couldn't win and then go all-out to win the races they thought they could. The result? They were fresh and I would lose to them and have to run yet again.

I lost over and over and over again. Matter of fact, I stayed in to damn near the last guy. It was the closest I have ever come to crying from physical activity in my life. It was demoralizing. I started to feel as if I could never win, and out of the entire course, it was the closest I came to saying "Fuck it" and quitting. When I finally won a race and was cleared to go eat, I may have been the happiest I've ever been outside of becoming a daddy.

As is the case with any good infantry school, road marching was a staple of the training. I'd go as far as to say it was one of the focal points of the training. "How far can you walk and with how much weight, all while still being combat-effective at the destination?" remains the most important question an infantryman is expected to answer.

One night, about halfway through the course and for reasons unknown to me, I got the worst blister of my entire life. Now, I ain't talking about some dime- or quarter-sized blister on my heel or big toe. No, I mean the entire sole of my heel was a blister. On top of that, I had several blisters between my toes.

Now, before I get all these cats talking shit, I did all the stuff you are supposed to do to take care of your feet. I had broken-in boots, changed into fresh socks, powdered my feet, so forth and so on. The reality is, if you walk far enough, long enough, with a heavy enough weight, sometimes your feet just get jacked up. It was an absolutely hellish walk and I was beyond happy when the movement stopped early the next morning.

When we stopped and removed our socks and boots, I was immediately sent to the aid station to get looked at. Now, I don't know if it was because I was delirious from sleep deprivation and being starved or if I just wanted to do something about the pain in my feet, but I completely glossed over what the medic said to me.

This motherfucker looked me right in the eyes and, with a straight face, said, "We are gonna inject acid into the blister." I don't think I even heard the guy. I just nodded my head in agreement, grateful for a chance to sit down and prop my feet up. I would realize in just a moment how ungrateful I was actually going to be.

The point of the acid injection is to cauterize the wound. Now, for some reason, they say this helps with pain and healing. "They" musta never got the procedure done because it didn't do either one of those things. What it did do was shoot a direct shot of pure fire into my heels that made it feel like my heel was going to melt off. To this day, I still rate it as one of the top-three most painful things I have felt. I have no shame at all in admitting I screamed out loud like a little kid.

Then this son of a bitch had the balls to say that he was going to go up and stick it in the other blisters as well. I looked him straight in the eyes and told him if he touched me with that needle one more time, I was going to beat him to death with my rifle. I grabbed my socks, my boots, and what was left of my pride and half-melted foot, and hobbled off back to the barracks. The worst part of it was this shit didn't help my feet heal at all. I am positive they just did this to fuck with me.

Everywhere you go and in anything you do, there remains a very high likelihood that you will run into someone you don't like or who doesn't like you. All of us have experienced simply not liking the look of someone's face, the way they walk, or the sound of their voice. It's not right and it's not fair, but we all do it. Truth be told, I don't know if the primordial part of our brain is responsible for it, but some motherfuckers you just don't like.

That was the case for me in ROP with one of the cadres. I can't remember the guy's name, but I absolutely hated him. He had a smartass tone to him that extended beyond the customary brusqueness of being Ranger Cadre. It's hard to explain, but sometimes you can feel that the guy isn't playing a role he's been assigned, but rather he's just a dickhead in real life.

I have always asked my guys (and so should anyone in a leadership position in a military or para-military origination) if they know what hazing is. Every time, I get some standard answer about mistreatment. To me, the alarmism around anything similar to hazing is the reason why we have gone soft when it comes to the training we are willing to put our people through.

You see, you can't nice your way out of bullets, ass-whoopings, raging house fires, and violent mental patients. Sometimes you must take an ass-beating to get the win. It's just the reality of life. If the first time you've ever gotten your ass beat is in a life-or-death situation, there's a strong chance you won't make it out of there alive. So, we need that hard training.

For me, the litmus test for hazing was always the following question: "Am I doing this for his benefit or my ego?" Far too many folks, especially junior leaders and frat boys, do it for their ego. They finally are "in charge" and can smoke someone, so they do it for no other reason than they can. That type of thrashing does nothing to make the individual better, and in truth, it breeds resentment and contempt for the leader.

However, I have found more times than not, sheepdogs want the hard training because they realize that it is preparing them for the reality they will face in combat and on the streets. Those shared moments of suffering not only teach the soldier what they have in them but strengthens the bond among their peers and even with the leader inflicting the pain.

This cadre dick that was helping facilitate the training was the kind that used it to feed his ego. And the guy hated me and my private, Holmes, who was with us. I am not sure what I did to this cadre. He messed with us relentlessly, and as much as I hate to admit it, I lost military bearing one night around 0200 in the morning.

He was tearing into Holmes for some shit that Holmes didn't even do. In that moment, tired as fuck and tired of this guy's shit, I stopped being a candidate for selection and reverted back to Holmes's Sgt. And as his sergeant, I wasn't going to let him get needlessly toyed with. Before I even realized what I was saying, I yelled in the bunk room, "Hey, why don't you leave him the fuck alone?"

What ensued next was wrong on my part. We got into a screaming match right there in the bunk room in front of everyone. I was out of line and had every right to get booted out of the program right then and there. I had forgotten my place and let my mouth move before I got my brain to filter what was taking place. Me and this guy were nose to nose and damn near ready to come to blows when the group separated us.

My buddy Pick took me outside and he, along with my new sworn enemy, smoked the shit out of me for hours. I mean I was absolutely thrashed. I couldn't have gotten my ass beat any worse if they physically attacked me. I was dead by the time they were done, but I was still in the course and so I counted my blessings.

At the end of the course, you are given the decision regarding your recommendation to take one of the slots to go to Ranger School. It came as no surprise to me that the dickhead didn't recommend me. He gave a long list of why I was a piece of shit, and while I stood there and took it, I just kept thinking to myself, *Right back at you, buddy.*

After his dissertation on my shit-bagness, it was Pick's turn to speak. He stood up and said right to that cadre, "Everyone knows Danny's my friend, and everyone knows you don't like him. Therefore, both of our evaluations have bias. I think we should cancel each other out and let the remaining members decide." He sat back down with little fanfare, and the group recommended that I take one of the slots to go to Ranger School.

Chapter Ten

Ranger School

"Discipline is the soul of an Army. It makes small numbers formidable; procures success to all of the weak, and esteem to all."
– George Washington

When we first signed up to go to Ranger School, we were told that we had to complete the course within one year. I was excited for the opportunity to check the next big box on my list to make the U.S. Army a career and rise through the ranks. But, as life had shown me in the past, sometimes it has a different plan for you.

As I was getting ready to ship out to Ranger School in the next couple weeks, I got another emergency Red Cross message. This time, Bobby had been cutting a tree down when a limb or portion of the tree had fallen and struck him in his head. He had to be rushed to the hospital and it wasn't clear at the moment if he would make it.

Now, for those of you unfamiliar with Ranger School, it's a sixty-one-day suckfest broken down over three phases: Darby, Mountains, and Swamp. It's a frequent occurrence that you get recycled and have to do a phase over again; what's not going to happen, however, is getting to leave and come back to resume the same day that you left, meaning that if you left on day thirty, you would have to start back on day zero when you returned.

That left me in quite the predicament. With the status of Bobby up in the air, it legitimately meant that I could get into Ranger School, make it several weeks, and then have to make a decision to either leave and start over, or not go to his funeral if he passed away. So, for me, I thought this was a no-brainer. I'd simply push my date to the next available class. I thought that was the common sense solution. I quickly learned my CO either lacked common sense or he was a bit of dick.

Captain Jansick, to this day, remains my most-hated leader I have ever had. He was a tall, red-headed-step-child motherfucker. He had a strong and pronounced jawline that always made him look pissed. Truth is, he probably was constantly pissed. He gave out Article 15s like candy. When one of the company's soldiers committed suicide, he came out and gave the least heartfelt talk to his men that I've ever heard. On top of that, he sent the guy's friends to his place to collect his TA-50 and help with clean up. He was an absolute piece of shit, and we all hated him.

Well, he called me into his office to talk with me about my situation. I explained to him that I had almost missed my mother's and brother's funerals and that I had no desire to see that play out again with my father. He didn't give a shit. He looked me right in the eyes and said, "If you don't go to this school, you will be refusing the offer of Army schools and you will never get a chance to go to another as long as I am here."

I was dumbfounded. I just stood there looking at him, waiting for him to say, "Psych, just kidding!" After a few moments, he realized that I hadn't quite processed what he had said. So, he asked, "What's it gonna be, sergeant?"

I snapped to attention and said, "If you think it's a choice between the Army and my family, it's not, sir. I will be a refusal of Army schools." I saluted him and walked out of his office.

To this day, I have only one real regret in my lifetime: that I let that asshole win. Not in that moment per se, but in the fact that I let his "No" mean no for the rest of my life. I didn't seek to find another way to get into Ranger School. I just got pissed off at him and said, "Fuck the Army." In that moment, with several years left on my contract, I made the conscious decision that I would be getting out at the end of this term.

I let a shitty leader (a temporary problem) affect me so much that I made a permanent decision. That decision has led to lasting ramifications; those fifteen minutes played out into a life that could potentially have been very different.

I work hard not to "what if" things to death. I very much believe you wind up where you were meant to be. So, it's not that I am sad about my current situation; rather, I just regret that I let that guy win by allowing his interference to be the final say in a dream I still wish could have come true today, especially given the fact Bobby made a full recovery.

I was pretty pissed at the clown and I knew that I was getting out of the Army at my ETS date, but I refused to stop caring about doing a good job. I did all I could to keep my guys focused on the mission at hand and their role as infantry soldiers. I wanted whatever team I was with to be first in all categories, and we worked hard to get there.

The hardest thing to do in a unit like the Old Guard is to remind them that they aren't just "toy soldiers." At any point in time, they can be called upon to close with, engage, and destroy the enemies of our country. Prior to 9/11, that was hard to remember. During peacetime in the dog-and-pony show, combat is the furthest thing from your mind. I mean, even if a war did break out, you're stuck in D.C. You're nowhere near the front line. As a matter of fact, I remember vividly talking to a group of young soldiers at the chow hall and trying to impart on them the truth of the matter: you never know when, where, who, or how the fight will come to you. There's always a chance that the wolf will come knocking at your front door.

Turns out, I didn't realize just how fortuitous those words would be. Just a few days after that chow hall dinner, the wolf showed up right in our backyard, and our innocence would be lost forever, along with the rest of the world's.

I was upstairs in the off-post locker room, getting ready for a cordon, when one of the guys walked in and nonchalantly said, "Hey, man, a plane has flown into the World Trade Center."

I didn't have any idea of the scope of the matter and even quipped back, "How in the fuck do you fly into one of the world's tallest buildings?"

I didn't think much of it beyond that. After all, accidents happen all the time, and in that moment, there was nothing I could do about it anyway. I had a task in front of me to knock out and I still needed to inspect my guys' uniforms prior to the cordon. I threw my uniform on and headed downstairs to the common area to watch the news and wait for my guys to come down for inspection before we headed out the door.

When I got downstairs, everyone was gathered around the big-screen TV in the lobby. No one was speaking, which was extremely odd given everyone was almost always busting balls or bitching about something. My eyes followed everyone else's and drifted up towards the TV, and I saw what held sway over the room. That was the first time I saw the smoke billowing out of the World Trade Center's North Tower and I realized that this wasn't just some small prop plane.

I stood there, frozen in time, and my mind drifted to the same initial thought I had, only this time, I wondered how a large plane could have messed it up that bad. My daydreaming was shattered when, on live television, we saw the second plane crash into the South Tower, and instantly, we all knew this wasn't an accident. We were under attack.

When the second plane hit, the once-quiet room erupted with

activity. Everyone was talking at the same time, trying to make sense of what in the hell was actually going on. We quickly got word that all events for the day had been canceled as this was a threat to national security. With nowhere else to go that day, we all stayed in the lobby, staring at the TV and wishing we could do something, but knowing we were far removed from the fight.

Well, that notion was quickly thwarted when all of a sudden, a soldier burst in the front door and yelled out franticly that the Pentagon had been attacked.

Everyone looked around at each other, confused. Had we all heard him correctly? Had the Pentagon, the very symbol of the U.S. military's might, really been attacked? If so, how?

"What happened?" someone asked.

And the other guy said that another plane had flown into it as well. The Pentagon was only a few miles away. If they had attacked that, what else was next? How many other planes were out there? Was there going to be a ground attack? Who was behind this? Were we getting ready to be invaded? What were we gonna do? At that point, we couldn't answer most of the questions, but we could answer one: we were going to the Pentagon.

While the Old Guard is known mostly for its ceremonial duties, it has another equally, if not more important role: defense of our nation's capital. It also happened to be that Charlie Guard was up in rotation to be the response in case something happened, and here we were standing in the epicenter of "something."

We immediately went back and changed out of our dress blues and jumped into our BDUs. We headed down to the arms room and drew out weapons and ammunition, all of which just seemed insane to me. We were literally getting prepared for war on our home soil. Even though I had been preparing my guys for scenarios just like this, it still caught me a little off guard.

After everyone got their gear, we all assembled loosely behind the barracks. The guys stood around and made small talk while the senior NCOs and officers were getting orders and drafting plans. Overhead, you could hear fighter jets streaking through the sky, providing defense in the event another plane was out to make another attack run. For me, I think about how those pilots must have felt in that moment, flying over the nation's capital, knowing full well they might have to shoot down and kill the very citizens they had sworn to protect in order to protect more. That is a burden I didn't envy and I am glad I didn't have. Those planes were filled with Americans, but those planes could be used to kill potentially thousands or more. You're literally damned if you do and damned if you don't.

Standing there in the back, my eyes continued to dart between the soldiers in our company and through the steel-barred fence that separated the base from the civilian world. Outside those gates, I saw people walking by with unease and uncertainty in their eyes. They were afraid, and who could blame them? I surely didn't. Inside that gate, the soldiers shared much of their uneasiness. They, too, were unsure of how this was all going to play out. The only thing we did know for fact was that we were going to take part.

At the time, so much remained unknown, and as a result, confusion ran amuck. Even over official lines of communication, there was confusion. It was like the worst game of telephone ever played. There were all sorts of rumors flying around. All of them sounded horrifying, but in light of what we had all just witnessed, quite plausible. Some said there was another plane out there (which turned out to be true), then someone said car bombs were going off throughout D.C., and that the White House had been attacked, and package bombs were going off in mailboxes. Luckily, at least 98 percent of the bullshit wasn't true.

After what seemed like hours, we were given the green light to head to the crash site. We loaded up in LMTVs (Light Medium

Tactical Vehicles)—basically, big dump trucks that the military uses to haul everything from gear to troops—and made our way to the Pentagon. You could see the smoke in the skyline as we made our way down the highway. We took Boundary Channel Drive and got off on Connector Road. We exited onto North Rotary Road, and that was when I could start to smell it: fire and ash.

We continued down the road and rounded the southwestern corner of the building, and it was then that I first laid eyes on the carnage. The smoke was still billowing out of the structure and emergency response crews were running to and fro across the grounds in front of the building. Pentagon personnel, still in dress uniforms, and Class Bs were covered in soot, dirt, and blood as they were trying to tend to the wounded.

Firefighters were at the base of the building and on the roof. Huge jets of water were being sprayed into the building, while EMS crews were in a constant rotation of arriving, transporting the wounded to local area hospitals, and returning. News crews were already busy getting set up on a grassy knoll just beside South Washington Boulevard, overlooking the crash site.

With so many people converging on the same place at the same time, coupled with the enormity of what was going on, the tension was thick and hanging in the air. Everyone was on edge and there was immense pressure to do the right thing and uphold your weight. The LMTVs came to a halt and we all jumped out the back and lined up in formation, awaiting the next set of orders.

Very quickly, it was determined that we would be used to help augment the security of the building. Our company was dispatched to various checkpoints along the way. From there, we were set up in a tent that would serve as our base, and we began shiftwork, running security along the lines. Typically, security isn't a very exciting job, but when you have a fucking airplane that was used as a missile sitting inside the building behind you, let's just say it ups the ante quite a bit.

Now, since I brought up the whole rocket/missile thing, let me take the time to dispel a little conspiracy theory. It wasn't a rocket that hit the Pentagon. That is, unless your rocket comes with twin turbine engines, seats, seatbelts, birthday cards, wallets, bodies, and stuffed animals. I swear, it pisses me off so bad to hear folks say this dumbass shit.

It's just like when they say that no plane wreckage was pulled from the site. I'm like, "Who the fuck told you that, Kyle?" There absolutely was wreckage pulled from the site. I know, I watched it. I pulled security on it in the parking lot adjacent to the Pentagon where they collected and cataloged it. So please, put your tinfoil hat down, get back to your mom's basement, and resume *Dungeons & Dragons* from where you left off.

People often ask me, "What is the most scared you've ever been?" Truthfully, the answer is that it wasn't in combat. The most frightened I have ever been in my life was at the Pentagon. I was waking up after dozing off from 'round-the-clock work, and I saw firefighters running off the roof. They were sliding down the aerial tower ladder in a fast, frantic way. All of a sudden, the air siren went off and that wail shook everyone to their core. Now, if you've ever seen a *Nat Geo* show, you'll understand what I saw next.

Just like when a herd of any wild creatures is startled, all of the people inside the compound moved in a wave. The entire body of people within the fenced-in perimeter responded at once, and moved in the same direction, towards the one opening in the fence. It remains one of the most unnerving things I have ever seen. No one spoke, no one took charge, everyone just moved at once. It was like getting sucked up by undertow. You just felt compelled to move by some external force that you couldn't see, only feel.

Before I knew it, I was up and running with the herd. In all honesty, it was embarrassing. I didn't even think about it—I just reacted. Far from the hero I wanted to be. I didn't even snap out of it until we got outside and one of the other NCOs asked for a headcount. I quickly realized I needed to regain my bearings and get accountability for my men. Luckily for me, they had been swept up in the same wave and were outside the wire next to me. Turns out it was just a false alarm. They had thought that another plane was inbound. Thank God for everyone that turned out not to be the case.

If not for pure exhaustion, sleep would've been hard to come by. Instead of the normal routine of work all day and sleep all night, we all worked until we were relieved and slept when we could. The humming of heavy equipment and bright flood lights made any sleep we got pretty light.

The following day, us Old Guardsmen were pulled off the security side. The firefighters had gained control of the blaze and things had stabilized enough to begin the process of removing the remains of the fallen. That task, unbeknownst to us at the time, would fall to us, which, in hindsight, makes perfect sense since we were the ones who conducted the burials in Arlington National Cemetery day in and day out.

An NCO approached and called for a sergeant and his team, and although it's an old line not to volunteer for anything in the military, this situation was too serious for those classic jokes. I followed him to the staging area. I was instructed my men and I wouldn't need any of our gear, so I assumed we'd be doing some basic physical labor. We sat with people from various organizations until another officer and a civilian counterpart came up and began the brief of what our next task would be. They said that with the fire now under control and security established, the next phase of the operation could begin. That next phase would be the investigation, which was spearheaded by the FBI, and remains removal, which would fall to the Old Guard.

As we stood there and got prepped for what was going to happen, the enormity of the moment washed over me. I was going to go inside the Pentagon and look for bodies of my countrymen. I would be a leader of this mission. I had never experienced anything close to this, and my "men," who were boys younger than me, were in the same boat.

I realized I didn't have the luxury of needing a moment. I didn't have time to try and wrap my head around all that was going on around me. Most importantly, I couldn't show my trepidation, or any of my emotions, really.

Then the senior NCO said, "Follow me," and I knew I needed to remain steadfast and stoic. As we stepped off, I sent up a prayer that I could do just that.

The excerpt below from the book *Pentagon 9/11*, which I am quoted in, paints the bleak reality that we faced in that job. We would be required to sift through the rubble and debris and do our very best to find the remains of 189 people. That was no small task, given the magnitude of the explosion the plane caused.

American Flight 77 smashed into the west side of the Pentagon, bringing great damage to the building and death and injury to many of its inhabitants.

Despite the fortuitous circumstance that only 3,800 of the 4,500-5,000 intended occupants had moved into newly renovated Wedge 1 with its strengthened walls and windows and that Wedge 2 had been largely emptied of personnel (about 700 remained) as renovation began there, the exploding airliner exacted a heavy toll of dead and injured. Of the 125 Department of Defense fatalities in the Pentagon, 92 occurred on the 1st Floor, 31 on the 2nd Floor, and 2 on the 3rd Floor, all between Corridors 4 and 5. The dead included 70 civilians (10 of them contractor employees) and 55 military. The Army incurred the greatest loss—75 men and women. Another 106 injured were taken to area hospitals.

On the airliner, all 64 people died, including the 5 hijackers, most of them instantly. Among the six crew members were a husband and wife pair of flight attendants. A party of eight from the Washington area-three teachers, three 11-year-old students, and two escorts from the National Geographic Society had looked forward to a field trip to the Channel Island Marine Sanctuary in California. One of the children was the son of a Navy chief petty officer on duty in the Pentagon. A family of four, including two small children, and a honeymoon couple bound for Hawaii were among the victims. What befell two passengers--William Caswell and Bryan Jack--was especially ironic. Both were Department of Defense employees on official business trips and had offices in the Pentagon.

The attack killed 189 people, all of whom, with a few exceptions, died within minutes. Antoinette Sherman, an Army employee, died six days later in the hospital. Caswell and Jack on Flight 77 brought the total of DoD-affiliated fatalities in the Pentagon to 127.[3]

We were going to enter the Pentagon through the southwest corner of the building. If you look at a picture of where the plane hit, we entered through a door to the far right of the contact point, almost on the corner of the west side. To get there, we had to weave our way through a maze of volunteers that had set up base inside the fenced-in perimeter. There were literally hundreds of people and dozens of outside organizations on site to help support the effort.

Matter of fact, one of the most amazing things about that day to me was the sheer amount of support that came onsite. Everything you could need was there: cell phones for free phone calls, mobile kitchens set up by food vendors such as Burger King and Outback

Steakhouse to feed the responders for free 'round the clock, toiletries and socks handed out without charge by the Salvation Army, and a portable clothes-washing station set up by Tide. It truly was an amazing display of unity and community. In that regard, I always wish it was 9/12.

We finally cut through the maze, and as we were getting ready to head in, I saw firefighters headed out. It was at that moment that I realized there was one major difference between them and us: the amount of protective gear they had on.

All my men and I were simply given work gloves, a basic face mask like everyone wore during COVID, and a pair of muck boots. We wore that in conjunction with our BDUs. We had very little, if any, protection from the atmosphere within the building.

We were exposed to the fumes, the burnt and shredded wreckage, the fuel floating in the water from the fire hoses, and the remains themselves. The scents and vapors were heavy from all the moisture and smoke in the air. We didn't think about it much at the time, but seventeen years later at our first reunion, we realized that we are all seeing ramifications to our health from that exposure. Skin conditions, gut issues, and autoimmune disorders, to name a few. Regardless of what's not working with our bodies now, we would do it all over again in a heartbeat. We took on the storm head-on, embracing and enduring the raging world around us.

As we waited for the last member of the group to arrive, the darkness of the door stood out in stark contrast to the bright blue skies of the day. Looking at it, the old Rolling Stones song "Paint it Black" started playing in my head.

I see a red door and I want to paint it black.
I wanna see it painted
Painted black
Black as night

Black as coal
I wanna see the sun
Blotted out from the sky
I wanna see it painted, painted, painted
Painted black, yeah

Stepping in through the door, that is exactly what happened: I stepped out of the sunlight and into darkness. Flashlights had to be used in certain parts of the building to be able to navigate along the hallways and corridors. The quick transition from light to dark, coupled with the state of the building, threw off my equilibrium and made me unstable; I doubted that my next step would be on solid ground.

After a few moments, my eyes adjusted to the low light, and for the first time, I was able to start making sense of my surroundings. What I saw didn't seem real. I thought to myself, *There is no way this is really happening. This is some shit out of a* Die Hard *movie.* At any point now, Bruce Willis would come through yelling, "Yippee-Ki-Yay, motherfucker!" and the director would yell out, "CUT!" But the film star never showed and the building continued to smolder.

As we made our way down the hallway, I kept my eyes on the ground. Not only was it dark, but everything was sodden, and the floor was flooded. The water could vary from an inch to ankle deep. In many places, it hid debris and rubble; I almost face-planted on several occasions.

The walls were stained and buckled along the hallway, which spoke to the magnitude of the blast from the crash. The airplane's fuel reserves were in the wings and the fuselage was filled in preparation for a long flight to L.A. Flight 77 took off from Washington D.C.'s Dulles International Airport at 0820 hours on its way to Los Angeles with heavy tanks of fuel for the cross-country journey. Most of that fuel was still unspent when the jetliner struck the Pentagon.

As a matter of fact, Donald Dusenberry, the structural engineer who co-authored *SPECIAL SECTION: PERFORMANCE OF THE PENTAGON: TERRORIST ATTACK OF SEPTEMBER 11, 2001,* said, "The lightweight wings and non-fuel sections of the plane sheared off almost immediately upon impact, but the heavy fuel tanks barreled through the first floor, creating a flow of debris that tore through the building like an avalanche, leaving a path of destruction twice the length of the aircraft."[4]

That path of destruction extended far beyond the visible collapse from the outside. Deep inside, much farther than one would anticipate, the evidence of the attack was burnt into walls and buckled ceilings. I fully expected that, as I walked through interior doors, quite a ways from the actual structural collapse, I'd walk into a normal room. The jarring reality, coupled with continued darkness, knocked me back a step or two and left me unsure of what to do next.

Luckily for us, we had our Pentagon guide, and that made it pretty simple. Just follow him in, deeper into the abyss. Then, as we walked forward, the darkness began to give way to light and I found myself wondering where the source was. It wasn't long before I found it, and we made a right turn into an open area that had been completely destroyed by the blast radius.

Looking out across the space, it resembled a scene from some dystopian future in a video game. Furniture and equipment lay covered in rubble and debris. Over to the right was an eviscerated body laying across a desk. To my left, I saw members of the FBI with pens and pads in hand, doing all the heavy lifting in terms of detective work. Strewn across the rubble were those little yellow numbered placards, and camera flashes continued to streak out like lighting.

At the base of the feet of a small gaggle of agents, there lay the body of one of the fallen. I watched as they sifted through his pants to find his wallet. Once found, they pulled it out and opened it up, looking for a means of identification. They found his license and I heard the gentleman read the name. Out of respect, I won't include it here. He placed the license back in the wallet and handed it to another agent, who bagged it.

Years later, I looked him up on the DOD's Pentagon Memorial site. There I found out that he was fifty-eight years old and was from Dumfries, Virginia. He was born and raised in Illinois and served in the Army from 1964 to 1966. He met his wife, Peggy, while assigned to Fort Myer, Virginia, and they were married in 1968. The website included a kindhearted description: "His innate honesty, love of God, and generous spirit made him a friend to everyone. He was an avid fisherman, inventor, and artist. He was very interested in Republican politics and was a true patriot."

A beautiful life that had been ruthlessly taken before the got to enjoy the retirement he earned.

From there, more photos were taken as we stood there, staring in disbelief at all that was going on around us. Hands in pockets, mouths agape, wearing a hodgepodge of gear, we were far from the fearsome-looking soldiers we intended to be. After what seemed like an eternity, we were told that we were free to move the remains.

Now, this fellow wasn't a small man. I am assuming he was at least six feet tall, maybe more so, with wide girth around his waist. Judging from the way he was dressed, I am assuming (though I don't know) that he was a groundskeeper or maintenance man for the Pentagon. He would not be easy to transport.

For anyone who has ever attempted a barbell deadlift, you likely know what 200-plus pounds feels like. However, when you transfer that to a body that is limp and awkward due to arms and legs, 200 pounds begins to feel more like 400. Just moving him over to the gurney in and of itself was quite a bit of work.

We were finally able to get him on the stretcher and ready to move him out of the building. With one of us on each handle, we steadied ourselves as best we could and counted to three.

"One, two, three, lift!"

We picked him up and began the cumbersome journey back out the way we came in. Walking in had already proven difficult enough when it was just carrying ourselves. With the full weight of the man on the stretcher, the strain of the walk took its toll. Every step sloshed the liquid that covered the ground. The rubble, jagged and deformed, was slick from the water and foam used to smother out the jet fuel fire.

Unable to see through the water, each of us took turns slipping and rolling our ankles as we walked. The sharp, quick drops came at unexpected and inopportune times, causing the other three stretcher bearers to carry the full weight of the man. This, in turn, caused them to slip themselves and move forward in a jerking manner that exhausted our grip strength and taxed our knees and backs.

It was during one of those moments where we slipped that the man's hand rolled over and struck mine. I looked down to see that he was wearing a wedding ring, and in that moment, my heart sank faster than it did tripping over the rubble. Of course, we knew that everyone we were carrying out had families who loved them. But seeing that wedding band on his finger made it real for me. I knew that somewhere, at that very moment, someone was on their knees, sick with worry and wishing in vain that their loved one wasn't the body on this stretcher.

And in the not-so-distant future, someone in a clean and pressed uniform, hat in hand with a chaplain by their side, would pull up in an unmarked car and knock on their door. They'd say their rehearsed lines, "Ma'am, I regret to inform you that your husband was lost tragically in the attacks on the Pentagon."

The wife would stand there in shock, despite knowing in her heart that a knock might come. I imagined how she may handle it. Would she remain quiet and unresponsive, not fully able to comprehend what had happened to the man she loved, or would she collapse, face in hands, stricken by the horrible tragedy that had befallen her husband?

What would follow? Did he have children? How would they deal with the loss of their father? What about grandkids and friends and family? To think that all of this would begin playing out in the very near future angered me greatly, and every step I took, I felt that fire in my belly grow. This man, like all of those who lost their lives that day, was guilty of one thing: going to work. I, along with countless other Americans, vowed that day, someone was going to pay for the load we were carrying.

The work was slow and cumbersome. To find remains and then notify the proper authorities to come catalog the scene, do the paperwork, and then be cleared to remove them was a tedious process. We found victims in all sorts of places and ways.

Digging through the rubble, my hand once jutted inside someone's skull. On another occasion, half of a person sat in the corner. I have no clue where his legs were, but he stared at me, mouth open, as I continued to dig. Another time, I found a hand, and when I picked it up, the arm came out with a long strap of skin that had once covered the shoulder.

What makes the dead so horrific in cases like this is that not only are they dead, but they are horrifically mangled and dirty. You want desperately to clean them, almost as if somehow washing the dirt and grime away would make it better, or even bring them back to life.

As horrible as all this was, what countered it was the outstanding professionalism and fortitude of the men working the scene. No one panicked. No one puked. No one complained about the work or the conditions. We all just did our job. After all, it's hard to bitch when your standing in Hell and realizing that your life could be much, much worse.

In a weird way, you could almost compartmentalize being around the bodies. As sad as it is to say, after you see a few, you start to become desensitized to it, almost numb to the reality that this person's life has been snuffed out. At least, in the moment you do. I guess that's how you cope with it.

But proof of life—things like wallets, birthday cards, and teddy bears—hit me the hardest. It reminded me that the lifeless corpses, those that looked like props from *The Walking Dead*, were indeed so much more than that. They were lives snuffed out in an instant. They had families and dreams. They had just woken up to go to work and give a solid day's effort, or were headed to some much-needed and deserved R&R. Many weren't even what someone could ever feasibly classify as an "enemy." They weren't soldiers or actively involved in any "fight" against Islam.

And yet, on a clear blue September morning, their lives were wiped away. Dreams dashed and hearts broken. Many spent their last waking moments terrified and dismayed. Realizing that there was nothing they could do other than hold on to the person next to them and send a prayer up. They died unable to make peace with the family they'd leave behind.

I have often wondered how that moment must have felt. The sheer helplessness of it. To know that your fate is out of your hands. Do you wonder, *Why me?* Do you even have the capacity to process it at that time? Are you filled with guilt for the things you didn't do or left unsaid? Do you cry or pray? Do you say, "Fuck it," and sit back as you face it head-on? I am sure it probably varies from person to person. No matter how it ended, it was fucked up, and someone was going to pay for it.

While we were doing remains removal, we began assisting in

another job: shoring up the structure of the building. Now, what a lot of folks don't know is that the construction of the Pentagon years earlier would literally be the very thing that saved thousands of lives that day.

> *When the Pentagon was built, no one knew that it would become an iconic monument to U.S. military power—or a target. In fact, the architects thought it would be abandoned after the war and turned into a massive record storage depot. Their prediction was wrong, but fortuitous.*
>
> *Thinking the Pentagon would need to store heavy caches of records for the long haul, the U.S. Army Corps of Engineers built in excess strength and structural redundancies that would end up saving hundreds and potentially thousands of lives on 9/11.* [4]

On top of that, the wing that was actually hit had just recently undergone further refurbishing. In an odd twist of fate, the plane struck the best side it could have to limit casualty totals, and on a day that makes you ask, "God, why?" I am grateful for that hidden blessing.

Still, even with that blessing in mind, when a mammoth jetliner filled with fuel and traveling in a excess of 500 miles per hour slams into a structure, that structure is going to need work done in order for it to be safe to inhabit again. That job had fallen to the premier urban search and rescue team in the country, if not the world, the FEMA Urban Search and Rescue Task Force, Maryland Task Force 1.

The book on urban search and rescue was literally written right here in Montgomery County. They have been deployed all over the United States and the world to assist those in their most dire time of need. Furthermore, this sadly wouldn't be their first rodeo in dealing with the difficulty of navigating a terrorist attack on our home soil, as they had previously responded to the Oklahoma City Bombing in April of 1995. They were highly respected professionals and an amazing asset of steady hands that ensured the mission was completed in both a timely and honorable manner.

While they provided the technical know-how (and busted their asses the same as us), the task ahead was just so large that the team needed some pack mules to help get it done. As infantry soldiers, we gladly fit that bill. The task they needed us to do was pretty simple and straightforward, consisting of two primary functions: remove rubble and haul in the 4x4s that they used to create support structures to shore up damaged walls and render them safe to work beneath.

The structures that they built resembled a large Jenga game. Around columns and under ceilings, they built up two 4x4s at a time until the weight of the building was once again supported with a strong foundation. This was backbreaking work done round the clock. No matter how tiring it was, everyone drew inspiration from the fact that the Pentagon, built during wartime urgency, was completed at a breakneck pace—just sixteen months and only using 15,000 workers. If they could do that, then getting the place safe was a task we could tackle.

All of this work meant that the days flew by. After the initial shock of the moment wears off, you find yourself lost in a rhythm. Get dressed, go inside, come out, decon, eat at a vendor, talk on a phone, get dressed, go inside, come out, decon, eat, get dressed, go inside, come out, decon, and go to sleep. Wake up and do it all over again. You kept this up until shift change, when another company would come replace you and you'd head back to the base.

Of all the bad that came out of that day, Lord knows there is one thing I miss, and miss dearly. That is the unity of 9/12. I was there the day they unfurled that gigantic American flag from the top of the Pentagon. I remember standing ramrod straight with pride in my belly and tears streaming down my face as it floated down the side of the building. It was big and beautiful, crisp and clean. It stood in stark contrast to the dust and grime of that crime scene, a reminder that they hadn't broken us—no, far from it; they had united the most powerful nation on earth.

Almost in unison, the rest of Arlington and D.C. did the same thing; large American flags were draped down the sides of buildings, large and small. It seemed everywhere you went, Old Glory was waving. On our trips back to the barracks after shift change, horns would honk and drivers and passengers alike would wave and cheer. It remains a sad fact of the day that, for many of us, we only remember we are Americans, joined by more than an imaginary line, when we are attacked. But in those moments when we bring it back to center, we see the future our forefathers hoped for, one where our collected talents and reserves are aimed toward one common goal. When we use the strength and ingenuity of our people, we do amazing things. We beat the largest empire on the planet, end world wars, and put men on the moon. And now, we were going to focus all of that energy on one mission: making those responsible for 9/11 pay.

Chapter Eleven

War

*The cost of freedom is always high, but Americans have always paid it.
And one path we shall never choose, and that is the path of surrender,
or submission.*
—John F. Kennedy

The years that followed my experience at the Pentagon weighed heavily on my mind and soul. I felt in so many ways that I had failed as a soldier. That anger that I held that day carrying that man out of the Pentagon hadn't waned. In fact, it had festered, fueled by the guilt I felt that many of my guys in my unit and even guys I had been in charge of, such as Holmes, had deployed to fight the enemy and I had not. These men were facing the enemy while I stayed safe at home.

What's worse is that, as the fighting raged on, first in Afghanistan, and then later in Iraq, we started to bury those fallen heroes in Arlington. Up until this point, we had spent our days primarily interring World War II and Vietnam vets. There was great pride to be held in that, because we were paying the proper respects to those long-forgotten heroes of yesterday, but there was no guilt with them. Their war wasn't in our time, and there was no way for us to do our part then. That wasn't the case now. There was war going on, and for those stateside, we weren't the ones fighting it.

That's why I personally believe the most coveted award you can earn is the Combat Infantryman's Badge (CIB.). It tells the world that you were in combat and returned fire towards the enemy. You have been tested and passed muster. You didn't just talk the talk, you walked the walk, and for infantrymen, who pride themselves on walking far as fuck with a ruck as big a Mack truck, walking the walk means everything.

So, as the years went on, I began to doubt that I would ever get the "opportunity" to go fight, and if need be, die for my country. I am sure for many of you reading this it may seem like me bitching about a blessing. "You were lucky enough to have missed war." To be truthful, I myself say that to our veterans who didn't deploy. But the logic never reasoned well with emotion.

That's why many veterans languish in the mental anguish of either not being able to save a battle buddy, or knowing friends (or even strangers, for that matter) perished while you did nothing. In no logical way does it make sense to "what if" to death how it may have turned out differently if only it'd been you rather than them. That spawns guilt that will eat men up inside. And yet, to know that you were living in a major historical time, that you could have played a role in a fight that mattered, to only find yourself sitting on the sidelines feels like a travesty of justice.

That's why, when the opportunity came for me to volunteer to go, it was a no-brainer. I had become aware that a single billet needed to be filled to replace a soldier who had been injured and pulled off the line. A request went out over the net that they were looking for an infantry Sgt. or SSG to volunteer to fill that billet. On top of all of this was the timing. The request came down right after Thanksgiving. That meant that the soldier who raised their hand would miss the holidays with their family.

For me, that just made the decision that much easier. I wouldn't have passed up this opportunity anyway, but now that it meant that if I didn't do it, some other soldier might get pulled up. One who had a wife and kids at home, who would have to see their holiday wrecked by the worry of having Daddy deploy to war when they should have been sharing yuletide cheer, was more than I could stand. I immediately replied back, "Send me."

Now, I knew that I had just volunteered for arguably the two most dangerous jobs in Iraq—either MiTT team or convoy escort. I wouldn't know which one I would be assigned to until I got in-country. The bad news was that the unknown is never fun to deal with, but the good news was I wouldn't have to deal with it for long—they had given me orders to ship out in just two weeks' time. When you know you're about to get on a potential one-way ticket to a combat zone, the last two weeks stateside, especially since this wasn't on the radar the day before, become extremely important.

I have always said that I hope when my times comes, I know that it's coming, because I want to make sure I get to dot my i's and cross my t's. I want to make sure I have said my final I-love-yous and gotten my affairs in order. Now, I know a lot of people will say if you live your life in the proper manner, you should be at peace and ready to go at any time. Respectfully, I think that's a crock of shit. There will never be a time that I wouldn't want just one more chance to tell my daughters and my friends that I loved them if given that opportunity before I passed on.

So, while there was a certain level of anxiety in prepping for deployment, there was also a certain level of relief that came with knowing I had the time to say my potential final goodbyes, or at least I thought there would be. Sadly, in some cases, it would be the final straw that broke the camel's back for me and "family."

As luck would have it (and oddly enough the same way I found out about the deployment), Debbie had found me again. This time it was through a soldier who had bumped into her at work somehow, and in the process struck up a conversation that found its way to me. Evidently, she had mentioned that she had a son in the Army but didn't know where. This soldier, feeling that she could be reuniting a mother with her long-lost son, took the initiative to find me using the search portal.

She reached out and told me that my mother had expressed interest in reconnecting with me, and to be honest, it almost seemed like divine intervention. Perhaps God, knowing what lay ahead for me, was giving us both one last opportunity to make things right here in this world. I should have known better than to expect that much from her.

At the same time, I had also reached out to my adopted father, Bobby. I can't even justify why I did it. I think at the time I thought that this would be the thing that finally made him proud. I mean, what could prove I was a man more than volunteering to go to war to fight those who had attacked us? Surely, this would be the thing that finally made him say, "I am proud of you, son."

So, with two weeks left, and in two separate conversations, I explained to them both the seriousness of what lay ahead. I would be leaving for Iraq on just two weeks' notice to replace a casualty of war, on a team I hadn't worked with at all, in a country I'd never seen, doing one of the most dangerous jobs you could do. IEDs were wreaking havoc on our forces and there was a high probability that I would be killed or seriously injured in a foreign country.

Both times, I relayed to individuals who were supposed to be my parents the very real possibility that their son was going to die in combat, and that if they wanted to see me, this might very well be their last opportunity to do so while I was alive. I let them know I would be leaving in a little less than two weeks, and if they wanted to see me they would need to come up before then. I was only a four-hour drive away. Both declined.

Neither one felt like making the drive. They offered up they'd love to see me, and I was welcome to come down. All I could think to myself was, what the actual fuck? Your son calls you up, says "Hey, Mom/Dad, guess what? I am going to war and I am gonna be doing one of the most dangerous jobs you can do! Real good chance I'll get blown up and come back maimed for life, or better yet, dead!" And your response is, "Oh, cool. Feel free to visit if you have time."

I don't know why I was shocked and hurt by their decline. I mean, after all, this wasn't a new thing. They each had a proven track record of this. Both had spent years failing to check in on me or ask how I was. Neither called on Christmas or my birthday. Neither kept tabs, so why did I expect them to care now?

I guess in my eyes, I felt like this was such an extreme situation that it would force them to open up to the reality that we didn't have a relationship, and that they'd want to use this "one last chance" to make things right. I figured if they loved me at all, even if it was just a little, that they'd jump on the opportunity to come see me before I went to war. So telling me "No" solidified to me that they didn't love me at all, and I made the promise right then and there to never love them back.

It was in that moment that I came to terms with the knowledge that blood doesn't mean shit. I know a lot of folks will say "family over everything" or "blood is thicker than water," but I am here to say that is situational as fuck. Not everyone is going to ascribe to that. Family is just like any other relationship on earth; both sides have to want it and both sides have to work on it. You'll spend a lot of time spinning your wheels, lonely, crazy, and depressed if you go through life thinking you can automatically (or even should) trust everybody you share DNA with.

It has been my experience that the best family to have is the family you choose. It could be your brother or your cousin. It could also be some guy or girl you meet at age thirty-five who actually gives a damn about you. It happens for all of us at different times, but we all eventually reach the point in time where we have to be selfish with our love. We have to decide who we are going to give our attention, effort, and loyalty to, because not everyone deserves it. Bobby and Debbie didn't teach me much, but I learned that lesson from them, and I am forever grateful for it, at least now I have no doubt about where I stood with "family" even though it hurt like hell at the time.

With the two of them clearly out of the picture, I turned my attention to getting my affairs in order and focused on those who had been there for me. I spent the next two weeks setting up direct deposits, making sure my roommate was taken care of, and getting my stuff out of said roommate's house. I made the rounds to see the friends I wanted to spend time with and even had dinner at a local Ruby Tuesday where we joked and told stories.

After dinner, we went back to the apartment with some folks, had some drinks, watched some TV, and then the time came to say goodbye. I put on my BDUs, grabbed my duffle bag, said my goodbyes, and headed off to the airport. As I pulled up to BWI, I couldn't help but think about all the plane songs where you leave and don't come back. Mostly I kept singing Elton John's "Daniel."

Daniel, my brother, you are older than me
Do you still feel the pain of the scars that won't heal?
Your eyes have died but you see more than I
Daniel, you're a star in the face of the sky

Was this going to be it for me? Was I going to die and become "a star in the face of the sky" like Daniel? Would I become just a story a few people told until they died, then wiped away from conversation forever? I didn't know the answer to any of those questions. The only thing I did know was that I was about to go on the next big adventure of my life, and with that, I slung my duffle across my back and headed to the counter to get my ticket.

My first stop en-route to Iraq was Fort Bliss, TX. Now, I love everything about Texas except Ft. Bliss. It sits right beside El Paso, which sits right on the border of Mexico, and while I got no issue with Mexico, the reality is that a lot of shadiness takes place at the border, and that meant that the area was a breeding ground for soldiers to fuck up. Anytime you put soldiers in a location with a list of places they can't go or things they shouldn't do, you can bet your bottom dollar that they are going to do both. I had a couple friends stationed there and let's just say El Paso is ripe for poor decision-making.

My visit there, however, was to be short-lived; just enough time to get in and do the most minimal of checking the box to say it was okay to deploy me. During that time, I got all administrative work knocked out. I set up wills, secured direct deposits, got my shots, issued my gear, and attended things like cultural sensitivity training. Which, in my humble personal opinion, was a waste of time because based on my encounters with the Iraqis, they by far did the very shit we were told would piss 'em off, but I digress.

After all the briefs were complete, we were issued all our gear, and we had successfully passed the "don't offend the locals" training, the day came to ship out. Everyone was pulled into a room and they spent time playing funny videos to lighten the mood. In one clip they showed this disgruntled-looking dude standing in the grocery store while his terrible-ass, Dennis the Menace look-alike son destroyed the grocery store and did his best *Exorcist* impersonation on the aisle floor. The commercial faded into a picture of Trojan condoms and the room erupted in laughter. Score one for the Army: tension relieved.

Then, as is always the case in the military, "Captain Motivation" enters the room. This is often preceded by at least one playing of (if you're lucky) the Lee Greenwood song, "God Bless the U.S.A." Now, listen, I love me some 'merica. I am literally covered in red, white, and blue, but for fuck's sake, I can't take that song anymore. It's like the military thinks it's the only patriotic song ever written, and they play that shit ad nauseam. Stepping up to take its place was, naturally, "Courtesy of the Red, White, and Blue," by Toby Keith.

After they felt they had thoroughly soaked you in the required level of patriotic bass, then it was time to remind you that you were doing this for your country and your brothers beside you! Now, I am all for reminding folks of the importance of the mission, but these cookie-cutter, boilerplate "hoooaaaah" speeches always fell flat for me, and in truth, for the other soldiers standing around. Listen, we know why we are here, we know where we are headed, and we know what we gotta go do. So how 'bout we just shut up and board the plane already?

The plane ride to the Middle East took forever. Though, I am sure the folks who took months to cross on a ship think I should just stop bitching. Anyway, we arrived in Kuwait so we could get ready to catch our rides to our respective new units. Kuwait is like Disney Word for the military. It's chuck-full of POGs (People Other than Grunts) who tell everyone they are "deployed" while they sit around and drink Green Bean Coffee all day long. The biggest kicker of it all? They aren't in the least bit of danger but they get hazardous duty pay. I ain't sure who came up with the idea for this racket, but I bet you a paycheck they were a POG too.

Once we got off the plane, they loaded us onto these commercial busses with curtains, closed all the drapes, and then issued three bullets to the one person who sat up front. I, for one, was wondering, *Why in the fuck did you give me three bullets? What am I supposed to do with this shit? Like what's the point?* What's worse is people were acting like we were about to get ambushed on the way.

We didn't spend much time there and I was told that I was gonna catch a hopper the next day out to Taji. Now, once we touched down there, I got offloaded from the bird and we got in a big up-armored transport vehicle that made it abundantly clear for the first time that I was in a combat zone. They took us from Taji to the Green Zone, a trip I didn't know at the time I would make countless more of over the next year in the country.

The official name under the interim government was the International Zone, but the name Green Zone, *al-Mintaqa al-Khadraa* in Arabic, was more commonly used because the area was safer than the rest of Baghdad (the Red Zone), which was where explosions, kidnappings, sectarian killings, and shootings were common. This Green Zone was a heavily fortified area in the center of the Iraqi capital that served as the headquarters of successive Iraqi regimes.

The centerpiece of the Green Zone was Saddam's former palace, and let me tell you, it was huge. The military had made the call not to bomb the shit out of it like they did to the many surrounding buildings because they knew they could use it for a far greater purpose than Saddam had ever dreamed of: salsa night.

You see, many of the bigwigs were stationed in the Green Zone, and Lord knows how many contractors. Black Water had mercs for hire and they had Oakleys, beards, and time for babes. Across from the palace was the pool, and let me tell you, that place was rocking at night. It was such a weird world to live in at times, to see all of this shit going on in the Green Zone when, outside of the wire, it was a very real and dangerous place to be.

But inside, it was almost like being back home. KBR made sure to provide the locals with lots of work opportunities (though I am sure they paid 'em shit). You could get your laundry done, uniforms stitched up, haircuts, and of course, buy Green Bean Coffee. They also worked to keep the grounds clean so that we could focus on the mission at hand.

The other pretty amazing thing about the Green Zone was it really was the International Zone. There were soldiers, sailors, airmen, and marines from every nation that was participating in the effort to restore power back to the people. This made for colorful exchanges and friendly ribbing, most of which climaxed during the World Cup. To be in a warzone and see soldiers from opposing nations gathered 'round was a life experience I am glad I got to have.

Across the street from the palace were the trailers that housed many of the soldiers who stayed in the Green Zone. I was taken there and assigned to a trailer that would become my home for the remainder of my deployment. I have often said that, in terms of a combat deployment, I got arguably the best setup you could get. I patrolled outside the wire but always came back home to my little trailer park in the Green Zone, and to be honest, it was quite nice, especially compared to what my brothers-in-arms were getting stuck in throughout Iraq and Afghanistan.

These little trailers each held four individuals split between two rooms. Bisecting the rooms was a shared bathroom. The trailers came equipped with AC, a small bunk fridge, and a closet for your gear. They were rectangular and stacked closely side by side. On any given night, you'd hear soldiers inside laughing and talking shit or standing outside in the walkway "smoking and joking." In the center of trailer city was a makeshift laundromat.

If not for the occasional incoming mortar attack, one could forget they were in a combat zone. And after the first one you lived through, you really didn't even pay that much attention to those anymore. I was lying in bed one night and heard the boom of one hitting and figured, *Well, it's already over. Might as well go back to sleep.* I rolled over and did just that.

After I was initially shown my trailer and instructed to unpack my gear, I was told I could wait around until someone came and got me, but I asked if I could just get a lift to the motor pool of the unit I'd be working with. I didn't come all the way over here to sit on my hands. I was given the OK and hopped in the back for the ride to meet my new crew.

I pulled into the motor pool and meet my new PSG (Platoon Sergeant). He was an old guy, had actually served in Vietnam, and was happy and proud to be in Iraq now. He asked me if I was ready to head out and I said, "Most certainly." They assigned me a rifle with an M203 (grenade launcher attatchment), so I jumped in the back of the Humvee and locked and loaded my weapon.

Oh, I guess it's probably important to point out that an honest assessment of the current situation would have rendered to any sane person I was not really "ready" at all. I had never trained with these guys; truth be told, I had never even trained in convoy operations in my life. Looking back now, it was a travesty that I was allowed outside the wire. I didn't know any of the SOPs (Standard Operating Procedures) for the unit, and I hadn't drilled what would happen if my vehicle or any other vehicle would be incapacitated, nor did I know where or what all gear was on mine or any other Humvee in the convoy.

I didn't know where we were going and I didn't know who was in charge. Hell, I wasn't even sure if my rifle was zeroed. But, like I said, I didn't come here to sit on my hands and I didn't know what I didn't know, and so I jumped in the back, and out the gate we went. It was time for me to see Baghdad up close and personal.

The first time you head towards the gate is a surreal moment. You see the sign that says "You are entering the Red Zone. Lock and load." Suddenly you realize that this isn't a game anymore. You're not playing in the woods out behind your house. There will be no debating whether or not they "got you." If they did, it would be very clear, and very bloody.

We rolled outside the wire and for the first time, I was in "combat."

Years later, sitting around a dinner table as a rookie firefighter, my captain at the time (an old Vietnam veteran named Moody) looked at me and said, "I don't know how you guys did it."

I looked back at him inquisitively and asked, "Did what?"

He said, "Roll out down the streets just waiting for shit to blow up. Every piece of trash could be a bomb."

I was stunned. I said in response, "I don't know how you guys did it. Walking through bush so thick that you can't see the man in front of you, just waiting to step on a booby trap."

We kinda looked at each other, realizing that no matter the generation, no matter how the war is waged, it all sucks.

What Captain Moody was talking about all those years later was the cold, hard reality of life outside the wire. You never knew who the enemy was. You never knew what would blow up on the side of the road or which car might be VBED. You never knew if a suicide bomber was waiting at the intersection or if they might be standing next to you on the street at the local vendor.

All of this made for a very interesting dichotomy: anyone could be the enemy, but you couldn't act like they were because that would result in them (or a family member) 100 percent becoming the enemy. On top of this were countless stories where the locals, Iraqi police, and army turned on the very soldiers training them or providing them with employment on the bases. These insidious attacks caused many to doubt the purpose of the mission and ask, "Why even bother?"

I mean, if these guys are here beside us and can clearly see that we are trying our best to help and they are still willing to kill us, what hope do we have of winning the hearts and minds of the locals?

This led to a very high likelihood of burnout because you were always "on," even back in the fortified Greene Zone or other bases and FOBs scattered throughout the country. You carried misgivings and second-guessed people who should be on your team, and when it comes to something as serious as war, there is no space or time for hesitation. But even the ones who didn't turn on you still came with other potential issues.

Many lacked discipline. The Iraqis wore no standard uniform and their PT standards were a joke. I still don't know if I have ever seen anything as pathetic as watching them attempt to do the side-straddle hop (military lingo for jumping jacks). They'd just flop around like a wounded fucking duck turning to and fro while their arms flailed wildly by their sides.

Often, this lack of discipline caused a myriad of issues, and further cause for soldiers of other countries to doubt them. They couldn't shoot, they couldn't communicate, and they were always quick to pass the buck onto any number of excuses. That made many of the ones who stayed combat ineffective. I point out "stayed" because it was not a rare occurrence for them to go AWOL. At the end of the day, they were more soldiers of fortune than patriots; the only problem was that they were shitty soldiers.

To me, this made it horrible for the guys who were there for the right reasons. Guys who saw it as an opportunity to save their country. To build it up and leave a safer, more stable nation-state for the kids and grandkids. Those who fit that mold had my undying respect. In so many ways, they reminded me of our founding fathers. They knew the risk they took serving in the military or police; risk not just for themselves, but for their families as well.

Just like the men who stood up to Britain in the early dates of the United States, fighting for independence in Iraq was about more than picking up a rifle and standing guard. It was about knowing that your family could be targeted. It was about knowing that if you backed the wrong horse and lost, it was the end of the line for your entire bloodline. You had to weigh trying to provide a better future for your children with the cost of their life if you failed. That is a heavy burden to take on, and one that, until you've carried it, you don't know if you would.

While I respected the reality of that world, I also felt that it was the failure of final, full commitment to the cause was the reason they struggled to find lasting success. So many of the soldiers and police wore ski masks to hide their faces. Again, I understand why they did that. Lord knows you can't fault them for it, but how can a citizenry trust police and soldiers who hide their faces? Those who come like boogeymen in the middle of the night and steal your neighbor? Especially since similar things happened under the previous regime.

Now, don't freak out. Again, I am not saying that these raids weren't justified or that I have no empathy. I do. I just know that those things taking place in a world where trust is already in short supply only leads to an ever-widening gap between the civilian population and those who are trying to protect them, and the insurgency exploited that every chance that they got.

On my first mission out of the wire, I got a taste of just how easy it would be to play on that trust. We were escorting a group of Marines from a Forward Operating Base somewhere in the country to go to a local bank and secure the money to pay the Iraqi soldiers they were training and patrolling with. I rolled out with a weapon I had never fired once and found myself in the heart of downtown Baghdad. Now, I know what a lot of you may be thinking: why are we escorting Marines? Aren't they supposed to be badasses? Why are we going to the bank? Why aren't the Iraqis getting their own money? Why are we paying them? Who provides the money?

All of these are very valid questions and I am here to tell you that I have zero clue the answer to any of them, other than we escorted the Marines because A. they are no badder than anyone else, and B. we knew the AO (well, at least my team did) and they didn't.

To this day, it remains the harshest cultural shock of my life, not because of how different it was per se, but rather how similar it was.

In so many ways it was just like any bustling city here in the States. Sidewalks packed with people and storefronts along busy streets. Street vendors sold goods (many of them sold the exact same thing, just a few feet apart) and police helped funnel traffic in a hopeless attempt to stop gridlocks.

In truth, outside of really, really shitty traffic—way worse than anything I've seen in the States (and as a DMV resident that's saying a fuckton)—and bullet holes and bomb craters, it was not that different-looking than any major city here. But the things that made it different made it another world, one where it felt like I was a Martian.

Being surrounded by that many people in gridlocked traffic, all while shoved in like anchovies in a tin can, made for an extremely claustrophobic feeling. That's compounded and multiplied by the fact that the primary weapon of choice, the IED, was devastatingly effective against coalition forces. You could very well be riding in your coffin.

All that up-armor that was meant to leave you feeling protected, in many ways, exposed you more. It made the Humvee top-heavy and cumbersome. That additional weight made you slower and more likely to roll over (another major killer of American forces) and it wore the hell out of the vehicles, making them susceptible to frequent breakdowns, something you absolutely didn't want to happen while you were outside the wire.

As we made our way through downtown, I realized for the first time the sheer amount of information you have to try to process when operating in an urban environment. There are potential threats literally everywhere you look. In asymmetrical warfare, and in particular with guerrilla warfare, you have to deal with the fact that there are no "frontlines." There is no clearly defined (and uniformed) enemy. Anyone and everyone could be part of the plan to kill you.

In many ways, the concrete jungle is the worst environment for a military force, particularly a large one, to work in. It is easy for our enemies to predict the route that the main force needs to take. The advent of cell phones makes it easy for lookouts to advise on troop movement and help coordinate an ambush.

The city itself provides multiple chokepoints and hide-sites from which to attack. Tall city buildings make it easy to get the high ground and rain down rounds on convoys. Overpasses allow for ease of dropping grenades down on passing convoys. Narrow alleyways are the perfect place to deploy thin wires across the street at head level to decapitate the exposed gunners. Buildings easily hide insurgent forces that lie in wait to launch attacks with RPGs and small-arms fire, and of course, the streets always hide the dreaded IED.

Improvised Explosive Devices accounted for approximately 63 percent of all coalition deaths in Iraq and over 66 percent of casualties in Afghanistan. They say that necessity is the mother of all invention, and Lord knows that they got extremely creative in their ability to deal death with them. Often the IEDs were constructed of conventional military explosives, such as artillery shells, that would then be attached to a detonating mechanism. They fell into three primary categories based on how they were detonated: Time, Command, and Victim-operated.

- TIME IED – uses a time switch. It creates a countdown timer using a mechanical or digital clock.
- COMMAND IED – operated by the bomber himself. They may be tethered or non-tethered. In the tethered iteration, they could use fishing wire or some other pull string to detonate it. In the remote-controlled option, RICED (Remote-Control Improvised Explosive Device), they may use a cell phone, Wi-Fi connection, key fob, or any similar mechanism.

- VICTIM-OPERATED IED – the name says it all. It is designed to explode when operated by the victim. Amazingly, no one in the bad guys' leadership position volunteered for that role.

No matter how they were detonated, the results remained the same: devastating. And I am not just talking about the physical destruction it caused. The mental toll it took—simply waiting for the road, rock, or building to blow up on you—was heavy. Knowing that the vehicle you were in offered little in the way of protection kept you on high alert and operating in the red at all times. What's worse is that it was very difficult to be proactive in facing them.

Sure, you could be on the lookout for telltale signs that one was there. Yes, you could look at the trunks of cars to see if they were riding low. You also had a pretty strong indication of where they might be, and you absolutely knew which routes were notorious for them. Still, even with knowing all of that, you simply rode down the road, teeth and asscheeks clenched tight, waiting for the bomb to blow . . . and it did, over and over again, all across the Middle East.

Every time that it did, soldiers had to watch their mangled brothers- and sisters-in-arms deal with the damage left in its wake. Lives ended in an instant, or at the bare minimum, were irrevocably changed forever. That is a heavy burden to bear, for both the soldiers it happened to and for their buddies left wondering, *Why not me?*

As we drove through the zigzag maze that sits at the entry and exit points of any base, you can't help but wonder, is this it for you? Will today be the day that you die? I can't speak for anyone else, but that never stopped for me. You learn to deal with it, maybe even suppress it a bit, but I always found myself wondering if today would be the day that I died.

We drove through the heart of the city, people and cars surrounding us at every turn. You start to feel like you are in a cage, and on display. You feel the eyes of every citizen drilling holes in your soul. Some seem to like you, but by and large, you feel the resentment that the average citizen harbors.

For me, I found a certain dichotomy in it. On one hand, I understood their frustration. Here we are, a foreign force that patrolled their streets, smashed their cars, shot up their streets, and bombed their buildings. I can get the resentment that they felt.

On the other hand, I was pissed the fuck off. Like, why didn't you stand up for yourself, your family, and your country? Saddam was an absolute despot. He was a tyrant. He stole your women from the streets in broad daylight and raped and killed them. You NEVER FUCKING STOOD UP! But now, now you're mad we are here? How fucking dare you? Why not simply say, "Thank you very much," and be on your way?

But that is how life is: full of contradictions. It's always shades of gray, never black and white like so many wish that it could be. That's how you get Americans patrolling the streets of foreign lands, trying to do good and not die. Some assholes fly planes into American buildings and the next thing you know, we now have operations all over the Middle East trying to "win hearts and minds" by dropping bombs over Baghdad. At least it made a catchy song.

When we finally got to the bank, I was told to dismount and block off an intersection. Now, if you ever want to feel exposed in life, do the following: go to a warzone, get issued a weapon that you have never fired, ride out into the heart of one of the biggest cities, and then go stand your dumb ass dead center in the middle of a major intersection, providing security for a medium-sized convoy that is forced to park on the street with raised concrete guard rails preventing you from going left and buildings preventing you from going right.

I remember sitting there in the street feeling like we were sitting ducks. To be completely honest, the only reason we didn't get torn up had to be because we weren't fighting a competent force. I mean, it was the perfect place for an ambush. Anyone who had any combat sense at all could have put us in a meatgrinder.

We were surrounded by buildings several stories high. We were bottlenecked in on one road that would only allow us to go forward or backward. At any point, they could have opened fire from a roof and/or blocked us on the street in front the bank by parking vehicles at the ends of the convoy. Given their penchant for suicide bombers, they could have walked someone right up and detonated the bomb, causing major damage and loss of life.

Standing in that intersection, I just couldn't help but wonder who was watching me or who had their sights on me. Was I literally in the crosshairs of an insurgent fighter? Who was my friend? Who was my foe? More importantly, I just kept asking myself, *Is this motherfucking gun sighted in? Will I be able to hit the motherfucker I am aiming at if shit pops off?* Not knowing that answer haunts me to this day. That was a failure of my team's leadership and my own intelligence for being dumb enough to go outside the wire without proper knowledge.

Standing there took forever. I'm wondering to myself, *What the fuck is taking so long? Is everything okay in the bank? What's going on?* Then, all of a sudden, I got a call to come to the front of the bank.

The gunner in the Humvee took over my sector of security and I jogged up to the bank door. Once I got there, I was asked to come in and saw that banks in Iraq are set up very similarly to banks back in the States. I was directed to head back behind the counter and towards the safe area. There, inside the vault, were giant bags filled with money and stacked on top of each other. They reminded me of the cows' feed bags we would pick up from Southern States Co-op back when I was a kid.

I was motioned to grab a bag and take it back to the Humvee. I grabbed it and slung it over my shoulder and headed out the door. Now, remember how I said perception is a motherfucker? Imagine you're an Iraqi citizen and you see a convoy of armed soldiers pull up to your local bank, block off all the intersections by force, go into the bank, and walk out with bags full of money. What are you gonna think? Probably that these bastards are robbing the bank.

That's why I will never understand how we didn't get attacked there, especially since we made that same run on multiple occasions. But that was us; another team wasn't that lucky. On a very similar run, a team was set up just the same way we were. Soldiers were staged outside the door of the bank, guarding it, when one soldier was shot and killed right there on the spot.

Such is the crazy aspect of war. One team gets hit and another doesn't. One guy stepped right and is fine; the other guy stepped left and is killed. It makes no sense, and many times it had nothing to do with skill. Many a badass motherfuckin' dude has been killed, whereas less-skilled warriors made it home. I count myself as one of them. I mean, how many Delta, Green Berets, MARSOC Marines, and Navy SEALs were killed in combat while my bitch ass made it home?

In so many ways, the unfairness of that doesn't sit right with you. Now, don't get me wrong, I am not saying I wish I had died in combat; just rather, I wish those men who were better than me made it home, too. At the end of the day, "fair" says that the best and most-trained should win, and winning in war means coming home. Sadly, as we all know, life ain't fair.

After we made the first run, we pulled back into the motor pool and I met in earnest, for the first time, the men that I'd share my time in combat with. We were the "Rough Riders," a mixed services unit that served as convoy escort to the MNSTC-I J-3 section. Our job was to escort key personnel anywhere that they were required to go throughout the theater of operations.

We escorted people damn near everywhere you could go. We went to Tirkrit, Balad, Al Kut, Fallujah, Basar, and the Iranian border on several occasions, just to name a few. The far trips we did rather infrequently, and the bulk of our travels were really within the city itself, and to Taji, as well as frequent trips to Abu Ghraib warehouse. That was relatively close to the infamous prison that gave a black eye to the military operations in Iraq when the treatment of its inmates became national headline news.

All of those destinations meant that we spent a dick-ton of time on the road. In the year I was there, I took part in over 800 convoy missions. That meant we got really good at doing our job and really close with the guys in the platoon, although there was a high transition rate amongst the team since many of us were individual augmenters assigned on an as-needed basis. Nowhere was this more evident than at the commander position; we had three different OICs in the time I was there alone.

At various times throughout the tour, the unit consisted of service members from damn near every branch; however, it was predominantly made up of soldiers and marines. For the most part (outside of me) all the soldiers had deployed together and the other branches served as individual augmenters. Coming into the unit late (these guys had been in the country a few months and did damn near a year train-up prior to deployment) made me worry if I would be accepted.

I knew the fastest way to gain acceptance into anything is to do more than is expected and to volunteer for the most dangerous jobs often. In convoy security, the most dangerous job is to be the turret gunner. The only issue with this was that there are only four slots available in our team, and with them taken already, I thought it may be difficult to secure it. Luckily for me, one of the gunners (arguably the main gunner) was set to be rotating back stateside in the upcoming weeks.

To me, being a gunner was like being a linebacker on a football team. Your main job is to defend your people by knocking other people on their asses. Everything you are doing, you do to protect your team from the enemy's offense. But in order to do that, you had to expose yourself to most of those offensive attacks.

The risks to the gunners were as numerous as they were deadly. You were the only one in the convoy susceptible to small-arms fire. With any explosion, IED, or RPG, the risk was far greater to the gunner than those inside the vehicle. Wires would be strung across roads to decapitate you and you were by far the person with the greatest risk in the case of rollover. Saying that you wanted to be the gunner was announcing to your peers you not only wanted to do your part to protect them, but you wanted the most dangerous role in the most dangerous job in the country.

Luckily for me, I had a pretty solid mentor to look up to. Megasion "Megs" was one of the most unique soldiers I have ever met in my time in the Army. In so many ways, he reminded me Clint Eastwood in *The Good, The Bad, and the Ugly*. He wasn't what most would think of when drawing up their description of a badass soldier. He was kinda portly, and while we didn't take a PT test, he didn't strike me as the guy who would have aced it. He had a square head and no neck, and with his K-Pot on while riding in the turret, he looked like a thick Goomba from *Super Mario Bros*.

He lived, ate, and breathed that .50 cal, though. Damn near literally. You almost never saw him outside of it. From the time he got in the motor pool in the morning until we returned from last run, the guy never left the turret. Often when we'd arrive at FOBs and bases across Iraq, and our VIPs would go off doing what we brought them there to do, we'd run to the PX, find a computer lab, or go grab lunch. Not Megs, not ever. He'd just sit in that fuckin' turret, chain-smoke cigarettes, and drink Diet Pepsi. The most you'd see him ask for was a bowl of bacon from one of the guys grabbing chow.

He may not smoke you in the mile, but he could run circles around you on that .50. He'd also done several tours and was one of the guys who seemed to only feel at home in that country. Matter of fact, he was already planning on how he could get another tour after this one. He was the perfect person for me to learn under, and, after I got cleared to gun Truck Three, fight alongside.

Now, I say fight, but in truth, the very first ambush I was in I didn't do jack shit; at least nothing that made me feel like I was worth a fuck. We were on our way back from a run to Taji and were getting ready to come under a group of overpasses we called "Spaghetti Bridge."

Spaghetti Bridge was the perfect place for an ambush. There was an overpass that crossed over two highways that traveled in opposite directions. Anyone who lives in or has been to the D.C. Northern VA area has seen a similar setup lane-wise at the 95/39/495 exit. The biggest difference between the two was that backed right up to the road were buildings and houses. The problem for us (and an asset for the insurgency) was the overpasses hid the roofs of these buildings. Anyone on top could see us coming, but we couldn't see them.

On this particular day, we were escorting a bunch of Iraqi soldiers who were traveling in two NTVs (Non-Tactical Vehicles). In this case, they were those white Toyotas. The things had no armor on them and so to make it a little "safer," they draped bulletproof vests over the doors by rolling the windows down and dropping the vests out through the windows like horse saddles.

We were rolling six-deep in the convoy with two of these vehicles spaced in between four of our Humvees. Now, when it came to ambushing a convoy, there were all sorts of ways to do it. Sometimes the goal was to hit the lead vehicle in an effort to halt the entire thing right there in its tracks and create a kill box. Other times, the hope was to disable a trail vehicle to exploit the fact that they knew Americans wouldn't leave a fallen comrade behind, and therefore would circle back to rescue them, again putting us in the kill box.

In this particular case, however, given the absolute lack of armor on the Iraqi vehicles, it made the most sense to target them. With damn near zero protection, there was a high likelihood of killing them and an almost 100 percent certainty that we'd have to circle back to rescue them, if they could even be rescued at all.

The problem for some of the insurgency is, I swear, sometimes they just don't think shit through and they aren't all that skilled. Now, don't confuse this with me saying that there weren't any skilled insurgents. That is far from the case. But sometimes the shit they did was so inept and so stupid you couldn't help but wonder what were they thinking.

Professional soldiers, they were not. In almost every case that I was attacked, they never did it in shitty weather. Too cold, not gonna attack. Too hot, fuck that. Raining? Yeah, right, bro. But if it was a nice day outside, standby, because they are about to blow your shit the fuck up.

Being new to the country at that point, I hadn't learned that fact, or maybe I wouldn't have been as caught off guard as I was by that first ambush. Rolling up to the bridge, I was traversing and scanning my lane when, all of a sudden, I heard what sounded like a pop and saw a smoke trail extend from the rooftop out below the underhang of the overpass.

Then, moving just slowly enough to catch a glimpse of it, I saw a projectile streak across the lane, barely missing the NTV in front of me and exploding on the concrete barrier to the left. I would love to say that I was Captain America in that moment, but in truth, I was kind of confused. At first, I didn't really register what was happening. Again, here I am in this extreme situation, but it just didn't look or feel real to me. It looked like something I was watching on TV, and even worse, it looked fake. On top of this, we were fucking moving along at 50 mph, so it doesn't give you a ton of time to process what's going on.

The next thing I heard was them open up with small-arms fire. The sound of the guns firing isn't what catches your attention, though; it's the sound of the rounds cracking by your head as they zing past you, barely missing you. In that moment, I managed to orientate my turret towards the incoming fire and locate them on the roof line.

I grabbed my radio and said, "CONTACT RIGHT, ROOFLINE 200 METERS!" I was already out of range for hitting the target by this time I'd have had to rotate almost to my six to engage and risked putting rounds far too close to the trail vehicles. All I could do was watch the master, Megs, turn towards the roof line and engage the targets, making them regret their shitty aim on this beautiful day.

After a gunfight, the adrenaline dump isn't instantaneous. We still had about twenty-five to thirty minutes of city to drive through to get back to base, and who knows if you might get hit again; odds are pretty high that you could. So, you don't have time to count your blessings or process that you didn't die. Also, because of the nature of convoy escorts, you don't pull over to consolidate and reorganize because your mission is to get the PACs back to base safely—so you do it on the fly while you keep the pedal pressed to the floorboard.

But when you get back to base and you offload everything, it's a different story. Especially the first time. I got back to the base and started going through all the required tasks to get ready to make the next run: cleaning the weapon system, topping off water, inspecting the Humvee for any damage that may not have been seen from the attack, and a laundry list of other tasks a mile long.

As you start to go into your habit loop of your required to-do list, your brain is free and clear to begin to process what just happened—that some random motherfuckers just tried to murder you. I can't speak for how others view it, but for me, the first thought was, *Holy fuck, I am not dead.* I mean, I am sitting here doing tedious-ass tasks, but just forty-five minutes ago I was streaking through the city with

RPG and small-arms fire cracking by my head.

It's hard to process the randomness of that. Think about it: you're doing 50 mph and the bullets miss your head by mere inches. A smidge faster or slower and you're a corpse on your first attack. You start to run through your head the enormity of the fact that someone just tried to kill you. The fact is that probably somewhere around 90 percent of the American population never experience the fear and rush that comes from someone trying to take their life. And as odd as it is to say, I am not positive that's a good thing.

As you start to run all this through your head, you begin the secondary run on emotions. I have always said you will never be happier than you are right after someone or something tried to kill you and failed. It's coming face to face with your mortality that makes you feel the most alive. That's not just Edger Allen Poe shit; that's just a fact.

After you go through this intense rush of happiness, you begin to look at the absurdity of everything, and I mean EVERYTHING. Like how forty minutes ago, you were in a gunfight and now here you are at the motor pool buying bootleg DVDs with three movies on them that just released in the theaters in the States back home.

Or you think, *What are people back home bitching about with their normal lives? Why are they upset that McDonald's doesn't sell the McRib anymore when you are over here racing down RPG alley?* Little did you know at the time, but when you get back that normal life, this is going to really, really, really piss you off, like a lot.

After you run through all of that, it finally happens, the most exhausting thing that can: the full impact of an adrenaline dump. You sometimes see this happen with professional fighters after just a few minutes into a fight on a major promotion. They touch gloves, they come out swinging for the fences, and then out of the blue, halfway through round one, it starts to look like they are moving through mud.

It's not that these guys or girls aren't in great shape or that they didn't take the fight seriously. No, they are, and they absolutely did. But after a twelve-week camp, fight week, nerves being through the roof, a walk out to a packed venue, standing in a cage waiting for the announcer to finish, touching gloves, and a solid two minutes of "go," your adrenal system just shuts down.

The increased adrenaline production that occurs during combat can be a double-edged sword. On one hand, it can make us more aware, sharper, faster, and stronger. However, it can also affect our ability to think critically. When danger suddenly approaches, the last thing you want to do is overanalyze the situation. What's more important is that you make a decision (fight or flight) and do it quickly. Adrenaline is designed to give us about sixty seconds of superhuman strength, speed, and stamina. The problem is that combat lasts a lot longer than sixty seconds.

On top of that, all those goodies you got from the adrenaline rush have to be paid for later. Especially when it was called on over and over again because the event lasted longer than adrenaline was designed for. When the time finally arrives that you can drop the red alert, that's not the only thing that falls. You do, too.

By the time I got back to the trailer, I was absolutely done. It was the first time that I really understood why Ranger School sought to make the recruits so exhausted. I could have gone a week without sleep and wouldn't have been more exhausted than I was after that first ambush.

On top of that adrenaline dump, I also struggled with the fact that I didn't feel like I had done enough in the first place. I didn't respond fast enough or grasp an understanding of what I was facing as soon as I would have liked, and I knew that could have resulted in people dying. Knowing that I failed at that level was heartbreaking for me and made me doubt my worth as a soldier.

You go through these moments and process them the best way

you can. You do this through a formal process called AAR (After Action Review). The team gets together and everyone says what they saw, said, and did. You point out where you could have done those things better, as well as what worked. You ultimately burn down to one simple goal: improve so that you can live to do the next one.

But after that is done, you are left to your own devices and your own thoughts. You retire to your bunk, where it hits you like a brick: you're fucking exhausted. Like the worst level of exhaustion you could possibly feel. You are emotionally, physically, and mentally drained. You want nothing more than to crash, but that proves much more difficult than one would think given the way you feel.

Lying there in that bunk, you rehash it all in your own private AAR and you come to one final conclusion: *I almost fucking died.* Once I came to terms with that reality, I couldn't help but shake my head over the absurdity of it all. Here we are, in a land that has been at war since the dawn of time, somehow foolishly believing that we are doing anything to change that.

Now, don't get me wrong; I was (and still am) all for going to war to protect our nation and our interests. I even know that we absolutely did good while we were there. I've seen it firsthand. But I also know that, for the most part, it's all for naught.

In a culture that demands honor killings every time you take out one of their own, you've now made a new lifelong enemy. Even when that person was clearly doing wrong and you can prove that, some won't see it and that death demands to be avenged. Furthermore, a country that has been ruled under an iron fist (with no exposure to democracy and capitalism) doesn't know what to do with the "freedom" we gave them.

This leads to even more anger and resentment because nothing is more infuriating for the masses than confusion and uncertainty at how the rules of the game are played. You take that and throw in the fact that we completely disbanded Saddam's party, effectively firing all the military and police, and you now have the perfect ingredients for radicalization for the insurgency, who are unemployed military-aged men with nothing but time on their hands and resentment in their hearts.

Lying there, you know there will be no "winning." No way to defeat that idea. No way for you to make an enemy cry "Uncle!" because any one of the folks looking at you could be the "enemy." So, you close your eyes and drift off to sleep with one final thought lingering: *Will I survive the next one?*

The next one for me would come for me on a routine trip we made damn near every day. We frequently took personnel to a t-shaped Ministry of the Interior building just outside of the Green Zone. On average, it took probably twenty to thirty minutes to make the run; not because it was far, but trying to get anywhere in traffic in Iraq proved time consuming.

We would exit the fortification of the Green Zone and cross over the bridge to head into downtown Baghdad. Almost as soon as you passed the bridge, you rolled into a traffic circle that then dumped you onto the road that would take you to MOI. It was a simple and straightforward run that we did literally hundreds of times.

On this day, as my truck entered the circle, I rotated to pick up security at the next intersection when the building on the right side of the road blew up. I saw the shockwave as it slammed me back up against the turret. The only reason I am still alive today is the bomb went off on the third floor. As I looked up, I watched the building go from the right side of the road to the left side of the road, all of which took place over my head.

Time seemed to slow down. I could see individual blocks of concrete flying through the air. I could feel the chunks of debris raining down on me and the Humvee. I watched as local Iraqis ran for cover. I started to traverse for threats to see if anyone had weapons or if a second attack was coming.

For some reason, I zeroed in on this one floating piece of paper. It reminded me of the floating bag scene in *American Beauty*. Just like in that video, the piece of paper seemed to have a life of its own, dancing in the wind amid the chaos of war, so limp and light it was completely unafraid and unaffected by the shrapnel and rubble that exploded out in all directions.

Then, as if God hit fast-forward, everything speeded back up. Everyone started talking at once. "Who's up? Is anyone hurt? Keep your eyes peeled. Push through! Push through! Push through!" I brushed the rubble off the gun, spun around to cover the rear, and just like that, I had survived my second ambush.

The crazy thing about war, especially in an environment like Iraq, is that you can go several days to a few weeks and not experience anything. No bombs. No mortars. No bullets. No ambushes. Now, that didn't mean that all of those things weren't happening; they were. All over the country, and even along the routes we'd be running as the Blue Force tracking would tell us, but for some reason, we wouldn't get hit. The attacks would come before or after we rolled through.

Now, we had a belief that the way we rolled was the reasoning for that. Many convoy escorts or patrols rode slow and rode low. What I mean by that was that the gunner stayed down (seated) inside the turret. In order for him or her to engage effectively, they would need to stand up, find the target (no small feat, as turning the turret wasn't all that easy), and then engage the threat. That's a whole lot of fucking steps to pull off in ambush. Most importantly, it takes balls to stay standing when the bullets start coming in, but in my opinion, it takes bigger balls to stand up once the bullets are hitting the walls you're sitting in.

We felt that our aggressive style—standing up, turret on a constant swivel, weapon at the ready—gave the very clear impression that if you sent hot shit our way, you were going to get some hot shit right back. If you know anything about nature, the predator always goes for the easiest kill. Why try us when you can wait for a more laid-back convoy to come through?

For all the negatives that came with the war, there was one major benefit: life was extremely straightforward. It's surprising how quickly you settle into a routine in combat. You wake up, grab chow, head to the motor pool, load up the Humvee, check your gear, lock and load, head out the gate, make your run, come back, PT, eat, watch bootleg DVDs, rinse and repeat. Every single fucking day. It's like being in *Groundhog Day*, right up until it's not. Then all Hell breaks loose.

John H. Arnold once said, "War is sometimes described as long periods of boredom punctuated by short moments of excitement." I'd argue that sums it up pretty damn well.

We had to make a typical run out to Taji one day and the ride out was pretty uneventful. The thing that used to freak me out about that run was you had to ride over this super-high overpass. That thing had to be a few hundred feet up in the air. I was always worried they were gonna blow it while we rode over it one day, and if the bomb didn't kill you then you'd be alive while you fell to your death below. Fuck that. There are levels to shitty ways to die and that would be pretty high up on the spectrum of shitty.

Luckily for us, they never blew it up, but right past it was the second set of overpasses: Spaghetti Bridge. Yep, the exact same one that I got my first ambush at. This time we had passed under the overhang with no issues. I was facing the rear and providing security for our backside when I heard a heavy-duty machine gun open up.

Now, during my time in-country I had been blown up, I had been RPG'd, and I had been shot at, but up until that point no one had laid into us with heavy and sustained machine gun fire. So, when I heard it start up, I thought we were the ones shooting. I spun the turret around so I could see what I was about to ride into and to see who was shooting, and at what.

What I saw next surprised me. The NTV in front of me was getting absolutely lit the fuck up. I mean, rounds where just slamming into the side of this thing. Luckily for those inside the suburban, this thing was up-armored, or everyone inside would have been dead. It was one the most accurate ambushes I experienced in my entire time in Iraq.

Making this even worse was the fact that this ambush was coming from the left side of the road, and that meant that they were firing over the four lanes of traffic, with complete and total disregard for the innocent lives in jeopardy from their rounds. Again, this was a main highway, filled with traffic as one would expect—men, women, and children going out about their day and these motherfuckers just started shooting through them to hit us.

That's why when people say shit to me about how bad America and Americans are, I let 'em know real quick that they can kiss my ass. We don't do that shit. We don't open up on a random convoy across and through lanes of traffic with who knows how many innocents taking part in their daily commute. We may accidentally kill innocents (a sad reality of war) but we don't do it haphazardly just to hit a low-value target.

In that moment, though, I knew that if I didn't react fast enough, more innocents would die and we might just be joining them. Seeing that the rounds were coming from the left side of the road, I started to swing my turret toward the threat. It was at that point in time rounds started hitting my Humvee and cracking overhead. One of the bullets hit my turret right where my arm rested against.

That bullet hitting the steel, and feeling that vibration all the way up my arms, remains to this day the eeriest thing that ever happened to me. When the round struck there was a loud *ding* that echoed in my ear. Simultaneously, I felt the vibration from that impact run up my elbow, through my tricep, into my shoulder, and finally stop in my neck. Later on, back in my bunk, I couldn't help but imagine how painful it must be to be shot, especially by a large round. If I felt that much energy transfer through the steel, I have no clue how some people survive the shots that they take in combat.

In the heat of the fight, though, you don't have time to think about that. So, I turned my .50 towards the buildings that we were taking fire from and pressed down on the butterfly trigger. I wasn't too worried about hitting cars because I was perched above them. However, I was concerned with what was beyond the buildings I was laying into. But I had to end the ambush.

There was only one little problem: my gun jammed. Now, if you want your asshole to get tight, just go ahead and have your gun jam in the middle of an ambush. The good thing about all of this is that muscle memory takes over. I reached up, re-racked it, and pressed down on the butterfly trigger again. Much to my surprise (and dismay), it didn't fire again.

What followed is the most fucking boot thing I have ever done in my life. I kept my M203 in the turret beside me, secured in the other fabricated handle to my right. I reached over and grabbed it, pointed it towards the building we were taking fire from, and depressed the trigger. As the 203-grenade launched from my tube, in the loudest voice possible, I yelled out "TWOOOOOOOOO OOOOOHHHHHH THREEEEE!"

The grenade sailed through the air just slow enough for you to watch it head towards its target. It struck the building flush, blowing a huge hole where the attacks had been coming from. Not another shot was fired, the ambush had been halted, and we kept on about our merry way back to the barracks, grateful to have survived another close call.

Now, I had a pretty unique little tradition every time we'd survive an ambush or an IED. I'd have cheesecake. I did this for really one reason only. I LOVE cheesecake, and since I didn't die, why not? As soon as I got to the base we were headed to (or in some cases, I'd have to wait to get back to the Green Zone), I'd go right to the chow hall and grab me a piece of cheesecake. What our war lacked in booze, drugs, and prostitutes, it made up for in food. In fact, I don't think I ever ate as good as I did in Iraq, before or since.

Every time I walked into the chow hall, I couldn't believe we ate like we did. I mean these cats had prime rib and lobster night. If you were stationed in any of the major bases you had ZERO fucking things to complain about, especially regarding chow. Let's not even get started on the spread you got for holidays. There are a lot of ways we fail out soldiers in this country, but I promise feeding us ain't one.

Sitting at chow one night and enjoying another spectacular spread, I had an moment that turned out to be eerily similar to the talk I gave my guys a few days prior to 9/11. First platoon had been tasked to make a run to Habbaniyah, a city on the other side of Fallujah. We made a lot of dangerous runs during our tour, and in Iraq, you had to be careful everywhere you went, but this trip was by far our most dangerous.

Damn near every time we made the trip, we got hit. Matter of fact, we were attacked 90 percent of the times that we made that run. I have often said that you will never be happier than when you got shot at or blown up but didn't die. And as odd as it sounds, that feeling can become addictive. It's like swimming right up to the edge of an infinity pool on a high-rise. Nothing between you and the drop to your death but a few inches of plexiglass or concrete.

Sitting there, floating in the water, arms hanging over the edge, you start to get a weird tingling in your balls. It's both frightening and exhilarating. You want to get away from the edge as fast as you can, but at the same time, something's compelling you to stay. Combat is much the same way. You spend your time in it wanting to go home, and your time back home wanting to get back to combat. We humans are odd creatures.

So, it wasn't overly surprising to hear some guys (especially the young ones) saying they were pissed when we found out that 1st Platoon had been pulled from the run for another mission and 2nd Platoon would be tasked with it. Sitting at dinner, they went on and on about how they wished we'd gotten the run because we always get hit on it and it meant being able to get in on the action.

While I was willing and ready to make the run if it were assigned to us, and even willing to volunteer to do the run (just like I had volunteered to come to Iraq in the first place), I was never going to complain if we got removed from any mission. My personal philosophy is that whatever happens, happens for a reason. If I get stuck in traffic, for example, I always remind myself that's where I am supposed to be. Maybe being stuck in traffic kept me from getting injured or killed at an intersection someone just blew through. This line of thinking helps me deal with disappointment.

So, as the guys started bitching, I shared my line of thinking— that it's foolish to bitch about fate. That we didn't know what the hands of fate knew that we didn't. Maybe us not going was because we weren't supposed to go and that we'd be dodging a bullet, quite literally. Sad thing is, once again, I'd be proven right in my attempt to remind the younger guys about the reality of war.

The next day, we made our run as we were instructed and actually finished up early. I got a workout in, grabbed chow, and retired for the evening to my trailer. I was lying in my bunk watching an episode of *Married with Children* (my favorite TV show of all time) when there came a knock at my door. One of our senior NCOs opened it and said, "Second platoon has been hit and they have KIA. Everyone is meeting up now."

My heart sank instantly. Even though you are in war and you know that getting killed is a very real possibility, it still comes as a shock when it actually happens. You make so many runs, dodge so many rockets, bullets, and bombs that you start to believe that you are immune to it. You're just too good, too protected to be hit. Sure, it'll happen to someone on some other team, and that sucks for them. But you and your team are good. In reality, death is all around you. You see the reaper smiling, and as Marcus Aurelius once said, "All you can do is smile back."

Most of us, though (myself included), smile back because subconsciously, you think you're gonna win. The joke is on death, because it may get someone, but it won't get you. It's like the quote from *Game of Thrones*: "What do we say to the God of Death?" "Not today." The average soldier is convinced that is the truth, that death may get them, but it won't get them today. Sadly, we know that for far too many, today is, in fact, the day.

That day had now finally found the Rough Riders. We had taken a great deal of pride in saying that we were the only convoy team in the country to have not taken any causalities. Give credit to our aggressive nature or to luck, it makes no difference; one or both had run out that day. I kicked my feet over to the side of the bed and put my head in my hands. Never before in my life had I wished I was wrong more so than I did in that moment.

I rose to my feet and punched the wall, leaving a dent in it. I grabbed a shirt, socks, and shoes, got dressed, and made my way to the meet-up point outside another guy's trailer to meet the team as they came in. We stood there in awkward silence. We didn't even know what to say to each other—how were we gonna be of any use to the guys in 2nd platoon?

We looked over as 2nd Platoon rounded the corner and entered the trailer area. They walked forward, gear in hand, not saying a word. They walked towards us and I honestly don't know if we were more of a hindrance than helpful. Perhaps the feeling washed over them of, "Great, we gotta explain it all over again."

Some of the guys embraced and said hello. While I was close with the guys from First Platoon because we spent a ton of time together, I wasn't that close to Second. I hadn't deployed with these guys and so I missed all of the workup time (training) they got in prior to deployment, not to mention all the time they spent together back home in the unit before orders even came down. So, I did what I felt was most respectful: I stood there and kept my mouth shut.

We were all standing there when a straggler came up. He had been walking by himself and it was abundantly clear that he was despondent. He walked up to the group and looked everyone straight in the face and, until the day I die, I'll never forget what he said: "I don't want to ever hear one of you motherfuckers bitching about not going on a goddamn mission again. This isn't a fucking game. Hernandez is dead and he ain't ever coming back. You guys wanted this mission so bad and look what happened. Don't even bother saying a fucking word to me." With that, he walked off back to his bunk.

The guys had been hit pretty much at the same place we always got hit. The problem was it was one way in and one way out, so you had to make that pass, and the insurgents knew that. They kept those highways rigged all the time. In times past, they missed the Humvee. This time they didn't, and registered a direct hit on Truck Three.

Of all the people I knew in 2nd Platoon, Ryan was who I knew best. Years later, he would come visit me and stay at my house while getting work done at Walter Reed. What follows is what he shared with me about that day.

Romeo 2-2 was staffed with Jay Wilkerson (TC), Phillip Bell (Driver), Robert Hernandez (Scout-Left side), and Ryan Hallberg (Gunner). The convoy took two IEDs while conducting the mission. One touched off during our trip into Habbaniyah and blew up between truck four and the dignitary's truck. They had a multi-hour layover in Camp Habbaniyah where they conducted an AAR and decided to stay overnight due to intel that insurgents were setting up another IED for our return trip to Baghdad.

Once BG Bulger returned from his meeting and tour of the base, Romeo 2-2 informed the BG (Brigadier General) of their assessment of the situation and cautioned him of the potential danger of returning. The BG insisted that they return immediately. SFC Kelley attempted to reason with the BG, but to no avail. Much to their dismay, they remounted and headed out toward Baghdad.

They had received intel on a possible insurgent scout that was "clocking" convoys as they passed. This activity was sourced to a single train car sitting on the tracks to the right of the road on their return. Ryan was assigned to the one-to-five o'clock sector during our mission. As they entered what we believed to be the "kill zone," Ryan could see the train car sitting on the tracks. He started to get lightheaded and decided to get low in his stance and take an aimed shooting posture. Seconds after he got low and began leading the train car in his sights, the second IED touched off.

Ryan remembers thinking, *Fuck, that was close!* and then blacking out. Later, he remembered his M-4 falling out of the turret and hitting him in the head, hearing people screaming, and then smelling sulfur and waking up on the floor. Their truck was full of smoke, SSG Bell was slumped over the steering wheel, and the truck was still moving at a quick clip into the field next to the road. Ryan braced for rollover and remembered their truck hitting a berm and coming to a halt.

He tried to stand back up in the turret and then realized that something wasn't right. He sat up and did a self-assessment. That's when he realized that both legs were broken. His right leg was broken in the upper femur area and his left had a compound tib/fib fracture and was actively bleeding. After his assessment, he could hear small-arms fire from our driver's side and realized that the back driver's-side door was missing.

He propped himself up against the B pillar of the truck to try and shield himself from any incoming fire and attempted to render aid to SSG Bell and Sgt Wilkerson. SSG Bell had a giant hole in his back from a shrapnel wound and Sgt Wilkerson was fading in and out of consciousness due to a shrapnel wound to the brain. Shortly after the small-arms fire subsided, SSG MacKenzie arrived and began assessing the situation.

Due to his heightened mental state, Ryan had to explain the order of triage to him: Sgt Wilkerson first, SSG Bell second, with Ryan going last. At that point, Ryan didn't realize that SSG Hernandez had been ejected from the truck. They pulled Ryan out of truck on a shrapnel-resistant blanket, due to a lack of cots, his right femur bones banging together every time they took a step away from the truck. They dragged him up to the road as we awaited air support.

They weren't able to make a 9-line due to faulty comms, and had to send two trucks back to Habbaniah to get quick reaction force (QRF) and ground ambulance assets. He remembers being in the ambulance and trying to calm those that were screaming. The day before our attack, Hernandez and Ryan got into a pissing match that almost went to blows. So when we were in the ambulance together, Ryan apologized for yelling at him. Ryan looked down and saw that both of Hernandez's legs were missing.

As they got offloaded back at the base, Ryan saw the look on the cute nurse's face and watched her turn pale. The last thing he did was look at that nurse and say, "I'm not doing that well, am I?" Then he blacked out.

Ryan woke up in Balad and his entire body was swollen. He looked to his right and one of our chaplains, the MNSTC-I Senior NCO, and some light colonel were sitting next to his bed—all of them with tears in their eyes. They pinned the Purple Heart on him and talked to him for a while. It didn't make much sense to him then, but they pinned him at that moment, almost convinced that he wasn't going to make it.

They called his mom and asked her to get a passport so they could fly her to Germany to recieve Ryan's body if he didn't make it. A few days later, Ryan called his mom and told her he was fine. Needless to say, she was quite confused. Ryan didn't find out until after he got to Walter Reed and after Hernandez was buried, what we already knew: that his friend didn't make the flight to Balad.

A few days later, we would hold a memorial service for SSG. Hernandez. We'd hold it in a building that was adjacent to the famous "Crossed Swords" that almost every soldier who deployed to Baghdad got a picture under. Both First and Second Platoon lined our Humvees up and made the walk as a group into the building to find our seats near the front of the stage.

It felt very similar to every other funeral I had attended. We walked in as the "immediate family" members and every eye in the room turned to face us. They looked at us with sympathy and pity. Many of them had jobs that didn't take 'em outside the wire much, or at all. Their jobs weren't really that much more dangerous in Iraq than a civilian's back stateside. Also, regular infantry is looked upon with pity. If you have a "cool guy" tab like Ranger or Special Forces, folks look at you as badass. Oddly enough, if you are just infantry, you get looked at not as a badass, but rather as someone who couldn't get another job. Both assumptions are far from the truth.

Taking our first causalities from our own ranks struck the team extremely hard. I don't want to say that it made it more real, because after getting blown up and shot at as much as we had, war was pretty fucking real. But there was something about that loss that both humbled and enraged us. Right, wrong, or indifferent after that hit, after Hernandez died, leaving behind his children and fiancé, and after all of those guys were hit and their lives irrevocably changed forever, we wanted revenge. Little did we know at the moment that in just a few weeks, we were going to get that chance at the exact same place Hernandez was killed.

We spent the next few days amped up while out on missions. We were chomping at the bit for someone, anyone, to attack us and give us the opportunity to make someone pay for what they did to our guys. It didn't matter if it was the same guys or not. We just wanted to hit someone, and to hit them hard. However, much like had been the case the entire deployment, after that hit, things were quiet for a little while. All that did was leave us to stew in our anger.

The mood of the team remained professional but somber. After something like that, you're not quite sure when the right time is to get back to playing pranks and sharing dick jokes. So, we just kept going out on missions and doing whatever we could to remain occupied. It was one of the more somber times I have experienced in life.

I think what made it that way was the culmination of two facts. First, we'd lost one guy, but we didn't know if the other guys were going to make it for sure, as their injuries were life-threatening as well. On top of this fact, we found ourselves now quite aware of our vulnerability. Now it was clear that we could get killed. We had to come face to face with that reality. The problem with facing it is that we now knew the hole a death would leave, and we didn't want to feel that again.

Then the inevitable happened: the run came down again. This time it was tasked to First Platoon, and our desire for revenge had been answered. With that in mind, however, the reality was that we knew these guys had gotten better. After all, they had mistimed all the previous IEDs before Second Platoon took a direct hit. That meant that they had either gotten lucky or good, and there was no way for us to determine which.

It really didn't make any difference at the end of the day. As much as I believe in the hands of fate, I also won't just throw my hands in the air and say, "Fuck it, whatever happens, happens." No, I want to make sure that I've done all I can to help fate out.

For me, the first step was to make sure that there was zero chance in hell that my gun would jam. After it jammed in that one ambush and I had to revert back to my M203, I vowed to never let that happen again. More importantly, I knew that the likely place of the ambush would be out of range for it anyway. The day before we made the run, I broke down every single link in my possession. Literally thousands of rounds.

I cleaned each round and the linkage. I cleaned and the entire weapons system from front to back. I inspected every inch of my fighting position. I restacked my ammo for ease of access. I removed everything from my turret but my M203 and one crate of ammo.

From there, we started talking about the mission. We knew where they were most likely to hit us. There was one road in and one road out into Habbaniya, so they knew which way were coming from. We also knew where we typically got hit. We made the decision that headed out there, we would cross the dirt median to jump onto the oncoming traffic lane in order to throw them off.

The fact was that was a pretty risky move in and of itself. Jumping the median could have us roll right over a planted IED ourselves. Also, each truck must follow the exact track pattern of the lead truck to not expose us to any additional risk. Just going a foot over could mean that we triggered an IED that the lead truck missed. Everything in combat is a calculated risk. We also knew that if we did it on the way in, we couldn't do it on the way out. But you can't get to the way out if you don't make it in, so fuck it, it was time to send it.

The night before, I didn't sleep much. I was filled with just about every emotion you can think of. Even before 2nd Platoon had been hit and taken causalities, the run would give you the jitters. You knew that you were going to get hit. I mean, it was all but guaranteed. But up until Hernandez was killed, the bad guys hadn't gotten a win. Now with our underbelly exposed and the sting still burning, it upped the seriousness of the stakes.

While it had been made abundantly clear that we could die on this run, there still remained a side of you as a soldier that was excited to make it. Again, as an infantryman, this was what you signed up for. You wanted to make that run and stare death in the face (at least if you were tasked with it). What's more, we now had an added incentive to make it: we wanted to take the fight to those guys who were responsible for killing and injuring our brothers.

You lie there in your bunk and you play out just about every scenario imaginable for the run. Where will they hit you? How many? What will happen if a vehicle goes down? Who will step up if a PL or PSG goes down? I've got the big gun. What's my plan if it goes down? Who is gonna give me ammo? What if we get stuck in the kill zone? How long can I stay in the fight?

No matter how amped you are, sleep always wins in the end—at least it does for me—and I crashed sometime after midnight. Regardless of the time I drifted off, when the alarm went off, I shot out of bed like a cannon. There is no casual or gradual wake up when you know for a fact you are headed to the meat grinder that day. At the first *ding*, my eyes shot open and my feet were on the floor. It was killing time, either them or us, and there wasn't any point in dragging it out.

I grabbed my gear, chow, and made my way to the motor pool. There I linked up with the guys, but the normal banter was missing from this morning's PMCS. Each of us knew what lay ahead; the only question that remained was, "Who's it gonna be—them or us?"

We jumped in our Humvees and headed out to pick up the general and get our safety brief. SSG. Boose, the acting PSG, gave the safety brief. He went over the enemy's activity along our route over the last twenty-four hours and the expected likelihood of new attacks that day. From there, it's a simple: "Got any questions? No? Good. Mount up, and let's roll."

As was customary for us, we would play DMX's "Rough Ryders Anthem" on our way through the Green Zone headed to the gate. That day, it served as a shot of adrenaline and even pulled on our heartstrings as we thought about going to the exact same spot Hernandez had been killed. Typically, we talked shit and cracked jokes on that last little leg before we locked and loaded and made our way out into the city. This time, we didn't say a word and the silence was only broken when I pulled the charging handle on the .50, right before I grabbed grips and picked up my sector of fire as we pushed out through the checkpoint and into the heart of the city.

The ride from Baghdad to Habbaniya would last an hour and twenty-one minutes (if everything went as planned). Roughly fifty-six minutes into that ride, you have to go through Fallujah. Of all the cities in the country I had been through, Fallujah still creeps me out the most. In 2006, it was a different city than it was during the second Battle of Fallujah that took place during April of 2004, exactly two years beforehand. U.S., Iraqi, and British forces had totaled about 13,500 (the U.S. specifically had gathered some 6,500 Marines and 1,500 Army soldiers, along with about 2,500 Navy personnel in operational and support roles). when. While it wasn't the hornet's nest it was then, it was still a dangerous stretch of real estate.

To drive through it was like driving through some dystopian future. Every single building had bullet holes in it, even the "nice" ones. Many either had gaping holes in them or were bombed to the ground. It didn't look like a place anyone would live. It made it easy to understand how young men of fighting age were easily radicalized and transformed into an insurgency. I mean, if you grew up there, unexposed to the outside world, and watched these foreigners come through and fuck your town up, wouldn't you be pissed off, too?

While Fallujah wasn't what it used to be in terms of threat, it was a step up in danger along the route and was the final phase into "the shit's about to get real." We were now less than a half hour from Habbaniya, and roughly fifteen to twenty minutes from where we expected to get ambushed. No one said a word, but you knew everyone's heartbeats had picked up.

We had little to no support, as we learned the hard way when 2nd Platoon got hit; QRF was not quick at all. The reality was we were on our own, and if shit went south in the next three minutes, no one was coming.

It was up to us.

In a swivel of the turret, I saw the hill up ahead and the designated jump point. A moment later, Truck One had made the jump across the median unscathed, and now it was up to each driver that followed to hit those exact same tracks across the median. I hunkered down behind the .50, holding the grip with my right hand and my turret handle with my left, prepared to swing to engage any targets = that might present themselves.

We crested the hill and I found myself muttering under my breath, "Come on, just blow, come on, just blow." *I know we are going to get hit, so let's just go ahead and get it over with.*

Apparently, our plan to jump lanes had, in fact, thrown them off, and no IED blew. We did take some small-arms fire, but it was sporadic and not even enough to really determine where it was coming from. Round one had gone to us, and fifteen minutes later, we were pulling up to the base. The problem that lay ahead of us now was the same one that had done 2nd Platoon in: they knew we had gone in, they knew we had to come out, and now they had all day to plan for it.

On base, our heart rates returned to normal, but after we checked out vehicles for damage, did our AAR, and grabbed chow, we subjected ourselves to more pain—they still had the 2nd Platoon's Humvee that was hit on the base. This was the first time that we'd been near it, and so we were tasked with securing some gear and looking to see if any personal belongings had been left behind.

Walking up to it was a shock. Almost every inch was covered in shrapnel damage. The charge had blown clear through the bulletproof glass, which was several inches thick. The turret was peppered with shrapnel as well, and upon seeing some of the spots that it tore through, I have no clue how Ryan made it out alive.

The wheels were shredded down to just the rims. Inside, seats were torn apart and there was one huge gaping hole in the back of the driver's seat. Looking at what was left of the Humvee, you felt both a sense of awe and despair at the same time. On one hand, before you was the realization of just how effective guerrilla warfare and insurgency could be against an overwhelmingly superior force. On the other hand, you couldn't help but be impressed that the Humvee could provide enough protection that three out of four people inside could walk away with their lives after a blast of that magnitude. Only one question mattered at that moment: could we do it again?

We got the word that the general was done and ready to make the run back. We got our brief and loaded up and got ready to roll. We weren't going to make the jump this time. We were simply going to run the route as fast as we could and hope that they would mistime the detonation of the bomb. Rolling out the gate, you couldn't help but feel almost like you were running back into a bad dream. All of these things had happened to 2nd Platoon just a few weeks prior and we knew the outcome; now here we were on the same road tempting fate the exact same way. All you could do is throw up a prayer for safe passage and get ready to do work.

We were hauling ass and the berm was coming up in sight when it happened. Just between my truck and Joker's (Truck Three), a bomb went off. We were lucky in that their timing was imperfect and this thing detonated pretty much right in the middle, and thus missed both trucks. It also appeared to be smaller than the one that it 2nd Platoon; wins all around. However, it was deafening, and my world went silent. I remember saying over and over (rather loudly), "I'm fucking deaf, somebody say something to me!"

At that moment, unable to look down because bombs were always followed up with small-arms fire, I didn't know if anyone in the truck was hurt. Finally, the driver yelled back, "Nobody say anything!" That was immediately followed up with, "Contact right!" from the TC I looked to my front and saw that Joker had opened up on the train car, and that was all I needed to know.

I instantly locked in on his tracers and saw the fighting position they were fighting from. I opened fire and let that .50 eat. Honestly, I lost a little of my cool, and instead of a sustained burst, I just poured rounds into the enemy. One of them ran to the train car, but since I had slap rounds, I let him have it. Everyone that fucked with us that day, and in that position, had their family singing slow songs by nightfall. Immediately after killing that part of the ambush, I heard, "Contact left," come across the radio and saw Joker sending rounds over the left side of the berm into a car parked in an open field. Again, I followed his tracers, and no one shot back after that.

We entered the village with my blood still pumping and my adrenaline through the roof. With my free hand, I started clearing the spent brass casings in my turret and could hear the clinking as they dropped into the inside of the truck. I was pissed off. These motherfuckers had tried to kill us once again and I knew the people in the village were aware of it. I knew that for us to get hit as much as we did in that area, they had to support it, or at the very least lacked the backbone to stand up to those conducting the attacks.

In my eyes, they were no better than the people pulling the trigger. They had allowed this to go on for years and were complicit in the deaths of service members that had come to this country in an attempt to help them. I had no love lost for anyone who lived there. Matter of fact, at that moment, I hated them.

What happened next was, in my opinion, God saving my soul. As we entered the village, I saw two military-aged men standing off to the side of the road. They looked at me with hate in their eyes. I had no doubt that they were involved with the bomb that just went off or with those individuals who had been shooting at us who now were no longer breathing. More importantly, I was certain that they were part of the group that had hit 2nd Platoon. I wanted to kill them to make sure that they couldn't hurt anyone else.

I went to rotate my turret but it was jammed. I tried several times to push my gun toward them, but no matter how hard I tried, I couldn't get my turret to move. I couldn't kill them. For the briefest of moments, we locked eyes. I knew they didn't like me. I hoped that they could feel my disgust for them. It was the briefest of encounters, but one that felt like it lasted a lifetime. It's funny how in moments like those, time feels as if it's standing still. It almost feels like you are in a Zach Snyder movie with an overabundance of still-frame shots to drive home the epicenes of the encounter. It's all going slow and then suddenly the frame speeds up and you're on to the next scene.

Our eyes were locked until life "sped back up." What's crazy is, soon as I was out of range, the turret moved again. It's why I say that God saved my soul that day. Was I justified to kill those guys? In my heart, I still say yes. I am sure they were tied into the attacks somehow, but no court on earth would have supported me killing them in that moment; earlier in the war, yes . . . then, no. They weren't armed. I didn't have physical proof of them shooting at us (or anyone else) and I didn't catch them in the act. In short, I would have been wrong to do what I felt was right.

That makes you look in the mirror and consider what it says about you. We think about morality when it comes to killing. That it must be a clear black-and-white issue. That the good guy always knows (and will act accordingly) when it is okay to take a life. I can tell you from personal experience, it's not always that easy.

The truth is that I didn't do anything wrong, but sometimes I look back and feel some semblance of shame. I didn't do anything wrong because I couldn't. If I would have been able to move that turret, I would 100 percent have killed them. To this day, in my mind, I argue about what is right legally, morally, and in reality. Because I have zero doubt that my inability to kill them that day meant that they killed other soldiers later on.

That day has conflicted me for so long. On one hand, I know I killed some of the people who were linked to past attacks on our team and others who had ran through that AO. I also hope and pray that I killed some of those directly responsible for the attack on 2nd Platoon that cost Hernandez his life and permanently injured others who were with him. But, at the end of the day, I realize that I have within me the capability to act as judge, jury, and executioner, and I don't know if that's a good thing. So, when it's all said and done, I am grateful that, as far I am concerned, God stepped in and stopped me and saved me from carrying the burden of one more trigger pull for the rest of my life.

The rest of the ride back to base was relatively uneventful, outside of the spare tire falling off and flying down the road for no real reason at all. I just looked back as it fell off the end of the Humvee and rolled off into the sunset like a cowboy at the end of a Western. Regardless of the reason, it wasn't worth stopping a convoy with a one-star general to retrieve, so we agreed to let it roam wild and free as we Charlie miked on back to base.

For me, that would be the last major conflict of the war. We'd soon be replaced by the follow-on forces and I would be given the honor of being one of the soldiers selected to conduct their training, to do the left seat/right seat ride to show them the ropes and ins and outs of the country and their job.

As all things seem to do, the end of my tour came surprisingly quick. At the start of anything with any sustained duration, the end seems so far away. But once the journey is complete, even if it was years in the making, you look back and feel like it was gone in the blink of an eye. As I said earlier, when in combat, you can't wait to get back home. But it's not until you get back home that you realize maybe combat wasn't so bad after all.

Chapter Twelve

Transitions

"If you don't take charge of your transition, it is a dark and lonely road."
—Captain Brian Stann

Looking back on it, perhaps the craziest part about transitioning back to stateside was the speed with which it took place. One day I was in Iraq, the next (after a one-beer pit stop in Germany) I was Stateside. It's hard to explain the feeling of stepping off that plane back home for the first time. To walk off the plane and know (well, to be relatively certain at least) that no one was going to try and shoot you or blow you up was a huge relief. A feeling you would assume would stay with you, but surprisingly, after those first few steps on American tarmac, you forget you're back home quite often. At least in those first few months.

I didn't re-deploy back close to home, so there wasn't any big fanfare waiting for us or for me (not that I expected to have a huge personal crowd anyway). So, I just got off the plane and walked to my bus to be trucked over to the base. I went through out-processing, turned in all my gear, did all my medicals, checked all the blocks, dotted my Is, crossed my Ts, and was bid *adieu*. I called my boy David Posin, aka DP, and told him I was headed home and asked if he could pick me up at Baltimore/Washington International.

My flight back was extremely humbling and flattering at the same time. Everyone would see the uniform and ask in an assuming manner if I were coming back from the sandbox. When that answer was yes, they'd follow up with how long was I gone and did I see combat, and the list goes on and on. When the answer was nearly a year and yes, it seemed that they felt an intense obligation to me in order to somehow make amends for the fact that they didn't go.

I was always (and still am) grateful when folks told me, "Thank you for your service," but the truth is, I am never quite sure how to respond, and I think most vets struggle with this. In a weird dichotomy, we don't want to be thanked, but we want to feel appreciated, and sometimes that gets lost in the civilian-military divide; which is a shame,because I am positive that society as a whole appreciates the fuck out of our military. We just don't speak the same language.

After I had as many free meals as a man can eat, I found myself walking through my last terminal toward the exit to baggage claims. As I approached the final corner, I found myself with an unexpected level of nerves. I started to wonder and worry what everyone would think of me. I had lost a dick-ton of weight since all I did while deployed was work out and run missions. As I rounded the corner, I was shocked to see just how many people were there to pick me up. Dave and his cousin Steve, Julie, a friend from my Army days, Antonio, my man with his one-hitter quitter, and then the girl I was not-so-secretly in love with at the time, Beth Vasquez. Oh, and Mauve Kat—she was a hottie too, and I thought we should probably go on a date or two.

As soon as we all saw each other, my nerves went by the wayside and we erupted in jubilant hugs and cheers. For a moment, everyone else in the airport disappeared and we had the baggage claim all to ourselves. It was crazy to have been gone so long and now to see these people was to pick up right back where we left off. We joked and everyone marveled at how "skinny" I had gotten. We took pictures, collected my duffel bag, and hit the road.

The ride home was the first time that I started to notice that I continued to act as if I were in Iraq. I scanned the side of the roads and felt uneasy going under overpasses. I am not sure why I felt this at that time. I had been outside and on the road prior to landing in BWI, and hadn't felt this way. Maybe it was because, for the first time, I wasn't with my guys I served with, but whatever the reason, I noticed my apprehension and being on edge and I didn't like it. I hoped that it would be fleeting.

We pulled up to Steve's house and as soon as I walked in the door, I was met with a thunderous, "WELCOME HOME!"

Lennie, who Dave had met and fallen madly in love with while I was in Iraq, had helped organize a surprise welcome-home party for me, and she had never even met me. Back then, Myspace was still a thing and I'll never forget that she created a countdown clock for me that served as a happy reminder of how many days I had left until I came home. Again, we hadn't ever met once; she was just that kind of woman, and I am grateful to this day not only for her kindness towards me but that Dave found that type of woman to share his life with. He most assuredly deserved her.

The party was a great time and it felt awesome to be back around civilization after a year of war. The first few days were cool, catching up with friends, partying, and sleeping in. After a few days, though (at least for me), that shit starts to lose its luster. What good is it to sleep in when you could be waking up and living your dreams? How can you call yourself a "go-getter" if all you're doing is sitting on your ass? So in my mind, the time had come to go to work.

So, I decided that I needed to get back to work. I started working at Fitness First as a sales rep. On the surface, it would appear that was the perfect job for me. However, I had such a horrible relationship with money that I wasn't confident enough to do the job. I never sold based on value; I always sold based on price. Dave was working at the same gym and was absolutely smoking me in the numbers and total contract value. He was charging more (justifiably so) and still signing up damn near three times the amount of people that I was.

The company had a hard-and-fast sales quota that had to be met each month, and I failed to meet it in back-to-back months. Looking back on it, I couldn't close a door. I was horrible and the worse I did, the worse I felt, and the worse I felt, the worse I did. Coming from the military where everything is about team, I started to really resent the job. I took a negative attitude toward the company. I didn't understand business yet and I constantly bitched that all the owner cared about was the money. I made myself a martyr instead of saying, "Hey, I don't know what I am doing, so why not ask for help? Ask for more training? Or invest in additional training myself?" Instead, I did what the vast majority of people in the U.S. do: I bitched, pointed fingers, and blamed everyone but myself.

When you do that, there is only one viable option, and that's to fail. You can do none of those things, you can do everything "right," and you can still fail. However, if you're a crybaby bitch and refuse to take accountability like I used to, failure is all you'll ever find. No success will come to you, except successfully getting fired.

Which is exactly what happened to me. Three months into this new job and here I was getting fired. I had gone from leading men in combat to packing my shit and doing the walk of shame in just three months' time. I remember walking out of the gym with a full cardboard box of my stuff—awards and citations I had been given in the military. Here I was thinking I had it all figured out, and just like that, the civilian world proved that it didn't care about what I had done in the military. And I took major offense to that.

To this day, I am not sure why. I couldn't see that the military and the civilian world actually cared about the same thing when you broke it down: they cared about results. I have found that veterans sometimes fail to see the forest for the trees once they get out. In the military, we believe that mission is for the greater good, but we fail to see that, for a business, making money is for the greater good. If the company doesn't make money, it can't offer its products, goods, or services to the community that needs to use them, and thus goes out of business. When that happens because you didn't charge shit or you sucked at sales, the end result is that you can't help anyone. You failed your mission.

As crazy as it sounds, many veterans are willing to lay down their lives for the greater good of God and country but refuse to charge what is needed to sustain their company for fear of looking greedy. The mind is a funny thing.

But back there, walking out of that gym, I didn't think of how getting fired was my fault. I blamed the company and all the people who worked in it (outside of Dave). What made matters worse, I got fired and Dave got promoted to general manager. Now, don't get me wrong, I wasn't jealous of Dave or mad that he got promoted and I got fired. That wasn't on him. I was just embarrassed because here he was, younger than I was, he didn't have some of the experiences that I had, experiences that were supposed to make you a man, and yet, in my eyes, he was more of a man than I was. He had his shit together. I looked at DP and thought, *This guy is the total package.* While I had no desire to make out with the guy, I can say he was a handsome fellow, about 5'11", athletic, with blond hair and blue eyes. I mean, if you liked muscular blond guys with blue eyes, you loved you some DP.

On top of that, he was fresh out of college and was killing the game. Here I was, supposedly a soldier who had been taught to be all I could be, and the only thing I accomplished was getting fired. What made matters worse was that I had no real clue what to do next. I didn't have another job lined up and I didn't see myself as posing any valuable skills to bring to bear. I saw no way to market myself. I didn't know how to write a resume and I didn't understand what soft skills were. So, in my eyes, I was a loser, again. Outside of the military I instantly felt like I didn't know what I was doing or if I had the talent to be anything worthwhile.

Now, without a job, and without any income, I was left wanting. I couldn't afford to pay rent and my roommate was already over me living at the house. I wasn't the neatest person at the time and he was OCD about cleanliness. We had already had a few verbal spats over the past few months, and so by the time it came for rent and I didn't have it, I had more than worn out my welcome, and the invitation to live there was revoked.

I had nowhere to go. I had no money. My credit was absolute shit. The result? I wound up homeless. I found myself living in my car. Luckily, Dave would find couches for me to crash on and that got me by. Again, I was still riding the pity party train. I found myself once again in the martyr role. How could he kick me out when he knew I had nowhere to go? How could that guy call himself a friend? What a dickhead!

Getting evicted only added to my shame. First I was fired, and now I was homeless! Absolutely nothing I was doing was working. I was failing on every level. But still I refused to see it as my fault. That narrow mindset put me on the road to becoming extremely bitter.

While it may seem like nothing being your fault is freeing, in actuality, it is binding and restrictive. As Jocko says, "When nothing is your fault, you are a victim to everyone and everything. You're no longer in control of your life, everything and everyone around you is." When that starts to happen, you begin to spiral out of control, and for me this was the start of the tailspin that almost cost me my life.

While I was bitter, I wasn't above working. I knew I had to make more money and so I started looking into several ways to get cash coming in. First up was going back and asking for a job as a personal trainer at the company that had just fired me. I also started working for a company called HomeSide that sold windows and siding. I would go work a shift in the morning at the gym and then go door to door with high school kids trying to book appointments for the sales reps to come out and give free estimates for windows and siding.

Neither job did shit for my ego. My job as a trainer was really just a glorified weight stacker. None of the trainers were certified and no one could request us directly anyway. Our job was simply to show new members around the gym, give 'em a free workout that demonstrated the equipment, and let 'em go on their way. During the times we weren't doing that, which admittedly was a lot, our job was to clean the gym, do bathroom checks, clean the cardio machines, and restack the dumbbells and put the plates back.

Anyone who's spent any time in the gym will tell you that the average meathead can lift every weight in the world except theirs when it's time to put the weight back on the rack. So these fuckers would come in, destroy the gym, spread their weights all over the place like they were dogs marking their territory, and then roll out to go hit on the girl working the front desk.

I hated these oiled bougie-as-fuck boys. Not because they wanted to holler at good-looking women—I mean, who doesn't want to holler at good-looking women? Hell, I think good-looking women want to holler at good-looking women, but at least have some class about it. Of all the mysteries, the one I'll never understand is why women put up with (or are attracted to) douchebag dudes. But over and over again, I'd be in there restacking weights and these fucksticks that treated the gym like a club would be upfront running wack-ass game, and somehow getting lucky here and there. I guess it all goes back to that Gretzky saying, "You miss 100% of the shots you don't take."

After cleaning up after these momma's boys, I'd go back, check the pisser, and then go do my most-hated job of all—clean cardio. Now, I have done a lot of shit jobs in my life, but for some reason I don't really understand myself, I have hated no job more than I did cleaning cardio. I mean, I have literally shoveled shit for a living and liked it better than cleaning the cardio machines in the gym.

So between stacking the weights, cleaning the cardio, and putting up with the fuckboys, along with the fact that I was to making minimum wage—meanwhile the freelance trainers were in the gym, utilizing it as they saw fit, having to do none of the grunt work, and making anywhere from four to ten times what I was making—you can understand why I had the breeding grounds for further discontent with my life. What took it over the top was I went to ask for a twenty-five cent raise from the manager of the gym, and I got turned down. It absolutely blew my mind.

Here I was, busting my ass, doing far more than anyone else in the gym, and I couldn't even get an extra twenty-five cents per hour. I just couldn't do it anymore. I didn't like the clientele that came to that gym, all the puffed-up meathead guys who thought they were too cool to speak to you, and all the superficial women who spent more time getting dolled up to go to the gym than they did actually working out at the gym. Too many women who looked like they were getting ready for a nightclub in D.C. rather than headed to the gym to get drenched in sweat. Truth be told, many of 'em never dropped one bead of sweat the entire time they were there. All I could wonder to myself was, *What was the fucking point of it all?*

Well, we all know the point. To get your dick wet. It was all peaCOCKing. To put on a show. To appear like you had something to offer the fairer sex. It wasn't about the work, it was about setting up the play for later that night. It was all a game, and your ability to "score" was the only thing most were thinking about.

My evening gig wasn't much better. At HomeSide, my job was to manage the team that went out to collect leads for the sales reps. The ethics of that job was borderline at best. It wasn't that they sold shitty products; they didn't. The windows were awesome, and the siding was great. The installation team killed it. But the way they generated leads was an outright lie.

Now, this isn't to say they were the only ones who did it this way. The truth, is the ENTIRE industry did things the exact same way. And not just windows and siding: roofing, security, driveway pavers, and insect repellents do this as well, just to name a few. They still do it this way. I often find myself giggling when I get a knock on my door or a ringing of my doorbell and look on my Ring camera to see a young high school or college kid standing there, polo and clipboard in hand. I know what they are going to say before I even open the door.

"Good evening sir, my name is X and I am with Company Y, and we just finished up work on your neighbor's house over on Street Name Y. Do you know him?"

They know you don't know him 'cause he doesn't fucking exist, but they also know you don't want to look unpopular, and besides, what are you going to do, call 'em a liar? You don't even know if the street they just listed even exists, but you don't want to look like a motherfucker who doesn't even know his own neighborhood.

Anyway, back to the pitch. "We just finished installing said product on an imaginary guy's house, and he loved it! Since we were already in the neighborhood, we are doing a courtesy to everyone who lives here and setting up appointments to give you a FREE no-obligation estimate!" On the surface, it makes sense. The guy's already in the neighborhood, and it's free, so why not?

The only catch is the guy isn't in the neighborhood at all. In many cases, there isn't even a job going on at that time. What is happening is the owner is sitting at his house waiting for the phone to ring to pretend that they are booked up with appointments and he needs to see if he can even get a rep out there. But wait, whoa-la, we did just have an appointment finish up early (see, I told you it was fast) and we can be over there within the hour. So, the appointment gets booked and the sales rep, who's probably drinking at the bar, gets called and told to head over to your house.

From there the dishonesty continues. He's not just a rep, he's the VP of the company (this was the only straight-up lie that was told) and it's your lucky day because he's there to extend to you a SPECIAL OFFER! If you will just let him leave his sign in your yard he'll take off 50 percent of the cost of your windows! Man, what a steal!

Two hours later, you have gone from not even thinking about windows or siding to buying anywhere from $15-40k worth. It sounds crazy to believe this works, but it works like an absolute charm. These industries are big and they have been killing the game for years, and I am sure they will continue to kill the game. With that said, it was just too much dishonesty for me to feel comfortable doing. That, and people are dickheads.

With all of that said, the last sentence sums up why I think it should be mandatory for everyone to do door-to-door sales. If you can learn to handle that level of rejection, everything else will fall in line. I didn't handle it well, and one day in particular, I knew I had to get out of that line of work before I killed someone.

I was already struggling enough as it was. I didn't have purpose, my life lacked passion, and I had absolutely zero direction. I was just an angry motherfucker floating through life, thinking nothing was my fault and that life had just continued to deal me shitty hands that were out of my control. What's worse is at that time, I wasn't even attempting to play them. I was getting pissed off, folding, slamming my cards down, flipping the table over, and walking away. In short,

I was really the dickhead and I was simply getting back what I was giving out.

Then one day, the world decided to give it back to me hard. I was out going door to door when I came upon a lady tending her flowerbed. As I approached her, I started my pitch. "Good evening, ma'am, my name is—" Before I could finish, she fired back, "I don't give a damn what your name is, get off of my property." I was flabbergasted. I had never been spoken to like that before, especially from some little petite lady who looked like she'd blow away if the wind picked up.

Now, for me, nothing is worse than unwarranted rudeness. You clearly have to go out of your way to be a dickhead. Being nice takes almost no effort at all. It's why I hate going out to the bars; people will bump into you just to be an asshole and then not even say, "Excuse me." You could punch me in the face but if you said, "Damn man, I'm sorry, I didn't see you there," I'd be cool. If you bump and keep on walking without an "excuse me," I'm ready to fight. Same goes for running off at your mouth in a smart-ass manner.

Had she been a he, I would have probably gone to jail that day. I can't hit a woman, but I also found it nigh impossible back then to not run my mouth straight back. I retorted that she didn't need to be a bitch about it. One thing I have learned over the years is that women hate a few words: "cunt," "moist," and "bitch." You let any of those words fly, they are going to do the best they can to cut you.

I followed up the bitch comment with the pathetic-ass "I'm a veteran" spiel. To which she came back with something that pissed me off at the time, but later in life I learned was true: "So what?" Standing there on the sidewalk, feeling three feet tall and fuming inside, I had nothing to say back other than "Fuck you." It didn't make me feel any better.

As I walked away, tears of rage and embarrassment welled up in my eyes. My clipboard hung loose in my arm, my head was down, and my shoulders slumped. If I could have stuck my head in a hole, I would have; anything to get me off that street and away from the weight of the shame that hung heavy around my neck like a yoke on a mule.

I couldn't help but wonder, *How in the fuck did I get here? Has anything I've done mattered? What was the point of my service? Why didn't anyone care? Why wasn't the red carpet rolled out for me? Where was the ticker tape parade? Where were all the opportunities I was told would be presented to me because I decided to "be all that I could be"?*

The truth that I didn't know then, and wouldn't learn until quite some time later, is that I was being a bitch and I had completely failed to grasp the notion of selfless service. No one owed me shit for a choice I made of my own free will. No one twisted my arm and told me to join the Army. No one begged me to go overseas and fight. No one asked me to try and be a hero. I had made all those choices on my own.

Furthermore, plenty of people cared and wanted to help, but no one wants to help a malcontent. No one wants to help a dickhead with a shitty attitude who blames everyone for their fuckups besides themselves. I wasn't getting met with the bullshit in my life because life, or anyone for that matter, was out to get me. I was stuck in this rut because I continued to make dumb choices. I continued to be a dick for no reason to people, just because I was angry and hadn't processed my own shit, like a man is supposed to do.

Even then, people wanted to help me, just like there are people today who want to help veterans. But back then I was just like a lot of guys and girls I see now: I wasn't willing to let them. It's far easier to bitch and complain about what was going on. It's more comforting to say everyone else sucks and the world is out to get you than it is to step up and say one simple sentence: "It's my fault."

That mindset leads us to become the worst version of ourselves— the angry veteran. I know, because I have been there, and I know where that form leads you. It leaves you disillusioned, depressed, angry, and alone. It robs you of your joy for life and steals from you the passion to live it. I didn't know it then—I was too wrapped up in my how denial and self-pity—but walking away with that woman cussing me out, I was giving her power that she didn't possess on her own. I was giving her permission to steal my happiness. I was saying that her opinion of me mattered when it most assuredly did not. Since that day, that lady has not contributed to one of my successes. But in the state of mind I was in back then, she 100 percent put one more crack in my armor, and got me one step closer to trying to take my own life.

I said she hadn't done anything to contribute to my success, but thinking about it as I write this, that's not true. As I walked away that afternoon, I knew I couldn't do this job any-fucking-more. There was no way I could continue to clock in and do a job with teenage kids more concerned with getting high than performing at a high level.

Of all the things missing for me at HomeSide, the most important was a purpose. The company didn't have a mission or vision statement. It didn't contribute to a non-profit (at least none that I knew of). In my eyes (which admittedly was a narrow and skewed view), the only reason it existed was to make money for the owners. I thought that was villainous at the time. Now I realize that no matter how fancy or altruistic we try to make it, that is the sole purpose of business: to make money. Failure to make money means that no matter how profound your purpose is, you fail to achieve it, because you'll run out of money to operate the business long before you make a dent in your purpose.

After my run-in with that lady in her yard, I decided that the lack of purpose, shit work, and poor pay meant it was time for me to do something else with my life. I thought to myself, *How can I make some money in the short term also moving toward a job that I loved? And not just that, but it would also allow me to make a positive difference in someone's life?* Personal training seemed to fit that bill.

This led me to start looking into getting certified as a trainer. I found out that ACE had a certification program through the local college that was a semester long. On top of that, I realized I could get my associates in personal training, and that opened my mind up to using the GI bill to pay for it. On top of paying for college, it also gave me a monthly stipend to live on, so it was a no-brainer for me to enroll and go back to college.

I started going through the courses and I also begin to look to take on personal training clients of my own. Even though I wasn't certified at the time, there was no law or regulation stating that I had to be. I figured I had spent eight years working out in the Army, I had lost damn near a Backstreet Boy in my lifetime, (150lbs, ain't no lie, bye, bye, bye). Couple all of that with the fact that I was actively enrolled in fitness and nutrition certification courses at school and I was confident I knew more than most of these "bros" walking around the gym in their little brothers' spandex shirts.

While that may have been true, what I had absolutely no confidence in was myself or my ability to make a sale. Looking back now, I had the work ethic and the drive, but I did damn near nothing right in terms of establishing myself as an expert, providing value, learning about the potential client's needs or goals, and instead trying to do 100 percent price selling.

That meant that I was in a race to the bottom and the person getting screwed was me. I wasn't establishing any investment in the client. I was establishing that I was the least-valuable trainer in the gym because I was dirt cheap. The only thing I got was headache clients who didn't pay shit. These clients, for the most part, were paying ten to twenty bucks a session, if anything at all. Hell, some folks I agreed to train for free just so it'd look like I had paying clients. Because they weren't invested and didn't take me seriously, they often missed sessions, leaving me at the gym wasting my time. Those who did show up often didn't pay on time, or at all. And they routinely canceled their training with me a week before the next payment was due, so the money I was counting on didn't come in.

All of this was a far cry from the $150k a year the personal trainer certification ad promised you'd make out the gate as a new trainer. What they failed to mention was the fact that you needed to have some clue on how to run a business if, in fact, you were going to be successful in business. As you can imagine, still stuck in the woe-is-me mentality, I quickly became disillusioned with being a personal trainer as a career and figured I'd better come up with something a bit more stable to offset my shaky start in the fitness industry.

But what should that be? What would give me the sense of purpose I was looking for, could play to my strengths, and give me the ability to remain physically active, which I liked, but just hadn't quite figured out how to make money in yet? I knew that I wanted to make a difference in people's lives. I've always wanted to do that and still do.

With all of that in mind, I started to consider what my other possibilities were. The first to come to mind was police officer, but in Montgomery County, you need an associate's degree to even apply in the first place, and once you did apply, you were looking for at least a year-long application process with zero guarantees that you'd get the job. That meant I was anywhere from three to four years away from a hire date in the best possible scenario. I couldn't hold out that long.

My next option was to become a firefighter. They didn't require a degree (many jokes would be made about that later by police officers) and while they too had about a year-long application process, they had just recently opened theirs up and were actively taking applicants for the next class. What made it even more appealing was thinking back to my time at the Pentagon on 9/11 and the sense of pride I got from working with the USAR team. More importantly, I remembered the pride and *esprit de corps* I had being part of that elite task force. The fact that the team came from the very department I was applying to was even more appealing.

I figured I would apply to the job, get on the USAR team, and because of the flex schedule, I would be able to maintain my trainer status and eventually grow clientele from there. So that's exactly what I decided to do. I was gonna be a career fighter who moonlighted as a personal trainer and life was going to be sweet!

For the next several months, I was finally motivated again. I was busy with both the college courses and my application process for the fire department. The department had a PT test you had to pass to even be considered for the chance to go to the academy, called the CPAT (Candidate Physical Ability Test).

The CPAT is an eight-event physical fitness test that each candidate must successfully complete in ten minutes to continue in the hiring process. MCFRS wanted applicants to pass and therefore offered an eight-week mentoring program to assist candidates to pass the CPAT. I was amazed at the number of people who failed to take advantage of this, or did so in a half-assed manner. The training included a combination of personalized fitness training and the opportunity to practice the skills they will be tested on.

The test itself consisted of eight evolutions, done back to back: the stair climb, equipment carry, forcible entry, dummy drag, hose drag, ladder raise and extension, the maze, and ceiling breach-and-pull. While these didn't require herculean feats of strength or marathon-level endurance, they were still very taxing when you stacked them on top of each other, and if you were out of shape and/or didn't take advantage of the practice run, there was a very real possibility that you would fail the test. I watched many, many people do just that and cost themselves a slot in the class.

For me, I took the shit deadly seriously. Even though I was

working out all the time in the gym. I made sure I adjusted my schedule to attend every single prep workout that I could. Looking around at the people who were trying to get into my class, it became apparent very quickly that I was one of the most, if not the most, in-shape member of this prospective recruit class. For the first time in a long time, I started to feel like maybe I wasn't a loser after all. Maybe, just maybe, I had found a place where I belonged and could once again thrive.

While I was killing on the PT field, I still wasn't doing all that great in the world of personal training. The confidence I was gaining by excelling in the fire recruitment process was not transferring over to the sales side of my business. I still had so much apprehension regarding asking for the sale. I couldn't stop putting my wallet in their pocket. I couldn't fathom how people would pay for personal training from me when I couldn't afford to pay for something I deemed as a luxury myself at the time.

Even knowing the value of their health, my relationship was so bad with money I couldn't justify in my own mind spending seventy bucks for an hour of coaching. Man, looking back, it's amazing how shortsighted I was at that time in my life. That is the destructive power of self-limitation. But in every setback, there is a solution to launch you forward if you are just willing to look and be honest with yourself.

The benefit of my self-deprecation was that I very quickly ascribed to the notion that I couldn't do it alone. This was my blessing in disguise. I didn't have the false bravado or arrogance that a lot of folks have when they start a business. I didn't think my shit didn't stink. I didn't think that I could do it alone; fuck, I knew I couldn't, and that was my leg up.

I looked around and thought to myself, *Well, why don't I get a partner to come on and help me in the areas that I'm weak?* I knew that my weakest areas at the time by far were money and sales. Luckily for me, I had the best sales and money guy I knew in the world as my best friend, Mr. Dave Posin.

Dave and I sat down and started talking about going into business together. At that point in time, he was managing Fitness First health clubs and was killing it. The beauty of this arrangement was that, as I mentioned earlier, they didn't have their own personal training department at the time and allowed freelancers full reign of their gyms. The thinking was that the trainers would bring clients in, the clients would get a gym membership, and life would be great for everyone; it was great for freelance trainers, but Fitness First was allowing hundreds of thousands of dollars to walk out their door each and every month.

One night over at his cousin's house, we sat down and began our plans for world domination. We started talking about what our company would be. We thought of the name SOLDIERFIT, and while knew the name was gold, at the time we were focused on what we thought the big money was: personal training. SOLDIERFIT could be a summer boot camp outdoors, but nothing more than that. That was a stupid, stupid, stupid idea, but so goes things when you are trying to create something from scratch.

I was so broke at the time, we agreed I would do the all the training and Dave would handle putting the money up to do things like get our LLC established and get the credit card reader. Not a monumental investment by any means, but back then, for me, it might as well have been ponying up a million dollars, 'cause I didn't have a pot to piss in.

Because we were positive that personal training was the way to go, we decided that since Dave wouldn't be training, we'd better get another guy to come on as a trainer. During that time, another guy (also a former soldier) named Troy was working at Fitness First. We approached him and he was all in. We forgot about the name SOLDIERFIT completely and decided that we would call our newly found company DDT Fitness, short for Danny, Dave, and Troy.

Now let that sink in. We had a name like SOLDIERFIT, and our dumb asses went with a name that made people think we were a wrestling move or a rat poison. But, like I said, you make a lot of dumbass decisions at the start when you think you are so smart. Everything was going great until Troy got worried that there might be a conflict of interest and decided to back out of the company; the only issue was Dave had already paid for the LLC, so, still to this day, we remain DDT Fitness DBA SOLDIERFIT, but we've got a long ways to go before we get there.

Now, you may be asking yourself, "Why did a company that came to be the best boot camp brand in the world start off focusing on personal training?" The answer is simple: I didn't believe in myself for shit. I thought I had to be someone else, and to me that someone else was easily identified: EATS. Elite Athletic Training Systems.

In my eyes, at that time, they were the baddest motherfuckers on planet Earth. They were all the good-looking people. I literally never saw an ugly trainer amongst them. The dudes looked like thunder gods and the women looked like Amazonians. They were the type of folks who made you feel ugly standing beside them, and when I stood on the same gym floor as them, I was honestly extremely intimidated.

They were (at least in my understanding) all former collegiate and professional athletes. They all had a uniform (and a clipboard, which I thought was pretty gangster at the time). They would come walking in looking like they absolutely belonged in the gym—Hell, the gym looked like it belonged to *them*. They were everywhere. I felt like I was in *Dodgeball*; they were GloboGym trainers, and here I was doing the best I could with the Average Joes.

I thought everything they did was perfect. Their logo, their uniforms, and their swag. It was jet-black and looked like it belonged streaking down the field scoring a touchdown to a standing ovation of the home crowd. No doubt after that was done, the star QB and the head cheerleader would walk into the after-party, chug a beer, and remind everyone why they were perfect.

Then there was me. We had this ugly-ass gray shirt. I mean, it was *ugly*. Our logo was dumb and now that Troy had backed out, the shit didn't even make sense anymore. I was far from the dream trainer. I could argue I was in shape, but I never kidded myself; I wasn't super-model hot, and I damn sure didn't look like a thunder god. I had a helluva success story thanks to my weight loss journey, but at that point I couldn't tell it for shit and I didn't understand the power that lay within being able to.

The result? I was embarrassed to be a trainer. I kept wondering how many people must be looking at me and thinking to themselves, *Why is that guy a trainer? He isn't yoked. He isn't good looking. He isn't even all that impressive in the gym. So who the fuck is he?*

That made getting clients hard—extremely hard. But for some reason, even though I had next to zero faith in myself, I never quit. I just kept getting up every single day, going to the gym, being embarrassed but doing the best that I could. One of the first things I did was go around to people in the gym and give them our DDT Fitness shirts for free.

Daily I would approach members, "Hey, if I give you this shirt, are you gonna wear it?"

They'd always say something along the lines of, "Yeah, man, of course."

I didn't understand what I was doing at the time, but I'd always make them commit with a follow-up question: "Are you absolutely sure? 'Cause if you ain't gonna wear it, I don't wanna give it to you."

To which they'd shoot back, "Hell yeah, man, I'd love to wear it."

Every single person I knew in the gym got the same pitch, and I always did it one on one so that no one else could see me doing it. Now, I can't say for a fact that folks didn't talk to each other and find out that everyone was being given these for free, but the fact is, it didn't matter. Within a few weeks, so many people had a shirt at the gym that it looked like half the members of Fitness First were getting trained by DDT Fitness.

But looks can be deceiving, and without any confidence or follow-up plan to turn people into members, I spent more money on shirts than I was bringing back in. Again, I felt like I was failing, and my lack of confidence was to blame. I was great at talking to people, right up until the point I had to ask for money. When I arrived, my hands got sweaty, I couldn't maintain eye contact, I'd slouch, and talk them and myself out of making a decision right then and there. That meant no one bought shit.

The truth was, I was going find myself in quite the bind if not for one saving grace: I had been selected to attend the next recruit class for Montgomery County Fire and Rescue. I was going to get a chance to be a firefighter and I was going to get another chance to serve.

Right then and there I made the decision that I was going to give all I had to do both things. I would go to the academy during the day and I would train clients at night. I knew I wanted to do a bang-up job at the academy, but I also didn't want to abandon DDT Fitness and have to come back and try to start that process all over again. Somehow, I had to figure out a way to do both, and to do both well.

Becoming a full firefighter would be no small feat. There's no single training or hiring process in America. Each of the departments throughout counties in the U.S. are different, so some will require you to become a paramedic or get other qualifications. After all, the demands of a firefighter in Southern California are much different than the suburbs of Alabama. Anyway, I was looking at six months of EMT school, along with six months of fire academy and a year of fire science education. After that, I'd be assigned to a station and be a probie for another six months. As a probie, you're the lowest on the totem pole. Everyone is watching you the whole time, waiting for you to inevitably screw up and then see how you respond and recover from those mistakes.

Instinctively I knew that the key to crushing the academy was to show up first, stay last, volunteer for all the shit details, take care of my fellow recruits, and do my best to out-work everyone else in the room. The first day we were told to be there at 0530. I was standing outside with all my gear at 0500, beating even the cadre in that morning. They opened the door and told me to report to the classroom and find my seat with my nametag. I did and awaited the rest of the class.

As everyone started to arrive, they migrated to the classroom and found their seats as well. One by one, the room filled up with men and women with anxious looks on their faces, ready to start the next several months in our preparation to become career firefighters. Looking around the room, I saw a diverse group of individuals from all different backgrounds, but the easiest to pick out by far were the former soldiers, sailors, and Marines.

They all arrived earlier than the rest. They were fit and had fresh, close-cropped haircuts. Their uniforms were ironed and wrinkle-free, with creases starched in. Their shoes were spit-shined to a high gloss. They sat in their chairs ramrod straight with their eyes focused on the front of the room, stoic and with minimal movement or talking. This wasn't their first rodeo, and they had a pretty good inkling of what they thought was to come next.

The civilian counterparts, however, came in a wide variety of appearances. Many were overweight, some seriously so. I found myself wondering how they allowed that to happen given the competitiveness of this job (MCFRS only hired 45 out of around 2,500 applicants). On top of that, the road to the seats that morning was almost a full year's journey. Few, if any, had fresh haircuts, many of them had wrinkles in their uniforms, and they came untucked when they walked. They slouched in their chairs and talked, seemingly oblivious to the fact that they had entered a paramilitary organization. Almost all of them were the last to arrive. It was my first real taste of the difference between civilians and the military after getting out.

Then there was a hybrid group that was made up of those who were firefighters in some capacity already. Some had been career in other, smaller departments and were looking for a pay raise. Others had spent time as volunteers in other jurisdictions or in Montgomery County itself. They seemed to walk a line more akin to the reality of the job. They took the job seriously, but they weren't nearly as rigid as those who came from the military. Their haircuts might not have been fresh but their uniforms were ironed, albeit not starched. Shoes were a solid black and well taken care of, but by no means were they spit-shined. Those who had experience in the field understood what I would come to realize too: that firefighters, by and large, aren't like the other sheepdogs.

They aren't commandos at all; they are blue-collar heroes. They are jack-of-all-trades, master of none. They need to understand building construction and vehicle mechanics. They have to be able to cut you out of a car and then provide lifesaving aid once you are out. They have to know how to get water to the twentieth story of a high-rise and how to get it miles from a pond to your farmhouse. They must run into a house on fire or dive into a raging river. There's a unique type of stress to being a firefighter.

Firefighters don't exist to close in on, engage, and destroy the enemies of their nation. They don't go in to hunt down criminals hellbent on breaking legal and moral law. They exist to protect life and property against the forces of nature, fire, wind, rain, disease, and age. It is a proud profession, and one no one really understands fully until they have done it.

All of us in that room had been selected to try and earn the rank to join those who had come before us. Men and women like those who climbed those ill-fated steps in the World Trade Center on 9/11. Each of whom knew the reality of entering those buildings likely meant they weren't coming back out. Climbing up with full kit, hundreds of flights, while frightened employees sprinted down the steps as they calmly climbed in the opposite direction, determined to save the buildings themselves and the lives still trapped inside.

Sitting in that classroom on September 7, 2007, a few days before the anniversary of 9/11, and a year after my tour in Iraq, the importance of this job was not lost on me, and I was determined to do it well. Our first day was spent doing what is typical of any new school you attend: you get a lay of the land, meet your cadre, and have the expectations and standards explained to you. It was like drinking from a firehose, pun intended, but as the first day always goes, it was over quickly. There wasn't much of an opportunity to shine on day one, but day two would be a different story. It was time to see who put in the past year in preparation for the physicality of the job.

Like all academies, physical fitness was a foundational part of the process. Now, you may be surprised to hear me say this, but I think they fuck it all up. I understand why the military utilizes fitness in a negative manner, whether it be as a corrective punishment or measurement in their elite schools such as Ranger or Special Forces Selection. These schools are doing so to select the literal best of the best to go and face the worst of the worst, and that is war. The benefit of working with the best of the best is that those individuals are so highly motivated (and in good shape by the time they do the schools anyway) that they aren't going to form a negative connotation with fitness. However, for the average person on the streets, if you punish them with PT, they are going to start to generate a hatred for working out. As soon as they think about it, they are going to remember how bad it was (instead of the joy in growing stronger and being fit) and they are gonna say, "Fuck that."

I've seen it happen again and again. Folks who started out of shape prior to the academy got in shape during all the training, only to fall back out of shape after the academy. They put them and their team at risk. What's more, it cost the taxpayers a lot of money to care for them in light of injury and death that could have been avoided if we'd just made them appreciate, rather than loathe, PT.

On day one, it was clear that many of them in the class already hated PT. Our first workout consisted of doing, in order: twenty-five push-ups, twenty-five sit-ups, five pull-ups, and a run from the gym to the top of the burn building (a six-story structure) and back to the gym, where we repeated everything six times. Out the gate, it wasn't even close. Some folks were strong, but weak runners. Some were strong runners, but weak pound-for-pound. But by and large, most of the class was out of shape.

That meant that those of us who were in shape stood out like sore thumbs, but in a good way. And out of that group, I was far ahead of the pack. So far that when I began my second lap, Captain Brown, the OIC for the class, looked and me and said, "Lap 'em." That was all I needed to hear. I turned on the afterburners and blew past the group, lapping every single member of the class, even the folks in good shape.

The Navy SEALs have a saying: "It pays to be a winner," and while I'd never claim to be close to being a SEAL, I learned long ago that they are absolutely correct. That first PT session set the tone and the standard for the rest of the recruit class. First, I earned the respect of my classmates. They knew I had taken it seriously (even if they didn't put in the same work in terms of fitness), and most importantly, they knew that I had, at the very least, the physical chops to do the job.

When we made our way back to the classroom and took our seats, it became apparent that the cadre took notice too. Captain

Brown stood up in front of everyone and said, "Only one person in here took this recruit class seriously, and that was recruit Farrar." I knew in that moment that I had led by example. It proved that you don't need to kiss ass to get noticed; you just need to excel when given the opportunity. Exceed the standard every single time and no one will be able to ignore you. You won't need to ask the spotlight to shine on you; it'll find its way to you all on its own.

Now that I had established a positive name for myself, I was committed to keeping it. I doubled down on my commitment to lead the way in every aspect. I was always first to show up and remained the last to leave every single day. On every training evaluation, I volunteered to go first. I always helped people when they were struggling. I volunteered to do the bitch work that no one wanted to do, and I always volunteered to do the heavy lifting.

It was hard work. Firefighting is easily one of the most physically demanding jobs I have ever done. It is hot, and while you might think to yourself, *Well, no shit, Danny*, until you've done the job, you really just don't know. It's hot in Iraq, trust me. But being in a house fire is an entirely different thing. Back in the day, firemen used to literally have their ears melt. You may think you're tough, but are you ear-melting tough? The answer is, more than likely, no.

I have never sweated so much in my life. I used to take my boots off and wring sweat out of my socks. It looked like I had dunked the socks underwater, left them there for a day, pulled them upright, and gave 'em a good twist. Sweat poured from them. What made it worse was the amount of physical work you had to do in those conditions.

Your uniform with gear easily went over one hundred pounds, and that's just what you wore. We aren't counting the ladders, saws, axes, Halligan bars, feet of hose you carried, or the fully charged hose line you drag behind you. On top of this, real life isn't like the movies. You aren't walking around a fully lit room fighting a hose monster like they did in *Backdraft*.

No, you are doing all of this on your knees. You find yourself there because of a couple reasons. First, the heat drives you down. Heat rises, so the "coolest" place to be is on the floor, and that's hot as hell, too. So not only are you dealing with crawling around, but you're burning your knees while doing it. Secondly, in a real fire, you can't see shit. You have to crawl on the ground so you can check the floor in front of you, and use your hands to trace the wall so you can find yourself around as you either make your way to the fire to put it out or search for victims.

All of this is extremely taxing, and that is the best-case scenario. The worst-case scenario is a firefighter goes down and you need to send in the rapid response team to try to save them, and in many cases, those on the rescue team become causalities themselves, also in need of rescue. That's why physical fitness is paramount for firefighters: your greatest chance of survival was self-rescue.

Being in shape as a firefighter wasn't about looks. It wasn't about posing for the calendar. It was about being able to do your job, save someone's life, and most importantly, not endangering your fellow firefighters because you couldn't do the job. As someone who came from a profession where the same held true, and, understanding the enormity of that, I didn't take kindly to people who couldn't pull their weight.

For example, we had a female who had been recycled three times and still couldn't do a pull-up with just her body weight. Not one single pull-up. This mattered because one of the most likely ways a firefighter could find themselves in need of rescue was to fall through the floor to the basement. In the event that took place, your best option would be to push your body through the opening and pull yourself up and out. If you can't pull your body weight up in PT shorts, then how in the hell are you going to pull yourself plus the weight of your uniform and gear? The short answer is, you can't. So now you just put your brothers and sisters at risk because you couldn't be motivated enough to be able to meet the standard of the job. For me, that is a huge "fuck you" to everyone on your team.

But, as is the case for most things, I knew there was nothing I could do about that, and so even though I was pissed off every time she failed to do a pull-up or every time she fell out of a run and needed to be picked up by trail truck, I knew it was above my paygrade and out of my lane to bitch or worry about it. There was nothing I could do to fix it and so I just focused on putting my head down and being the best I could.

I really didn't have much of a choice. In the academy, you are taught a skill during the day, given the night to study it, and tested on the following day. While the academy is six months long, it is very similar to boot camp in that you learn just enough to go downtown and get your ass kicked.

Firefighting in and of itself is a very challenging career. While it may seem like it's pretty straightforward—put the wet stuff on the hot stuff—it's actually very, very nuanced. There is so much science that goes into it. Understanding BTUs and how much water it takes to put it out. How much water can you dump on a structure and still expect it to stand. The formulas to understand the water pressure needed to get hundreds of gallons of water up a standpipe to the thirteenth floor of a high-rise at just the right pressure to make sure it puts the fire out but isn't so powerful the firefighter on the end of the line can't handle it. Knowing what materials will give off toxic fumes when burning—good thing all our shit is made out of plastic and synthetic fibers these days. All of that is just scratching the surface of what you need to know on the fireside.

The reality is that most of the calls you run are medical, as much as 75 percent when I was in. So half of the academy is spent learning medical as well so that you also graduate a certified EMT. This portion of the academy was run in a similar fashion as the fire side. You would be instructed on a particular task, given twenty-four hours to study for it, and tested the next day. The biggest difference here was that what really mattered were the tests from MFRI (Maryland Fire and Rescue Institute), all of which culminated with a practical evaluation at the end of the course administered by reps from MFRI. You had to pass in order to graduate.

As you can imagine, all of this made for long-ass days and a ton of stress and pressure to get it right. On top of all that, I had committed to continue to train clients to keep DDT Fitness alive. That meant that when we were released for the day from the academy, I was really just getting started on my second half.

A typical day for me consisted of getting up at 0400 and studying over breakfast. I would then head out the door to arrive at the academy between 0500-0515. I would make sure that everything was set up and ready for the day, and if someone was missing prior to class, I and the other students would shoot out phone calls and texts to make sure they were up. Around 0600 we'd start heading to the gym to get ready for morning PT, which would last an hour or so and consist of running, lifting, or calisthenics.

After PT was complete, we'd head back to the locker room, shower, grab breakfast (or breakfast number two if you were me), clean the locker room up, head to the classroom, and do some more review before the day got underway. Depending on what was on the agenda, the class was responsible to set up gear, move the guidon, and ensure the water coolers were topped off.

Then, again depending on the day, you would begin morning instruction between 0830-0900, either in class, in the field, or up on the training grounds. You'd break for lunch for an hour (if no one had screwed up), eat in the cafeteria, and then come back for afternoon instruction in the same manner as the morning. At the end of the day, you'd police the grounds, put the gear away, clean the classroom, and be dismissed between 1630-1730 depending on the day. I'd always stay late to make sure everything was ship-shape so that we wouldn't get in trouble the next day, and as soon as that was done, I would beat feet to the gym just as fast as I could to start my side hustle.

I'd arrive at the gym, get changed, and get ready for my first client of the afternoon. During my time at the academy, I carried about a dozen or so clients, and since I wouldn't be ready for the first one for sure until 1830, that meant that I was going to be in the gym till at least 2030 every night. I'd give everything I had to make sure that they were getting their money's worth. They were paying me for a service, and they didn't care if I was tired. I don't blame 'em.

No one made me come train clients at the end of the day. No one made me sign up to be a firefighter. I was a big boy and I took on those challenges, so no complaining. I gave 100 percent of myself to each session, and when the last one was booked, my day still wasn't done. I wanted to be number one and so I would wrap up at the gym and then head back to the house for dinner and more studying.

I would study till at least 2200 every night. I knew that if I was in bed by then, I could get six hours of sleep and be ready to go again at 0400. I have long held the belief that the worst thing I can do for myself is to not be busy. My mind and my emotions get the best of me when I am sitting around with nothing to do but think.

To a lot of people, that type of day sounds horrible. They will cry and scream about quality of life, but if I am honest, I am at my happiest when my schedule is that full. I don't like to say "busy" because busy people tend to be miserable. They feel busy 'cause they are doing shit that doesn't move their needle, so they feel no real value for all the time they spent at work. All of that changes if you have a clear-cut mission and objective to accomplish in mind, and I had that in spades. I wanted to be the best and I was going to do everything I could to accomplish it.

It has been said that with children, days are long and years are short. I think we feel that way because kids are a lot of nonstop hard work. As a result, the same applies to anything you spend a great deal of time working hard on. Mornings that start at 0400 and run into nights that end at 2200 definitely make for long days, but they also make for equally short years, and before I knew it, family day had arrived and graduation was just a few days away.

It would be the first time that I would have anyone show up for a "family" day in my life. While most had mothers and fathers, brothers and sisters, and (I don't mean this rudely, but I can't think of another way to say it) very plain Janes girlfriends or wives, I had Chrissy show up, who was anything but "plain Jane."

I had met her at the gym and she was hands down the sexiest woman I had ever been with. She was the kind of pretty that made you feel ugly just standing next to her. We had been dating for about six months and had started living together. I had moved into her house soon after starting the academy.

She was one of the most beautiful women I have ever seen in my life. She was Asian, about my height, with long jet-black hair. She had a confidence about her that instantly created a bubble wherever she went. She was the kind of woman who made the average dude feel ugly, like she was a 12 out of 10 and he was just a 5. It wasn't that she set out to do that, she was just beyond-approach beautiful.

She worked in the bar scene in D.C. and managed the VIP tables in one of the premier nightclubs in the area. That meant she was not going to take anyone's shit and she was keen on fashion. She wore the latest designer clothes and was always put together. While she was a hard worker and busted her ass to afford her look and lifestyle, to say she stuck out amidst the blue-collar lifestyle that produced firefighters was an understatement.

I'll never forget when she walked into the room; I couldn't help but smile. It was like the music stopped. Every man's mouth hit the floor. They couldn't stop staring. I watched the eyes of every single one of them follow her every move throughout the room. It was like she was the lead actress in a romantic comedy and every guy in the place was hearing a different love song as she walked by. To her credit, she didn't even notice it. She was oblivious to their stares. She embodied the Sammy Kershaw song, "She Don't Know She's Beautiful." All I can tell you was having her show up made me feel like a king for the day, and when you've felt as bottom-of-the-barrel as I have in my life, that's a feeling worth its weight in gold.

With family day over, all that was left was the usual out-processing that you need to do to clear any school. We made sure we cleaned all the equipment and returned it to inventory storage, primed and ready for the next recruit class that would follow us. But most importantly, the moment arrived that everyone had eagerly been waiting for over the last few weeks: station assignments.

Everyone who wanted to get after it wanted to be stationed in Battalion 1, at Station 16. It was easily one of the busiest battalions in the county. Regardless of where you ended up, you just wanted a house with lots of opportunities to do your job and learn.

When the assignments came out, I was excited to hear that I had landed in Battalion 1. I was chomping at the bit to get into the field and the only thing that remained for us to do was graduate.

The day that we graduated, I invited all those folks who had become my family; Dave Posin and all of his family, the Glasgows, my girlfriend, and those friends who had supported me when my own flesh and blood had abandoned me. I wanted so desperately to make them proud of me. I wanted to make anyone proud, but especially those guys.

Walking into the auditorium in my dress uniform, my chest was puffed up, my march was crisp and in step, and my face beamed with pride. I looked over and saw all of my friends seated and smiling back at me and waving as I marched by on my way to the stage where we all would be seated.

The command to "take seats" was given and I found myself seated near the front row with the ability to see the entire crew in the audience. The cadre talked about all the things that we had learned as recruits and the importance of the work we had been trained to do. The chief and the mayor shared their appreciation for all the hard work we had done, and all the hard work we were going to have to do in the future.

When they were done, it was time to issue out the awards for Recruit Class 31. I knew I was in the running for the physical fitness award, but I was completely caught off guard when they called my name for the firefighter award. I scored the highest on the combined scores of practical and written evaluations. I snapped to attention and made my way to the podium to receive handshakes from the COC and be handed my award. I stood there beaming with pride as they took our photos.

I marched smartly back and once again took my seat as they called out the winner of the EMT award. I had done pretty well on the test, but I knew I was no match for the guys who had prior experience and knowledge. I applauded loudly when the recruit's name was called and he made his way, just as I had, to the front of the stage. I sat there staring at my award, in complete disbelief that I had earned it. I was snapped out of my daze when I heard them say my name again.

Turns out, I had taken the physical fitness award after all. Again, I quickly jumped to my feet and hurried to the front of the stage to shake hands and take photos. Beyond excited that I had taken two awards home in front of everyone I loved, it dawned on me that I had received two out of three awards and that had to mean that I was possibly going to earn the top award of them all, the Chief Graitz Award for top overall recruit!

At this point, I was speed-walking back to my seat. I was gushing with pride and couldn't believe that this was happening. This time

I wouldn't make it back to my seat before they called my name for a third time. I had indeed won the award for overall top recruit. I quickly placed my fitness award in the chair and hurried back to the front of the stage.

In the audience, my crew erupted. They were cheering and clapping so loudly, I was starting to blush. Standing up there, I felt like I had finally made it. That life was going to start going my way. That nothing could stop me now.

I didn't know it back then, but life was soon to remind me that there is no such thing as "making it." There is no such thing as arriving at the top of the mountain. There will always be another worst day of your life, another problem to solve, and another mountain to climb. As Mike Tyson once said, "Man isn't meant to be humble, he's meant to be humbled."

And life had a whole lot more humbling in store for me.

Chapter Thirteen

The American Dream

"The faith that anyone could move from rags to riches—with enough guts and gumption, hard work and nose to the grindstone—was once at the core of the American Dream."
—Robert Reich

As soon as the after-party was over, it was time to turn my attention and focus on becoming the best firefighter I could be, and also expanding my side hustle. If I am being honest with everyone, I think I ultimately benefited from the low pay of firefighting. At the time, I lived in Montgomery County, and even renting a one-bedroom wasn't feasible to do on that salary. Two things became abundantly clear rather quickly. One, I had to generate more income to cover my bills, so shutting down DDT Fitness wasn't an option; and two, I had to move, because I couldn't afford to live on my own, and Chrissy and I had suddenly split up.

At the time when I was busy going to clubs in D.C. and Bethesda, the last thing I wanted to was move to Frederick, which was roughly forty-five minutes north of Montgomery County. It had been (and remains so) dubbed "Fredneck." I assumed it was a backwoods hick-town and I wasn't thrilled about the idea of moving to it. But the plain and simple truth was I didn't have a choice.

Around this time, I was running with a buddy of mine who was a Montgomery County police officer. The dude was easily one of the best-looking guys I've ever met in real life, and while I didn't grab his ass, I could easily see why women did. We used to spend our nights out at the bars in Bethesda talking to every pretty woman we could find. Somewhere along the lines, he started dating this local girl who had a girlfriend in town, visiting. We all went out one night and I fell in love damn near instantly.

She was in great shape, with an amazing body and long straight brown hair. She had grown up in the South after her parents had moved down there when she was a young girl, and as a result, she had a subtle Southern accent. She walked into my life after I had just exited my previous relationship, which had ended poorly.

She was also getting out of a bad relationship and I think that played a major role in why we hit it off so fast. She would drive up from South Carolina often, and when she wasn't up, we were on the phone every night. She was ready to get out of SC and I was ready to move to Frederick. It seemed like the stars had aligned and, at the time, it seemed like it only made sense to move in together.

Now, I had mentioned earlier that staying busy and proactive is the best medicine for me. But now that the academy was over, life actually slowed down quite a bit. Now, instead of going to work every day, I only worked nine days a month. This left me with a bunch of free time, which should have been a good thing because it should have let me expand my business. But life was about to throw me another curveball.

Remember when I said Fitness First was fucking up by allowing independent trainers to use their gym for free? That they were literally letting hundreds of thousands of dollars walk out the door? Well, they wisened up to that and decided to put an end to it themselves. In its wake, they created what I called the "Redshirt

Program." It really wasn't all that creative of a name, they just happened to wear red shirts, but it was a slow death for me.

The first major hit was that Dave was going to have to step away from DDT Fitness, as it was now officially a conflict of interest. Now, before some of you in the cheap seats start casting stones, it absolutely was the right call for him to make. The company was making shit money. It was all work and no reward for Dave. Every month, he ran the cards by manually entering in the billing information, digit by digit. He was taking zero dollars from the company because it made so little, but I needed that little to sustain it. On top of all of this, he was killing it in his role as GM.

Dave was first in sales for the company almost every single month. He was clearly a leader in the brand and Dave took that role seriously, just as he always does. It's one of the things I admire most of all about him. I have never asked him, but I assume the truth of the matter is that in the early go of things, Dave held on as long as he did out of loyalty and friendship. He knew he was helping me, and Dave always put others (especially friends) above himself.

But when the time came that it could be seen as unethical, he did the right thing and stepped away. There was zero animosity on my part. As a matter of fact, I told him when he said he had to step back that if the day ever came that it became profitable, I would give him a chance to come back on as a full 50/50 partner. I'm sure he thought the gesture was a kind one, but I doubt, if he's honest with himself, that he believed for even a moment that I'd make good on that promise. Hell, I am not sure I even believed it myself.

That's why, when coupled with the fire department, I wasn't too pressed about what was going on with DDT Fitness. I figured that if I liked firefighting and DDT was giving me some spending cash, who was I to bitch and look a gift horse in the mouth? Don't get me wrong, I still worked a ton. I would leave the house the morning I was on shift around 0500, get to the station at 0600, pull a twenty-four-hour shift, get off, and head to the gym. I'd work at the gym until early or late afternoon and then drive the up-to-three hour drive home (depending on traffic) to get home and hang out with the girlfriend.

Now, my greatest strength is also my Achilles heel. I jump into shit without really weighing the pros and cons of what I am about to do. With my girlfriend now living with me just a couple months after we met, we started to realize that outside of physical attraction, we weren't as compatible. We fought like cats and dogs, and I mean we argued constantly. I didn't know it at the time, but I was about to go real dark, real fast.

My life was starting to go to hell in a handbasket. I wasn't happy at home, but I wanted a family so bad. I didn't know how to fix our issues. At the time, I thought she was the bad guy, but if I am objective and honest about it, I was an asshole. Honestly, I was the kind of guy back then I never want my daughters to meet. I am ashamed of the way I spoke and the way I acted toward her. Nothing I can say ever will, or should, justify it, and I ain't trying to.

With that said, I was battling a lot of shit. I was angry and my PTS was through the roof because I hadn't learned how to channel it all at that point. At times I thought I wanted my girlfriend, and at other times I couldn't stand the sight of her. To her credit, she tried to be good to me and stand by me.

I knew that what I wanted more than anything else was a family. I just couldn't figure out how to build one the right way. That led to me making the same mistake countless people make over and over: I figured the best thing I could do was get married.

I mean, how stupid was I? Not only was I stupid, but I was an asshole, too. I remember asking her on the way back from South Carolina: "If we got married, would it fix your issues?" Like, how unromantic is that? I was a failure of a partner, but sadly, it only got worse.

The way I asked her to marry me was pathetic. We were living in a condominium at the time, and she followed me outside to where we let the dogs go to take a shit. There, between the two buildings, with zero creativity and no real thought put into it, I asked her if she would marry me. She said yes, and if I am honest, I don't know why. I dunno . . . Maybe she was just as lost as I was at the time and that's why she took my shit. Maybe she did love me, but I just wasn't ready to receive it. But again, I just couldn't get anything to line up, and my next attempt at a family was headed to failure. Just like every time before it.

We were scheduled to get married down in South Carolina, and in truth, we did have an awesome party. But when it came time for the wedding, I knew I was making a mistake, but it was like I was caught up in the gravitational pull of a black hole. I desperately wanted to get out, but it was too late. I was already sucked too far in.

Nowadays, I often joke that if you look down the aisle and think, If this doesn't work out, it won't be so bad, fucking run. If you're thinking that it's not gonna work out and it's gonna be bad. But it was too late; she was standing in front of me, and before I knew it, I'd said "I do," and she did too.

In a very short time frame, my entire world crashed to the ground and I hit rock-bottom. While I had loved the academy, I found that I wasn't as thrilled with the actual job. I still contend that if we ran real emergencies, I would have loved being a fire fighter, but in my experience, that just wasn't the case.

Here I was in one of the busiest houses in the entire county, working in the city, and 95 percent of my call load was bullshit, plain and simple. I already mentioned that over 75 percent of our calls were EMS-related, but what I failed to mention is 95 percent of that 75 percent was just bullshit. Things I'd never call the ambulance for. People with upset tummies and headaches. And Lord, don't get me started on the drunk calls we ran, over and over and over again.

The county had no drunk tank. So, the police would get called, who'd in turn call EMS, who would take them to the hospital, who'd keep them until he was sober enough to be let out, who'd then go get drunk again and do the entire process over again, only this time at 0230. I couldn't help but get pissed off. One, because I was an angry son of a bitch during that time, and two, I couldn't help but think about the resources these guys were wasting. I mean, what would happen if a real emergency took place and it cost someone their life because we had to dispatch an ambulance or engine from farther away because we were busy dealing with the same drunk motherfucker for the hundredth time?

I also couldn't wrap my head around the notion of "staging." The idea of staging is to keep EMS providers safe until police secure a scene that's either violent or potentially violent. I was of the ilk that we signed up to risk our lives, but the department ran under the premise that you can't save anyone if you're dead. Which, to be clear, I understand and respect the intent and purpose of it, so much so that I quote it in coaching all the time. With that said, however, I didn't agree with how restrictive that policy was when it came to doing our job.

I'll never forget one of the worst calls I ran: a shooting that involved teenagers. We were dispatched but were told to stage in place one mile away from the scene. We sat there for what seemed like hours, waiting to be given the all-clear to proceed to the scene to render aid. We had been told in the original dispatch that there were multiple victims, all of whom were minors. We sat there in the engine just waiting as the clock slowly ticked by. Minute after agonizing minute waned until we were finally told we could proceed to the scene.

We arrived to find the police swarming a bus. While they were just trying to do all they could to help these young victims, the truth was they were in the way. They weren't qualified to render the aid these guys needed. In fact, at one point, one of the officers was slapping a kid in the face to get him to wake up. The kid, a young African American, had been shot in the aorta, was bleeding out, and his skin had already started to take on an ashen appearance.

He needed real medical treatment, not well-meaning slaps in the face. The truth is, I can't tell you if we would have been able to save him if we got there faster; honestly, probably not. But I do know that he died on the operating table a few minutes later, and when that happens, especially when it's a kid, you're gonna "what if" that situation until the day you die.

But for many of us, our frustration didn't end on the EMS side. Compared to some other departments (Prince George's County comes to mind), Montgomery County seemed much more tepid in its firefighting protocols. Many of us felt that the department could be more aggressive in house fire situations. A lot of guys thought we should ventilate roofs and make entry more often. They didn't like the idea of spray-and-pray, where you just stood outside and sprayed water into the house through an open window, waiting to see if the fire would go out. It always did—after most of the house had burned to the ground.

While the department had many great leaders in it, I (along with others) was frustrated with the way promotions work. It was all book learning. Could you study the mounds and mounds of study material and pass a written test? If yes, then up the ladder you go. While I understand that there is no perfect way to promote—and yes, people will find faults in anything you do—it just seemed asinine that a job requiring navigating complex and dangerous scenarios while under extreme stress, where lives were on the line, required academic quizzes to advance as opposed to practical evaluation. Another issue I had with firefighting was that you had to learn to drive the engine to get promoted to Firefighter III. I can understand the reasoning behind it, but some of us hate to drive (a lot of us can't drive for shit) and here they were, forcing folks to have to drive this big-ass engine down tiny-ass streets. On top of that, if you hit something, it was (justifiably so) a huge-ass deal. Which made your life miserable.

It would have made more sense if you had to become a master before you became a lieutenant (something that, again, in my mind, made total sense and would have justified forcing everyone to drive) but you didn't. You could literally get your Firefighter III, drive next to never, depending on your house assignment and seniority, take your lieutenant test, be good at book learning and test taking, and then boom, you're a LT in charge of a wagon, and maybe even a house. That meant that I saw a decent amount of absolutely incompetent motherfuckers in charge.

My last beef with the department was the way some of these guys looked at side hustles. Now, damn near every single firefighter that I knew had some form of side hustle. That could be anything from a full-blown mortgage agency to doing oddball jobs here and there. But almost everyone did something. On top of this, almost none of them lived in-county. You couldn't afford to. Even with a side hustle, I had to move to Frederick, and I could barely afford to live *there*.

While it can vary based on volunteer status and how the house is run, in my experience, the shift was pretty consistent in terms of scheduling. I got to work around 0530, did shift change and line up between 0630 and 0700, checked out the rig, did PT, then did your day's training. You'd grab lunch and then your afternoon would consist of training, dinner, and then around 1730, it was considered "your time."

Most of the guys would go sit in the day room and watch TV or a movie or sit out in front of the station. I, on the other hand, would do things for work in my free time, and that rubbed some folks the wrong way. I never understood, and still don't, how it was okay in their eyes that they could go sit on their asses and watch *Married with Children* re-runs, but I couldn't work on my company in my free time; it just didn't add up, and it was a point of contention for me with some of the other guys in the department.

Now that I have gotten that little bitch session out of the way, let me state emphatically that's what it was. All of those things I just bitched about were molehills I made into mountains. Every job on earth has things you're not gonna like about it. Writing a book, serving as the president of a non-profit, and being CEO ain't no different. There's always gonna be some shit you don't like or wish you could do differently. I often look back and wish I hadn't quit the department, because the job was important, rewarding, and it mattered. But at the time, my mental state was absolutely wrecked. I was bitter, depressed, and angry. I felt like the world owed me a lot of shit.

I was upset at work and even more upset at home. I wasn't happy at home, the gym, or the station. I thought all of those things were letting me down, but the truth is, I was the one failing to do my part. I was the one failing to show and be truly present wherever I was. Every issue I had, each mistake I made, was everyone else's fault.

I was racing towards the cliff, and since I didn't have any brakes that I could find, I figured I might as well crush the gas pedal. If I was gonna crash, I might as well make it a royal fuck-up. And Lord knows I did everything in my power to ruin my life on the way down.

First and foremost, I was a horrible husband. I was mean shit. I was rude, uncouth, and disrespectful. My temper was a fuse just waiting to blow. I held so much resentment toward her for everything going wrong in my life, because I thought getting married could fix us and make her happy. On top of that, I had the feeling that I was financially responsible for her when I felt (wrongly) that she didn't do enough to pull her weight.

We were both volatile together and we were both unfaithful. I was all messed up in my head. PTS was through the roof and that just fueled my horrible attitude and decision-making process. Back then, I had none of the tools I have now for changing my head space. I just kept going deeper down the rabbit hole, all while stacking up dirt behind me so I couldn't get back out.

I am ashamed to admit it now, but I was always looking for someone to fight. I would go to downtown Frederick and try to fight anyone who looked at me wrong. I literally stood outside the bar in the streets and tried to fight a cop like a complete jackass. I was drunk and pissed off. The police officer had every single right to smash my face in. He was a big boy, so there was a really, really solid chance he could have done it with little fanfare. But luckily I had brothers in the Desert Knights Motorcycle Club who stepped in for me at that time.

Chapter Fourteen

Fight Your Way Out

"The harder the conflict, the more glorious the triumph."
– Thomas Paine

I didn't grow up on or around bikes. I couldn't wrench on 'em at all. I wasn't the ttypical biker by any definition. But as my world was falling apart, I knew I had to find some sense of what I'd lost. It all started when I heard about the Patriot Guard Riders, which was a volunteer organization founded in 2005 to attend the funerals of military and first responders at the family's request. Mostly, they shield families of fallen heroes from those that would disrupt the services of their loved ones. There had become a growing movement at the time of protesters showing up at the funerals of fallen service members to protest the war and other aspects of our society. The Patriot Guard would literally form a wall to block the protesters from getting close to the family and sometimes used their bikes to drown out the chants the protesters yelled during the services. The Patriot Guard Riders has grown to include thousands of members across all fifty states in the U.S.

As someone who had spent time in Arlington, the notion of someone disrespecting the final services of a veteran was something that made me furious. How dare anyone not only desecrate the service of a hero, but do so while the family—mothers and fathers, husbands and wives, sisters and brothers, sons and daughters— were in the middle of mourning. I was literally ready to fight.

I figured that would be a worthwhile organization to become a part of, a cause that would give me somewhere to focus my attention. Only issue was, I didn't know how to ride a motorcycle at all. By happenstance, I was driving to the station one morning when I heard that Frederick Harley Davidson was having a summer sale, and that was all it took. I decided right then and there that I was going to purchase a motorcycle. I went to their website and found a brand-new Sportster 883 and fell in love.

One of my biggest blessings and curses in life is that when I get something in my mind, it stays there and festers until it's satisfied. As Yelawolf said, there are "no brake lights in my life, I'm either rich or evicted." I, naturally, couldn't wait to get a license to purchase the bike, 'cause that meant I'd lose out on this awesome-ass deal, and that just wouldn't do.

So, instead, I asked a buddy of mine who lived in the neighborhood to come with me and ride it off the lot. What's kind of ironic is that we took it to the parking lot of what would become SOLDIERFIT so I could learn how to ride it. Of course, I had no idea at the time that this would eventually be my second home, but it's funny how life works out.

After I got my license, I started looking into vet organizations to ride with. The first one I found was a motorcycle club (MC) called the Warrior Brotherhood. I happened to find Matt "Hollywood" who said he had been riding with them but was looking to transfer to a different club—a new one started specifically for the Desert Era Veterans, The Desert Knights of America.

In another odd twist of fate, he gave me the contact information for the national president, who said that they were actually just starting up a new chapter, and that chapter was to be in Frederick, Maryland, of all places. He told me that they would be having the first meeting of the prospective chapter in a few days and invited me to attend it.

I showed up at a nice house in one of the communities in Frederick and was greeted by a man I came to absolutely love: K-Dub. K-Dub ended up becoming a father figure to me. He had a calm and quiet demeanor. I can't think of a better way to describe him than "soothing." No, we didn't hug longer than twenty seconds or stare longingly into each other's eyes, but he had a way about him that would calm me down and keep me level-headed. Which was needed back then, because I was reckless, hotheaded, and ill-tempered. I earned the road name "Mayhem" for a reason.

K-Dub invited me in and I met the rest of the guys in the prospective chapter, and to this day, I credit that night with being one of the main things that would save my life. The brotherhood that I found there was, in so many ways, what I had been missing in my life. The priorities of the Desert Knights MC were straightforward: family, work, club. But that didn't mean you could use family or work as an excuse to fail to do your duty as a brother, and your most sacred duty was simply to be a good brother.

That meant that we didn't judge our brother. We didn't care what he did wrong. We didn't help him continue to do wrong, but we didn't hold it against him or judge him for it either. We were there whenever he needed us, day or night. We lived and breathed, "I am my brother's keeper."

A lot of times folks ask me, how does that work? It sounds great in theory, but how does it happen in real life? I have seen brothers do amazing things for each other. I have been helped personally so many times, but the time that sticks out to me the most was when a member named Fratello went far, far above and beyond for me in the name of brotherhood.

I had posted on social media that my water heater had shit the bed. It wasn't really a bitch session, so to speak, just a matter-of-fact statement about what was going on in my life at the moment. Frat instantly hit me up and told me he would take care of it. Now, that in and of itself is awesome, but here's the kicker: he lived in Delaware and I lived in Maryland.

On a weekend—his time off—he went and purchased a brand-new water heater on his own dime to save me sales tax since he lived in Delaware. He then loaded it up and drove all the way to my house in Frederick, which was several hours away. He removed the old one and installed the new one, essentially by himself (remember I told you I ain't a mechanic) and took the old one off to discard it for me.

He did all of this without being asked. He refused to accept money for his time, gas, or labor. The only thing he would accept was money for the heater and homecooked meal. You want to talk about family, about brotherhood, about actually, truly taking care of someone? Then as far as I am concerned, you must be talking about the Desert Knights. I didn't know it when I came to that house that night, but these guys would keep me out of jail and save my life in just a few short months.

Despite all the belonging and appreciation I found when I started riding with the club, my marriage started to dissolve even more. I was continuing to find myself arguing with her, and my contempt for her, and my life, only grew. Despite all that, she continued to look out for me. I'd be out, drunk downtown, and she'd call the guys to come pick me up. One guy would throw me in the back of the truck and another guy would ride my bike home.

The guys did all that they could, but no matter how much they did or how great their intentions were, nothing was going to change until I decided to change it myself. They couldn't fix my attitude, lifestyle, or perspective. I needed a wake-up call, and my wife was about to give it to me. She had started seeing someone else, and as much as I continued to play the victim, the truth is, who the fuck could blame her?

I honestly don't understand why I was upset at the time. I was blaming her for a lot of my problems, and I clearly, intentionally, caused damn near all of ours, so one would have thought I would have been happy when she said was leaving me and wanted a divorce. But I was devastated.

I had spent all this time wishing she was gone or didn't live with me, but when she finally told me she was moving out, I panicked. Looking back at it now, I loved her, but I was in such a fucked up head space I couldn't handle the fact that I did. I almost resented that I loved her. I didn't have any faith that I could love someone or that they could actually love me in return. It's something I have struggled with my entire life, something I still struggle with, to be honest.

In counseling, my therapists have basically linked it to abandonment issues. From my birth mother to every woman I have ever been with, I get left. I always get left. I have so little faith in people that even when good folks are in my life and treating me proper, I end up treating them bad because I fear that they are gonna leave. The crazy part about it is in truth, many leave not because they don't love me, but rather because they get tired of my shit. It's a self-fulfilling prophecy, in a way, and a vicious cycle that's taken me ages to break.

When she packed her stuff and moved out, the house seemed cold and empty. It wasn't this sense of relief I thought I wanted and needed. Instead, even though it was clearly my fault, I took it as just another example of people abandoning me. I wish I could have understood at the time that I had abandoned myself. I had allowed the things done to me to dictate how I treated others. I had taken what happened to me as an excuse to repeat the cycle and hurt someone else. The sad part is we ended on horrible terms and I'll never get to tell her that now I am the man I've become, I am ashamed of the man I was. She deserved better, and it's my sincere hope she found better somewhere down the line.

Back at home and alone, I thought I just needed to get out of the house. I figured it'd be a good idea to go downtown and grab a beer in a crowded room. Hell, who knows, maybe I'd get lucky and pick up some chick at the bar so I could get laid. At least that way, I'd wake up next to someone warm, even if it was only a temporary fix; I've always heard the best way to get over someone is to get under someone else.

So, I grabbed my shit and headed downtown. Back then, I didn't know anyone in Frederick, whereas now I can't go downtown without running into an awesome local I know.

I got to the bar and found my place on a barstool at the end of the bar and ordered a round. I started to look around in hopes that I could find a pretty girl to make eye contact with and strike up a conversation. Maybe there'd be some other lost soul there like me, desperate to find someone to use to pass the time. Perhaps that's when we are in our saddest state: used people looking for other abused people to use.

The problem for me was that, at that moment, I didn't see anyone who looked abused. I didn't see anyone who looked sad or alone. No one there looked like they ran there to hide from the emptiness of home. From where I was sitting, slamming 'em back, everyone there was there with other people. Maybe a date, family, or group of friends. Everyone was too busy laughing and enjoying the company they came with to link eyes with the depressed lonely guy at the end of the bar. I started to feel insignificant, and the longer I sat there, the more I wanted to crawl under the bar.

This was back before I understood that people wear masks. While there is no doubt social media has exacerbated this with filters and only posting our life's highlight reels, it has always been there. We don't like to have our underbelly exposed. We don't want you to see us failing and falling down. We don't want the world to see us ugly-crying. Don't let it be known you got left for another man and don't let the world know you're broke.

Instead, spend more money than you got to go to the VIP room so you can get that selfie as the thousand-dollar bottle of vodka comes rolling in. Show everyone you're a boss bitch by spending $937 more on a bottle of Tito's you could have gotten at the store down the street from your house. We keep sharing lies about our lives and yet can't grasp the reason we're unhappy.

I see it now, but back then, on that night, I couldn't see it. All I saw was a room full of people who were getting it right. They were content. They were loved. They had money to go drink at the bar, which I did not. Hell, I was wondering if I could afford to be there in the first place.

I kept looking around and all I could see were people happier than me. I continued to feel worse and worse. The drinking wasn't helping any of those feelings; in fact, it was doing what it does—multiplying them. I didn't know much at the time, but I did know this: I had to get the fuck out of that bar. I had to leave all the perfect people with their perfect clothes and smiles. I had to run away from folks who had lives I wish I had. They stood in front of me as a constant reminder that what I longed for was real, it was possible, it just only seemed possible for everyone else but me.

I jumped in my car and drove home—a dumb move by any definition. I was staggering on my way out the door, drunk, disgruntled, and depressed. I somehow made it home without killing myself or anyone else. Thanks for the grace of God in moments like that. I staggered through the door and began to climb the steps one by one up to my condominium.

It felt like I traded one prison for another. Where the bar made me confront my failure at happiness, the house made me confront the ramifications of that failure. At home, at the end of the night, alone, I started to wonder who she was with and who might be holding her. I am a very visual person and can see anything my mind conjures up in vivid detail, be it a company or someone sleeping with my wife. It is another one of those parts of my life that serve as both a blessing and a curse.

Drunk me decided I needed to be drunker me, and so I went to the cabinet and poured me another drink. I sat back down on the couch and began to give into the depression. I decided that I just wanted to go to sleep and needed to find any way I could to do that. I had a bad back from jumping out of planes and so I had some pain meds in the house. In the past, I had used them on nights I couldn't sleep to take the edge off and help me crash out. I figured what the hell. Since the liquor wasn't getting the job done, why not take a few of them?

I am not totally sure how the next few minutes or hours played out, to be honest. Somewhere along the line, I assume that in a perfect storm of depression and depressants, I figured I had finally had enough. I had been battling suicide ideation my entire life, if I'm honest with myself.

This time, there was no one around to stop me. No one around to talk me out of it. So, sometime later that night, I decided that this was it. I was done. I wrote a sloppy suicide note. I apologized to the world, but most of all, I apologized to my wife. I took all the rest of the pills and then I tied a knot in my sheets and made a jump for it.

Now, I don't know why I am still here. I am not sure if my knot-tying skills were off due to intoxication. I don't know if I subconsciously sabotaged my own shit. I don't know if the Man Upstairs had bigger plans for me. All I do know is that I woke up strapped to a hospital bed the next morning, trying to figure out where I was and what the hell had just happened.

Waking up strapped to the bed with leather cuffs is a sobering experience (pun intended). At first, it's absolutely terrifying.

As I started to blearily blink myself awake, I lifted a hand to rub my face. I was groggy and everything was unfamiliar. But as the leather restraint around my wrist caught, the resulting rush of panic jolted me awake. My arms could only move a few inches off the bed.

Even though I woke up in a hospital room, I was absolutely petrified. The first thoughts that ran through my mind were: *What the fuck am I doing here? Why am I tied down? What's going on?* Slowly, as I gained more clarity over the situation, I began to recall the events of the night before. It occurred to me that I had attempted suicide and that I must have been sent to the hospital. It turns out my roommates found me and called 9-1-1, and that's who picked me up.

After the initial fear wore off, it was immediately followed up with embarrassment. *Who knows I'm here already? What's being said about me? How many folks must think I am such a bitch? When the fuck can I check out?* I needed to get out of here before anyone else found out.

Right about then, with all those thoughts racing through my mind, the curtain pulled back, and in walked the charge nurse. She greeted me with a warm and friendly smile, but I just wanted to crawl under the bed and die. My eyes quickly darted to my feet; anything to avoid making eye contact with her.

Back then I was still trying to be macho (kinda absurd when you think about me lying there in a gown, naked underneath, and strapped to a bed after trying to kill myself) so the fact that she was a cute petite blonde only exacerbated my embarrassment. She tried to ask me questions to get a better sense of what was going on, but I did my best to play the strong silent type.

All of that would fade away when she told me the reality of the situation. She tried to lead with it gently at first, recommending that I check into the psych ward in the hospital. I told her emphatically that wasn't going to happen and that I was ready to check out of the hospital right now! She gave me a look that said she knew that was what I'd say, took a deep breath, and placed her hand on mine.

"Sir," she said. "You attempted suicide last night. Therefore, you only have two choices: you can self-admit and be in the unit for a few days if everything checks out, or you can refuse and we will call cops back down here and they will issue you an emergency protective order for your own good and we will admit you to the unit against your will. That will reflect poorly on your record in the future and you will be in the unit for a minimum of several weeks. The choice is yours."

That was easily the most dejected and defeated I have ever felt in my entire life. It was made abundantly clear to me at that moment that I was not in charge. I had no say over my life. In fact, my life had been turned over to the state. Just like that, I had lost my freedom. I'd rather have been anywhere on earth than there in that hospital bed. Little did I know that I was about to go to a place that made me wish I had stayed right where I was.

With no other real option, I agreed to self-admit to the unit. It wasn't long after that an orderly arrived at my bed with a wheelchair and told me he was ready to give me a ride to my new room. I was released from the restraints, glumly got up out of bed and shuffled over to the wheelchair, where I slumped down in it and kept my eyes glued to the floor ahead of me. He backed me up and started pushing me through the cold and sterile hallways.

We worked our way through the labyrinth of corridors and elevators until we came to a door that was clearly meant to keep people in. He swiped his badge, and after a long buzzing sound, the doors opened and we passed through. He pushed me past the aid station where they looked me up and down, sizing up the fresh meat that had just rolled through the door.

The orderly waved at everyone behind the glass and they gave cordial smiles back. He rolled me into a small white room. It was very spartan—just a white bed in a white room with a white floor. It reminded me of something out of *A Clockwork Orange* or *One Flew Over the Cuckoo's Nest*. He asked me to get out of the wheelchair and take a seat on the bed. He backed the chair and himself out of the room and closed the door behind him.

I sat there on the bed, all alone. I found myself wondering why I wasn't in a straightjacket at this point. I mean, everything else played out pretty much exactly how you would imagine getting admitted to a psych ward would go—might as well roll out the straightjacket and electro-shock therapy while they were at it. I started to size up my situation and accept the enormity of it when I noticed one of the walls was covered with a painting of a lone palm tree on a small, deserted island.

Now, I do not doubt that whoever painted this mural did so in an effort to give a calming and soothing feeling to whosoever happened to be sitting on that bed. I mean, who doesn't want an idyllic Caribbean getaway with coconuts, cool water, and a warm breeze? So bless them for trying. But in my shitty, depressed, and miserable mood, all I could see was negativity. I looked at that palm tree and didn't see peace. I saw solitary confinement.

I looked at that painting and saw everything wrong with my life. I saw my failures and my loneliness. I saw a picture of my future. Me, alone, in some small, private Hell that I created because no one could love the wretched soul I had become. Hell, *I* didn't even love me. How could anyone else? I just slumped down on the bed, dropped my head in my hands, and cried.

I wasn't there long before someone came and got me and moved me to the main living quarters of the ward. Walking in, it was like a college dorm for the insane. You had to pass through double doors that remained locked at all times. On your left as you came in was the orderly station, where they did paperwork and could keep an eye on everyone. Directly in front of them, there was a large open area where everyone would mingle. It had tables where you could read magazines, solve word puzzles, or any number of things you could do to "safely" pass the time.

To the left, a hallway went down that had dorm rooms on either side of it. The rooms had two beds and a shared bathroom. You were issued a toothbrush and paste, and no razors were allowed. You walked around in either a gown or scrub-type tops and bottoms with those no-slip socks hospitals give you. Most people were on a variety of meds to keep them sedated, and it was odd for me to be stuck in there without being on anything.

I spent a dick-ton of time walking up and down the hallway. Often, I'd stop at the end and look out the window to watch ordinary life moving on, people milling about down on the street below. I grasped a new respect for freedom after being locked up and watching the birds fly off into the horizon. It was after my first trip to the window that I noticed the sound of the door locking behind the orderly, and it really hit me: this could my future.

I wasn't in charge in here. My freedom and my fate were absolutely 100 percent in these guys' hands. If this staff and this doctor didn't want to let me go, they didn't have to. If they felt that I was a danger to myself or to anyone else, they could keep me walking up and down that damn hallway until I was old and gray. Nothing, and I mean *nothing*, scared me as much as that.

The days are pretty much like clockwork when you're a patient, and I guess that's for good reason. You had your check-ins scheduled throughout the day. If you were medicated, you were placed on a schedule to line up and take your drugs, which, to me, was the scariest part of the whole damn program. I was petrified that I would be placed on the roster for individuals that had to start taking pills. When you are locked up in there, everyone seems crazier than you. Then you start wondering if you are crazy for thinking they are crazy, and what's even crazier is you start wondering if they are looking at you and feeling sorry for how crazy *you* are!

Every meeting with the staff is like a game where you are busy trying to convince them that you are sane and are okay to be released so that you can be like the birds you've been watching and just fly away from this fucking nightmare. So I attended every morning and afternoon group session. I participated and I did everything I thought I needed to do to get the hell out of there.

When you're locked up in there, you feel as if you are in suspended animation. There is no clear-cut way out. There is no promise. No sentence time. Just a vague and hazy, "Let's see how today goes" over and over. You start to feel like your chain is getting jerked, and at least for me, it eroded what little trust I already had. That meant that I didn't open up about shit. I said I was great. That everything was fine. That I had no issues. I musta just got drunk and acted stupid. Fuck help, I just wanted out.

It worked and I was cleared to get out. Walking out into the sunlight that morning is still, hands down, one of the best days in my life. If not for the fact that I knew I was still messed up walking out, I would be totally okay reliving that day over and over and over. But, as I rounded the corner leaving the hospital and broke into a jog, I knew I better start running towards something worth doing or I would be running right back to that hospital (or the grave) before I knew it.

As I have mentioned before, the worst thing I can do is nothing. Sitting around with time on my hands gets my mind racing and my nerves up. Neither are good for my mental health or happiness. I knew I needed to do some type of aggressive hobby to process all of this. I had to get my demons beat out of me. I decided that I would turn to fighting.

I figured fighting would check off a lot of blocks for me. It would let me get my anger out and keep me active, too. I knew it would humble me. It's impossible to be arrogant when you're getting your ass beat every day. More importantly, it would allow me to prove something to myself. To re-earn my worth as a human being. To stop being a loser and to literally step in the arena and lay it all out there with the ultimate prize on the line: redemption.

That's why I think fighting, for the most part, is a poor man's game. The vast majority (not all, because there is always an exception to the rule) are in the fight game because they are broke in some way, shape, or form; either finically, physically, or emotionally. Again, that's not always the case, but for most, there is this underlying pain that is driving them to prove something, either to themselves or the world that has written them off.

It is very rare that a rich kid, showered with love and attention, has any desire to go get beat up day in and day out for the hopes of making anywhere from zero to a couple thousand dollars in some old community rec-room somewhere, and that's where 99.9 percent of all fighters get their start. They have to have that chip on their shoulder and think the pain they're carrying every day is worse than the pain of getting their body pounded on daily.

I had that chip. Fuck, at that time, I had a boulder. I was mad at literally everyone and everything. I wanted to lash out at the world. I wanted to make someone else feel my pain. I thought at the time it was hurt somebody else or hurt myself. I failed to see that all I wanted was for someone to be proud of me. Someone to take notice of how hard I was willing to work. While I had the Knights to hang out with and would without a doubt help if I needed work done or my ass bailed out of jail, the dynamic of that relationship didn't lend itself to helping one feel accomplished or that others were proud of them.

So I was left wanting to have someone say they loved me or that they were proud of me. I didn't know at the time, but my hero was about to show up in the most unlikely of places.

There was a local martial arts academy that I had heard of called Evolve. A few of my personal clients trained there and had been raving about it. I figured this was the perfect time and place for me to go check it out. Now, I also knew that I wanted to have a buddy go with me, so I hit up Dave and pitched it as a good hobby for us to get into. Once I booked a trial, I showed up for my first PDS class (short for Personal Defense Systems). It was a mixture of boxing, Muay Thai, and traditional kickboxing.

The gym was in an old industrial complex and looked like everything you'd expect to find in a fight gym from the movies.. Just mats and mirrors. The main side was everyone who was starting off and there was another part, across the parking lot, known as Area 51. That's where the fighters trained. It was smaller, with just a couple thousand feet of mat space and two separate offices, one of which had been turned into a room from one of the fighters who lived there, a theme I've seen repeated numerous times at Evolve and other MMA training centers along the way.

I walked in the door and did the most douchebag thing you can do: I said, "I want to do a fight." I say it's a douchebag move because typically when folks do it they think they are badasses and that they are just going to whoop everyone's ass in the gym. They aren't there so much to learn as they are to prove how awesome they are. That desire is extremely short-lived because, within a few rounds of them getting their asses thoroughly kicked by someone they outweigh by thirty to forty pounds, they start to understand they don't know shit about fighting.

I began the training process and was showing up every day. I was putting in work and was benefiting not just physically, but emotionally as well. I met a girl and quickly became infatuated. She asked not to be mentioned too much, so I'll respect that, but I fell madly in love with her. I loved her completely, from the top of her head to the bottom of her feet. I loved her despite our differences and despite the fact that we honestly probably weren't the best fit for each other. This, in conjunction with having a cathartic outlet, put me on the right track. My plan was actually working. I was able to focus on one clear-cut goal—being able to fight—and I was so sore and exhausted that by the time I got home, the only thing I could do was crash out on the couch. I didn't have enough energy to focus on being depressed or angry.

After several months of training there and earning my green belt in PDS, there finally came the opportunity I was looking for: fight team tryouts. Tryouts consisted of several steps. One was a visual assessment of your skill level where you shadow-boxed and grappled. Next was a physical fitness test and a day where you got your ass handed to you with PT, and if you passed all of that, it culminated with three rounds with a new, fresh fighter each round. You would be cornered by one of the coaches and it was just like an MMA fight, only in headgear, shin pads, and boxing gloves.

My nerves were actually through the roof. The smoker (conditioning) took place after all the other classes were done, so we started at 2030. Master Mike, a former Marine, black belt in several arts, and owner of the academy, had a hard rule that beating each other up didn't take place in front of the other students. He knew not everyone wanted that and he didn't want to deter people from learning the arts out of fear of getting their face bashed in by some high-level fighter in front of a crowd.

The fact that only fighters and coaches were watching was

pressure enough, but on those nights, the man himself, Master Mike Moses, was in charge and ran the show. Just having him show up on the mats was enough to make me shit a brick. I hadn't really talked to him much but I already idolized the man and I wanted nothing more than to make him proud.

The time came for us to get the show on the road. Jason "J-Mo" Morris and Zac Davis were the coaches, and J-Mo was cornering me. The first guy I drew was Al Benjamin, a lanky fighter who loved to throw them things. He tore me apart on the standing exchanges, but I was able to shoot some takedowns and get in some ground-and-pound. All in all, it wasn't too bad of a showing on my part, and I did better than I expected, even though I wouldn't call it a win.

They rang the bell and it was time to go back to my corner. It was then I realized a major chink in my armor. I hadn't done anything with a mouthguard in since high school football. I had literally held my breath the entire time. Just completely forgot to actually breathe around the damn thing. By the time I got back to the stool in my corner, I thought I was having a full-blown asthma attack. J-Mo did his best to calm me down and offer coaching, but the only thing I could think of was how I couldn't breathe for shit.

After what seemed like five seconds, Master Mike said, "Let's go," and in stepped Gus. Now, Gus not only was a much, much, much better fighter than I was, but the guy had a gas tank that just didn't quit. Much later on when I was running conditioning for the fighters at Evolve, I did my damnedest to break the guy. It wasn't happening. There simply wasn't an off button on him.

We walk out and touch gloves and that was the last offensive thing that I did. Gus beat the living shit out of me. I didn't land one single punch. I didn't mount one offensive attack, at all. In fact, the only plus side that came out of the entire deal for me was I was able to catch my breath while he beat my ass. I have no doubt that a heavy bag put up more a fight against him than I did.

After the three minutes of being a piñata came to an end, I was back on the stool getting coached by J-Mo again. There really wasn't much to highlight from the last round. I got my ass beat; he knew it, everyone in the room knew it. No need to dwell on the negative. Let's move on, shall we?

The last guy up was a purple belt named Jordan. He was one of the top BJJ guys in the academy at the time and so there was good reason to believe that he was going to take me to the ground. J-Mo advised me to keep my distance and to keep the fight standing. Avoid the takedown at all costs.

Well, the bell rang, I walked out to the middle of the mats, we touched gloves, and instantly started beating the shit out of each other. I locked his head with my left and he did the same with his fist, and we literally stood there for the entire round and just punched each other in the head repeatedly until they broke up the fight. If you've ever seen Dan Frye vs Takayama, it went exactly like that. The entire room was losing its mind. I didn't prove I could fight that night, but I proved I wasn't scared to try. I proved I wouldn't quit. That was all Master Mike was looking for, and I earned my place on the team. To this day, it remains one of my proudest moments.

Making the team was an amazing accomplishment, but that was just the first step. Next up came the grueling part: going to practice every day. The truth of the matter was, I wasn't that good, at least not compared to the trained fighters. I was getting my ass kicked day in and day out. I had zero head movement, which meant I walked around with a black eye at all times.

One time, J-Mo kicked me in the side of the neck, and while it didn't knock me out, it shut my circuits down. I literally had no control over my body. In the mirror, I watched my body starch up and fall over like a tree a lumberjack had just chopped down. Another time, Zach hit a question-mark kick that broke my nose and certainly left me questioning why I was sparring him. It honestly got so bad that Master Mike told everyone I had to stop sparring. He assigned me to the heavy bag and I felt absolutely dejected. Instead of looking cool in front of him, I thought I looked like a loser.

What made it even worse was that he told me he wouldn't let me fight yet. This sucked because my entire reasoning for asking Dave to come train was for us to fight on the same night. Now, he was cleared to go and I was not. Once again, in my eyes, I had failed.

I had talked a big game and found myself unable to back it up. I had told everyone that Dave and I were going to fight on the same night. I didn't do it to be boastful; I did it to put it out in the universe so that I would be held accountable. I still do that to this day. I say publicly what I am gonna do because I know it'll keep me from giving up.

But in this instance, I didn't think I really had a choice. Master Mike was the coach and I had to listen to him. Shortly after getting told he wouldn't let me fight, I was at a pool party and everyone was shooting the shit and then the topic of the fights came up. Everyone was pumped and giving Dave major (deserved) kudos. Then they came to me and I had to say I was told I couldn't fight.

I'm not one to lie, so I told the truth: Master Mike said I wasn't ready yet. It was humiliating. There, in front of friends and hot girls, I had to say that Master Mike said I wasn't a good enough fighter to go out and fight the same time that my boy was. I wanted to just go drown myself in the deep end.

That humiliation led to me drinking a few more beers, and with beers comes liquid courage. Now, in almost every single situation you can imagine, liquid courage tends to get you in trouble. This may have gone down as the one time in history getting drunk actually changed a man's life for the better.

After leaving the party, I went home and was dejected. I was embarrassed by the situation but I really felt like I had let Dave down, too. I had recruited him under the premise that we would do this together. Now he was fighting, and the best I could do was get a ticket and cheer from the stands. Of course, I know Dave wouldn't judge me; he has never judged me, not back then and not today either. But that's probably why I felt the weight of letting him down, even if he wasn't.

As a man, I believe that the most important thing you can do is live up to your word. To follow through on your promises. For people to know that if you say you'll do something, it will get done, and here I was failing to do something I said I would.

Now, back to the whole liquid courage thing. When I got home, I just couldn't get it out of my head how I felt sitting at the pool while everyone was talking about how badass it was that Dave was fighting, and I was forced to say I wasn't cleared to fight. In that moment, I had what I thought was a genius idea that, in truth, was a stupid idea that just so happened to work out. I figured I would write Master Mike and plead my case to him.

Now, keep in mind, at that time, Master Mike didn't know me. I was just some kid who trained at his gym and appeared to be better as a punching bag than anything else. He had told me I couldn't fight because he was trying to look out for me. He was being a good coach, and here I was challenging his coaching with little to no relationship built at the time. In truth, I am lucky he didn't take it personally and tell me to kick rocks.

Either way, in my drunken state, I had decided the best course of action was to write a Facebook message to this man who barely knew me and plead my case for being able to fight. Since I was intoxicated, I can only imagine how poorly written this plea was, but it essentially amounted to the following:

Sir, I know I am a dumbass and I am not very good. I understand that you are trying to look out for me and that you also have a reputation to maintain. I know the importance of having people perform well from your gym in competitions. I understand that their performance is a direct reflection on your school, and ultimately, you. I know I am not the most talented. I understand I am not even close to being the best in your school. But what I lack in that I will make up for in heart. Nothing matters more to me than my word, and I gave my word that I would fight that night. I can't promise you I'll win, but I can promise you I will not embarrass you. Would you please reconsider letting me fight?

I hit send before I ever realized what I was doing, and in truth, the second I did, I almost shit my pants. I thought to myself, *This guy is going to kill me.* I thought, *Man, he's probably gonna be like, who the fuck does this kid think he is?* My heart rate skyrocketed as I saw that he was writing me back almost instantaneously. I was fully expecting him to lay into me about my insolence. Instead, he wrote back two sentences:

Okay. You can fight.

My mouth dropped wide open. If I am honest, I never thought that would be the response when I wrote to him. I was sure that the answer would be no. I just sat there, in my chair, staring at the screen for a few minutes. Finally, I was able to get myself together enough to respond to his message. All I could muster was a simple "Thank you, sir," and I went back to sitting there in silence.

After a few minutes, I finally came around to my senses and it dawned on me that I only had a few weeks left to go before the fight. My wish had been granted and now the reality of what I had asked for was taking hold. Luckily for me, I had continued to stay in shape, but I still had another twenty pounds to drop to make my fight weight. With the fight on, it was time for me to sober up quick and get my ass back in gear.

The next morning, I woke up with a renewed sense of purpose and vigor. I wrote the entire team and told them that I was cleared to fight by Master Mike, and I would be back in the gym that day. I also let Zac know that I was cleared for him to get me a match made for the event, which was the final piece of the puzzle I needed in order to close the deal.

I went back to training full-steam. I was so excited. No matter how tired or bruised I was, you couldn't get the smile off my face. A few days after resuming training, Zac informed me that they had an opponent for me lined up and we started getting ready to game plan. At the amateur level, they do their best to line you up with someone with your same skill set and experience. The guy I drew had already competed in, and won, his first fight.

Fighting is a pretty fluid thing. Sometimes wrestlers box each other and sometimes strikers shoot a takedown. So even with footage of one fight, there's not too much stock you can put in it. So, we really didn't work to break down his fight. We knew that my best assets were my gas tank and my grappling. So, the plan was to close the distance and grind him out.

The next several weeks revolved around that game plan. Training to push the pace, close the distance, get the fight down, and grind it out. The last hurdle left ahead of me (or so we thought) was the weight cut. If you have never cut weight before, it is, in my opinion, the most grueling shit you can do. How some of these guys out there at the pro level cut the amount of weight they do boggles my mind.

I entered the sauna with half of my twenty left to go. It was an absolutely miserable experience. You're already dehydrated to begin with and that just adds to the feeling of you cooking alive inside that plastic jumpsuit. Everything in your body and being is screaming to get the fuck out of the suit and out of the sauna. It is as much a mental game as it is physical. It felt like I was literally melting.

I had a couple of the guys in there with me. I'd sit until the allotted time and then I'd step out just long enough to wring the sweat out and step on the scale. Once completed, I'd head back into Hell for the next round. I did that over and over the day of weigh-ins. By the time we got to the final round, I could, no shit, see my heartbeat in my stomach. You could see my veins all over my body; my shreds had shreds. I was normally between 185 and 190 pounds, but there I stood, damn near bone dry and 145. It was time to head off to weigh-ins.

Dave and I got there and hit our weight like the professionals we are. Dave had made pretty drastic cuts himself, down from plus 200 to 170 . We'd checked off a pretty big milestone for ourselves, and that's when I got a big wrench thrown in my plan. My opponent had been switched out at the last minute.

Now, in and of itself, that's not that unusual; it happens all the time. However, what happened next proved to be a bit of a problem. First, the guy lied about his record. He said he had zero fights when in fact he had seven. Second, he didn't make weight. The guy came in at 165 pounds, which meant he hadn't undergone the process of the weight cut. He hadn't been depleted at all. What's more, at no point did he try to make weight. The day of the fight, he was walking around drinking Gatorade and shooting the shit. Lastly, and arguably the worst part, he was the head coach for the other team.

Zach and Master Mike didn't want me to fight him. Both of them were actually livid at the prospect of me fighting him. Zac even went off on the guy the before the fight and told him he was lucky I had the balls to fight him. I looked at Master Mike and said, "We knew there was a chance I was gonna get my ass beat here tonight. People already have their tickets and everyone else is lined up to fight. Just let me go." I reiterated the promise I made to him when I was drunk messaging him on Facebook: "I can't promise I'll win, but I promise I won't embarrass you."

And one more time, Master Mike said, "Okay."

We had four guys fighting out of the card that night, and I was slated to fight fourth. I can't remember who fought first that night, but he won his fight. That was followed up by Gus, who won his in an extremely convincing fashion, beating the guy up quickly and ending the fight in the first round. After that came Dave. I was sitting in the back warming up when I saw the ambulance pull up.

Looking out the window, I asked what was going on out there, and they told me that Dave beat the breaks off the kid he was fighting. Which, in all honesty, was karma, 'cause the kid had run his mouth nonstop on social media about Dave leading up to the fight and how he was going to fuck Dave up. Well, the kid learned that day that talking on the keyboard and backing it up in real life are worlds apart; all it took was a good ol' fashioned asswhooping to bring the lesson home.

Now, on one hand, I was extremely happy that my team had done well. That's what you want for them. On the other hand, the amount of pressure I felt to not be the first guy to get his ass beat was enormous. One of the things that surprised me the most was how bad my nerves were. I was sure that after combat, fighting wouldn't be that big of deal for me. Hell, I'd gotten in enough fights in bars since I'd been back that I felt fear wouldn't factor in.

The opposite was true. Donald Cerrone once talked about the walk to the cage. That when you're in the back, you feel like you're moving in quicksand. That you can't punch cause your hands feel heavy. Your stomach starts doing flip-flops and you gotta go to the bathroom to throw up. I literally did all of that.

In the back, I felt exhausted. I felt sick. I was trying to hide it. I felt like a little bitch. I wasn't afraid of getting hurt. I was petrified of getting embarrassed. It started to hit me that I was gonna be really outclassed out there and I didn't want to let everyone down. Most importantly, I didn't want to embarrass Master Mike.

Then, there he was, standing in front me. Him and Zac. They said, "Alright, it's time to go."

We left the room and headed down the hallway to the gymnasium.

There we stood outside the door and waited for our queue. I heard the song I had chosen for my walkout, "Forever" by Drake, Kanye West, Lil Wayne, and Eminem. To this day, that song still gives me goosebumps.

"Last name Ever, first name Greatest," pounded through the speakers and the double doors were thrown open. Instantly, the nerves went away and I went into the zone. I had my hair in a red mohawk. I had on a sleeveless muscle shirt, and in my hand I carried the American flag. Evolve had packed the house, so when I walked out, the place went ballistic. I marched to the cage, stripped of the shirt, hugged the team, and stomped into the cage. Master Mike followed me in as I made my trip around the cage.

When I came back around to my corner, he told me to press my back into the cage to get a feel for it. Up until that point, I had spoken very little to Master Mike, and I had never heard him cuss before (truthfully, I don't think I've heard him cuss since), but I'll never forget what he said. He stood in front of me and told me, "If it goes outside of round one, expect it to go the full three rounds. If you are losing after the round, I'll tell you. Now run cross the cage and punch that fucker in his face."

Mike exited the cage and I heard it lock. I looked across the cage and there he was, one of the smuggest son of a bitches I have ever seen in my life. He called himself "Prodigy" and had a look of assurance on his face that said he thought this was gonna be an easy money fight. The referee motioned us to the middle and I stormed to the center of the cage, and the ref stepped in to keep us separated.

Ol' Prodigy stood there, smirked at me, nodded his head and said, "Bring it on." The ref said a bunch of shit I didn't hear and then he motioned for us to get back to our corners. I didn't turn around; I just backpedaled to the cage and kept my eyes locked on his. The ref asked if Prodigy was ready, and then asked if I was ready. I nodded yes and did a knife hand towards the center of the cage and yelled

"Let's get it on!"

I ain't been much in life, but I've always been a good soldier. Master Mike said run across the cage and punch him in his face, and that's exactly what I tried to do. I came out of the corner at a dead fucking sprint. I had every intention of crashing into him and just going for broke. He looked at my dumb ass running full-steam ahead, dropped down, and shot a perfect double.

He picked me high above his head and slammed me into the mats. I remember thinking to myself that it didn't hurt, but in the time it took for me to register the lack of pain, he'd already slipped into full mount. He collected my arm and my head in a super-tight arm triangle and I knew right away I was screwed. This had gone just about as bad as a fight can go. In less than four seconds, I was slammed, mounted, and judging by how fast my world was going gray, I was about to be submitted.

As I watched the darkness start to creep in around my eyes, I thought for one second about how fucking embarrassing this was. I was gonna get beat within a few seconds of the start of the fight. The very next thought to enter my head, however, was, *You promised you weren't going to embarrass him.* I can't explain what happened next. It was as close to a real-life Hulkamania moment as you'll ever get, but somehow my body just came alive.

The gray instantly snapped back and I felt a surge of adrenaline run through my body. I managed to create space, enough to get out of the arm triangle. Then I collected his head as I tried to roll him over playground-fight style. I tried to fire off a punch and he took my back.

Soon as he got there, he started sliding his hands under my chin, going for a rear naked choke. Zac had asked me in training what positions I wanted to rehearse the most and I said, "The two worst I could get in: rear naked and mount." Well, the first thing that clicked into my head was from training: get my ass to the mat!

I managed to do that, but Prodigy, being a vet, seamlessly transitioned into full mount. He postured up and started raining down punches on my dome. Now, I didn't feel his punches at all. I don't know if it's 'cause he hit like the bitch that he was or if it was the adrenaline pumping that blocked out all feeling. Either way, the only thing going through my head was that if I didn't move, they were going to stop the fight.

I wasn't very effective. I didn't really use any type of technique. I just kinda flailed around leaving my arms exposed. Not one to pass up an easy opportunity, he scooped my arm and instantly jumped to a deep arm bar. I followed him around but I was in deep. I went to scoop him up to slam him, but as soon as I lifted him off the ground, the ref screamed out "NO SLAMMING!"

Well, fuck.

I am stuck there with him a few inches off the ground but unable to slam him down. I started shaking him, and eventually his grip loosened and his legs broke apart. I took that as my moment. I grabbed him by his throat and pinned him to the mat. I slammed my fist into his face over and over. All of a sudden, he realized he was in a real fight and started shrimping for dear life. I was chasing him and throwing punches every inch of the way. I over-committed to one of 'em and he swept me. As soon as I hit my back, I shrimped out, and for some reason, he folded over. I've always been good at taking the back for some reason, and without a second thought, I threw my leg around his back and hopped on. I slammed my arm around his neck and locked it in to my opposite elbow. Sliding my left hand behind his head, I grape-vined out his lower body while doing my absolute damnedest to rip his head from his shoulders. Instantaneously, he tapped.

And just like that, I beat him. The head coach of the other team. The guy who missed weight by twenty pounds. Who lied about his record. Who should have mopped the floor with me, and who was a way better fighter. He broke. And I was the one who broke him. I jumped up and the crowd went nuts. The referee raised my hand, declared me the winner, and my life was never the same after. I didn't know it at the time, but that was the night SOLDIERFIT was born.

A few days later, we were back at the academy finishing up a night of striking training. We all lined up like you do and waited for the instructor to do a recap of the class that had just taken place. Master Mike looked at the class with a sledgehammer in his hand, and asked the following question, "How many of you think I could hit you with this sledgehammer and you'd keep coming?"

The students looked around at each other, a bit perplexed, unsure of what the correct answer should be, and so he asked it again: "How many of you think I could hit you with this sledgehammer and you'd keep coming?" Again, silence, until one guy cracked a joke that he'd call the cops, but after a low chuckle, the room fell silent again.

Finally, Master Mike says, "I know two people that I could hit with the sledgehammer and they'd keep coming. One I've known about for a while, and that's Zac; the other is Danny. I have no doubt that I could hit either one of these guys with this sledgehammer and they'd keep coming. Danny had no right to win that fight. The guy was a better fighter, but he didn't have the one thing Danny had, and that was heart. Danny went out there and stole his soul that night."

I was speechless. My entire life, I had been looking for someone to notice me. To see that I was a good guy. To understand that, goddammit, I tried. That I was willing to die to do good. I felt ten feet tall standing in that room. To have everyone on the mats look at me with admiration, if even only for a moment, was a level of validation I had never experienced. It was life changing for me. But

Master Mike wasn't done yet.

A few days later, he asked me to meet him and his right hand, Mrs. Melissa, at a local Starbucks. I showed up, we grabbed a couple cups of coffee, and went to sit outside to enjoy the day. It was perfect weather. Bright clear blue sky with a subtle breeze. He then offered me the deal of a lifetime: I could bring SOLDIERFIT into his gym for free.

You read that correctly—for FREE. He opened his entire gym to me, literally charged me nothing for rent or utilities, and gave me free rein of the place outside of the times he ran his classes. Literally gave me a key to the place and said, "Have at it."

I jumped at the opportunity. I started running bootcamps all day long. I had come from the big box gym model and I thought to myself, if a big box gym can charge a low monthly rate, and has all that equipment and overhead and still make money, why couldn't a company only teaching classes do the same thing? After all, most people with a gym membership literally spend all their time in the classes!

So that's what I did. I started off running early morning, mid-morning, noon, and evening classes, because those were the times they didn't have any classes at Evolve. I was charging twenty-five bucks per month for unlimited access (absolute rookie mistake). I'll never forget the night I came in the door with a workout for three people and saw twenty-three people waiting for class. I knew in that moment I was onto something.

In the beginning, I had no budget. I built my workout equipment out of things I could find. For TRX straps, I used tow straps. For weights, I used tires, old dumbells laying around, rocks, and sledgehammers. I used old firehoses for battle ropes and even cut and attached pieces to big tires to use as handles to create deadlift and farmer's carries. I would cut tire tubes in half, fill them with sand, and duct tape the ends to create sandbags and Bulgarian bags. And of course, we often used good ol' bodyweight to get the job done.

I learned to do more with less. I did everything I could to make up for my lack of funding. Our marketing was word of mouth that was fueled by the fact that we issued shirts to the "troops," as we called them, that they had to wear to class. The premise being that in the military you wear uniforms, and we were going to carry that over into our culture.

To be honest, I think uniformity is important in certain settings. No team ever won the Superbowl with a shitty uniform. You look like shit, you play like shit. But more importantly, fitness is an industry that has sadly become less about the blessings of having a healthy body and more about how close you can get your workout on Instagram to look like Cinemax after midnight. Having everyone in a uniform took that away. The fact that everyone had to wear the same shirt, and that guys couldn't take their shirts off, or girls couldn't wear their little sister's sports bra, meant that the people we wanted to help—the overweight and out of shape—didn't feel self-conscious about workouts. As a former fat kid, I understood that.

The other benefit that came from it was free marketing. Not even free marketing, but marketing that actually paid us. Everyone who was a member was so proud to be members that they wore those shirts everywhere. To the store, church, work, parties—you name it. Hell, we even got pictures of people taking on vacation wearing it. Our members literally became walking billboards, and that made all the difference in the world.

From there, we absolutely exploded. That was January 2017. We ended that month with thirteen members and thirty classes per month. We now have thousands of members and hundreds of classes per month. We moved out of the Evolve academy space, and I no longer needed supplemental income from firefighting. We have won Small Business of the Year multiple times and at every level: county, state, and nationally. We have been INC. 5000 ranked twice. We accomplished all of this because one man believed in me and gave me a chance.

Yes, our team has done an amazing job. Yes, I have absolutely worked my ass off, and so has Dave, but make no mistake about it, if Master Mike didn't help me when no one else would, SOLDIERFIT would not be here today. I was close to giving up. In fact, I had thought about it several times, if I am honest. But he saw something no one else saw in me. Hell, I didn't even see it in myself.

He was the father I never had. He has backed me at every turn. He has mentored me and he has been an amazing friend. He has done all of this in spite of the fact that people have screwed him over time and time again. He has been taken advantage of and abused, not because he couldn't beat their ass (he could, easily), but because his heart is the biggest one I've ever seen. He'll just take it on the chin and offer his chin again to the next dreamer he meets down the line.

I don't know why he does it, but because he did, my ledger will never be clear. I will always owe him and I'll never be able to pay him back. No amount of money in the world I could give him would be worth what he has given me. I know he doesn't want it anyway. What he wants is for us all to pay it forward because we all drink deeply from a well not of our own creation. So, that's what I try to do. That's why our goal at SOLDIERFIT is to revitalize the American dream, 'cause Master Mike revitalized mine. So when you wonder if what you do matters, remember what Mike did for me, and know, without a shadow of a doubt, it does.

Chapter Fifteen

Paying It Back

*"The best way to find yourself is to lose yourself
in the service of others."*
—Mahatma Gandhi

SOLDIERFIT was gaining momentum. We were winning awards left and right and we were happy to be doing it. Getting honored over and over again as small business of the year meant so much to me, especially since I was coming from a place of self-doubt and deprecation. Owning my own business and changing lives for the better was doing the same for my own life. Quite literally, helping others was helping me.

I have often told people that I have done some of the most rewarding jobs on earth. Being both a soldier and a firefighter (since you never really stop even after the career ends) fills one with a sense of purpose that is hard to explain or replicate in other industries. You are literally fighting for others and saving lives. I am grateful for the opportunity to work in both career fields. With that being said, the fitness industry, if done correctly, provides you in many ways with even greater satisfaction.

In the military, you often don't get to see a mission's full success in the grand scheme of things. The men on your team get transferred out after weeks or months. As a first responder, you rarely get to see the person whose life you saved maximize the extra time they've been given. That's totally different in the fitness industry.

You get to see your clients weekly, and in some cases, daily, for years. In front of your eyes, you see their transformation. You watch them literally blossom into happy, confident, and content people. I've seen it time and time again. Fitness force multiplies their lives. They learn how to set a goal and then go execute it. Learning how to take control of their bodies more often than not empowers them to take charge of many other aspects of their lives. Have I seen out-of-shape successful people? Absolutely, but I have rarely seen an in-shape person who wasn't also successful in some other aspects of their lives.

While owning SOLDIERFIT is rewarding in so many ways, I still felt like I owed something more to those who were struggling in areas that I too had struggled. At the time, I didn't really think that many had struggled like I did. It was actually a source of great shame for me. I thought I was the only one, the weak link, who had failed to transition properly. I figured I was just one of the dumbasses that didn't navigate life well in any aspect. Little did I know at the time, but nothing was further from the truth.

Slowly but surely, it started to surface that there was a quiet and insidious storm brewing amongst our ranks. It was estimated that a whopping twenty-two veterans were taking their own lives each and every day.

A 2022 study by America's Warrior Partnership revealed up to 44 former service members take their life each day.[5] And according to the Annals of Epidemiology, a study of over 1.3 million veterans showed that those who've served have a 41–61 percent higher risk of suicide compared to the general U.S. population.[6]

It's clearly an epidemic. But, back then, over five years since

I started writing this book, no one beyond veterans and military families was talking about it. It wasn't until tragedies started striking communities that the word began to spread.

Personally, what hit home was a soldier from Frederick committing suicide. Sergeant Tyler Moore. As a fellow paratrooper, I felt a kinship to him. His father was a former Green Beret, a stoic barrel-chested man with gray hair and a square jawline. I remember meeting him and instantly felt immense sorrow for him. He carried his pain well, but you could see it in his eyes. His son had passed away far, far too soon. I saw Sgt. Moore do his best to comfort his wife, and I am sure it pained him to know that no matter how strong he was, there are just some mountains a man can't move.

I met his family when we dedicated our martial arts room to Sgt. Moore. At SOLDIERFIT, we dedicate every room to a fallen service member, and we dedicated our martial arts space to him in Frederick. This came shortly after Sgt. Moore was awarded his associate's degree posthumously by Frederick Community College, and a memorial was built to him (and other veterans who had passed away) on campus by the veterans club.

Listening to the family speak about the pain of the loss and the importance of his life touched me deeply and reminded me of my own struggles.

I was actually gearing up to go on my bachelor party for my second marriage when Robin Williams committed suicide. My news feed, of course, blew up. Everyone knew who Robin Williams was. He was easily one of the biggest A-list stars to take his own life. With so much talk about Robin's suicide and so little regarding the twenty-two vets per day, it was easy to understand why the veteran community was so upset. And upset they were.

My news feed literally erupted with friends and fellow Facebookers saying that everyone cared about Robin's suicide by no one gave a fuck about a veteran's life. There was this belief amongst many of my peer group that, again, civilians just didn't care about the warfighter. It would take years for me to know for sure (and to find out that we veterans are our own worst enemies at times), but I had a strong belief that civilians did in fact care very much about veterans. The problem was that no one knew about it.

It wasn't long after Robin's suicide that I was sitting at a bar having a beer. My soon-to-be wife had already left for her bachelorette party and I was scheduled to head out to mine the next day when a few mutual friends posted that a local veteran, Specialist Adam Richardson, had committed suicide. This would now make two that had taken their own lives from Frederick in just a matter of a few months. This was too close to home, and I knew, given my own issues, that this had to be just the tip of the iceberg.

Spc. Adam Richardson was well-known by several other veterans in our area, one of whom, Dominic Macnusso, was a close friend of mine. Hearing Dom share the news was a gut punch, and I knew I wanted to support the effort in some way. I reached out to Dom to ask if he had any point of contact with the family, to which he responded, yes, Adam's brother, Steel.

I reached out while sitting at the bar and began a conversation that would last my entire bachelor party and change the course of my life. The first thought that came to my mind was showing the family that people cared and that there shouldn't be a stigma associated with suicide. We should focus on helping people find the resources to combat PTS, depression, and other mental conditions that beat you down until you decide to make that permanent decision to end your life. To do that, we had to start with a show of support, rather than judgment, in the event of a tragedy such as this.

Instantly, I went to work creating a detail that would pull a twenty-four-hour vigil at the funeral home leading up to the service. Next, I recruited the Desert Knights to provide a motorcycle escort to his final resting place, and the boys didn't disappoint. At least forty bikes showed up. The family was overwhelmed with the outpouring of love and support from not just the veteran community, but the community as a whole. It was then that I knew what we had to do long term: we had to make this unknown problem known. I knew in my heart that if we did that, we could make a positive impact on the numbers.

I took the original idea and tried to put in into place, quite literally. I created a non-profit called "22 Needs a Face." The goal, I thought, was clear and apparent in the name: to put a face to the twenty-two veterans who were committing suicide each day. As long as we kept speaking in abstract numbers, no one we were speaking to was going to get it. Unless it happened to someone they knew, there wasn't a strong enough emotional connection to it to compel them to care enough to act.

That meant that we had to make it personal. We had to tell the stories of each individual, to break the twenty-two down to an individual story. I knew if we could do that, we could move people to act. But we ran into one big issue: the name that I thought explained what we were trying to do perfectly was confusing as hell to people.

As a side note, a non-profit organization is a business for a collective, public, or social benefit. Unfortunately, the name puts a lot of undue pressure, because the people running them (and much of the general public) thinks these organizations need to spend every single dollar that comes in on the services they are giving, or else they are a shitty non-profit. It's a horrible way of thinking, and one we'd do well to soon abandon.

Forgive that tangent, but it drives me nuts. Anyway, back to the point I was making. In business, you have what's called your elevator pitch. Opinions vary on how long it should take to give, but the consensus is between forty-five seconds to a minute, tops. If it takes you that long or longer to explain your name and purpose, you got a shitty name, no matter how good you think it is. The market dictates all and the market told us no one got our name.

The name didn't correlate to veterans at all. There was no quick connection. Furthermore, at the time "twenty-two" wasn't a well-known statistic yet, so that only led to more confusion. Despite the hindrance of the name, passion actually got us quite a bit of traction and the support was huge out of the gate. Even at that time, without any real clear mission outside of awareness, the support and the funding came rolling in! It confirmed what I had felt all along. The public, determined not to repeat the mistakes of the past in Vietnam with our service men and women, desperately wanted to take care of those who had worn the uniform.

While it felt good to have gained traction, the truth was, it was still extremely frustrating and difficult to explain who we were over and over again. I knew that if we were ever to find a way to scale this thing, we had to come up with a better way to articulate our point. Something that resonated with the viewer instantly. As luck would have it, I had recently read about how humans are visual creatures. That meant if we could come up with some way to visually represent what was happening within our ranks, we could touch the nerve needed to create an instant bond with the viewer and compel them to act.

Riding down the highway one morning, it hit me. A platoon is typically anywhere from twenty-five to fifty service members (staffing is almost never at the upper end) so at twenty-two a day, we were losing roughly a platoon a day. It also occurred to me that the recognizable battle cross memorial (consisting of all a soldier's belongings: boots, weapon, dog tags, and K-Pot helmet resting on top) existed to show that it was an individual, a single life that was lost amidst the massive casualties of battle. When people see that, they are moved. They feel it. So why not do the same thing for the twenty-two veterans? Sitting there stuck in traffic, Platoon 22 was born.

At first, my idea was to simply make a traveling memorial that was put on by 22 Needs a Face. We would set it up at whatever event we were at or at any event that requested the memorial to be present. We sent out an all-call for veterans to donate boots, and they poured in. Before we knew it, we had several sets of "platoons" and boots that represented every service branch from both the Vietnam and the Desert Era wars.

I made sure each pair of boots was laced up tight and would be placed in formation "dress right dressed." In the Platoon 22 leader position, we placed jungle boots to represent that our Vietnam service members were still in the fight, quite literally, as their generation actually made up the bulk of the twenty-two veterans who commit suicide each day. We wanted to make sure that they felt acknowledged and cared for, especially as I expected that their numbers would only increase as they aged out and needed more services.

As we started doing more and more, I learned that the rabbit hole only went deeper down. Our veterans were struggling mightily. These struggles manifested in so many ways: depression, anger, PTS, addiction, domestic violence, finical issues, and it felt like the list went on and on. My generation was outpacing our civilian counterparts in terms of rates of suicide, and the female veterans are nearly 250 percent more likely to kill themselves than civilian women.[7]

Over and over, I found myself going out and meeting veterans in distress at all hours of the night and in places throughout the area. One night I'd be going to a local bar, another night on the street in downtown Frederick, another I'd be sitting on the back steps of a veteran's house. I've talked 'em down and I've talked guns out of their hands. Over and over again, I saw these men and women in pain, and I started to notice a trend.

Over and over again, these veterans who were doing poorly

were doing so because they were failing to transition from military service to the civilian sector. Some of this, to be frank, is their fault. Veterans greatly overestimate and underestimate our worth at the exact same time. Let me give you an example.

I want you to think about that young person who joins the service with the eventual desire to be a police officer. They are sold a crock of shit from the recruiter: "If you do four years, you'll be better positioned in police academy." That just ain't true. So they join with the plan to do four years and bounce. They get in and life happens. The military is demanding—this ain't no forty-hour-a-week gig—and so, for the most part, these guys don't have/make time to get their degree in those four years (a major requirement to have in many, if not all, departments nationwide).

These guys do their four-year pump and think not only are they getting out and getting hired on a force, but because they were an MP, they are jumping to the front of the line. Hell, they'll probably even get picked up for SWAT. Nothing could be further from the truth. They aren't even competitive. Not with other, more-seasoned service members, nor the civilians who have a degree. Matter of fact, in most cases, they are less competitive than the civilian with a degree.

Now, while they don't have the hard skills needed to land the "dream job" they want right out of the military, they absolutely have the soft skills to land a long list of jobs (many that are actually high-paying). And lots of companies abide my regulations that prevent unequal hires in regards to military. But the problem here is twofold. Firstly, they spent absolutely no time prepping for the transition. This stems from the way the military handles transition, trying to cram it all in at the tail end of your stint. I don't care if you did four years or forty, no one is paying attention to shit those last couple weeks.

Secondly, they get out ill-prepared. They don't know how to

interview. They haven't learned how to sell themselves. After years of "we" instead of "me," it's completely foreign to them to try and highlight what they did. When you spend years getting it beat into your head that no one likes a "spotlight Ranger," you find it insanely difficult to put yourself in the spotlight, and that factors hard in your difficulty to navigate transition.

Lost in transition, they start to lose themselves. Some end up dead in jobs that crush their soul. Some get into drugs and alcohol. Others get addicted to illicit activities. The theme remains the same: they are looking for an adrenaline rush again. There's a pretty famous meme out there that shows a Marine shooting a machine gun around a corner with dust flying off the wall from bullets hitting it. The subheading says, "PTSD is realizing you'll never be this awesome again."

Like it or not, there is a lot of truth to that. What do you do when what you did is done? Furthermore, what do you do when what you did was arguably the absolute apex of what a human can do? As horrible as war is, as much as it can demonstrate all that is base in man, it does the opposite, too. It shows the absolute best of the human condition.

Men and women willing to lay down their lives for their fellow service members. Willing to endure all types of strife and suffering: hunger, pain, sleep deprivation, solitude, missing of important moments such as holidays, anniversaries, and even the births of their children, to serve and save their fellow man. How one can look at that type of devotion and not be moved is beyond me.

But when that is gone, when it's replaced with sales meetings, TPU reports, and new-member quotas, the passion behind a purpose is lost too. Sadly, more often than not, the service member isn't prepared for that reality at all.

The overwhelming majority of service members enter the service at a very young age, roughly eighteen years old. Well, our brains aren't even fully developed until around the age of twenty-five. That means that you become indoctrinated into an all-encompassing organization with a very clear mission and purpose: to close with, engage, and destroy the enemies of our nation.

After spending years in the military, many veterans are unequipped to go work for an organization without a clear mission, and sadly, most businesses out there lack a clear mission, vision, or sense of purpose. Everything revolves around the bottom line and that doesn't speak to veterans at all. But that isn't where the struggle stops.

Whenever the day comes that you get your DDT2-14, be it four years or twenty, it is a moment you have fantasized about for literally years. You look at it as you're finally free to go and do as you please. You finally clear CIF (Central Issuing Facility), which is a monumental task in itself, by the way, and you head to toward the gates for the final time. You drive through and think to yourself, *So long, suckers!*

The future looks bright. No shaving, no early morning wakeups, no more bullshit "fun runs," and most importantly, no one telling you what to do anymore. You can grow your hair long, put your hands in your pockets, and sleep in till noon. I mean, who is gonna stop you? Even better, work is gonna be GREAT. No more forced long days. If you make me stay late, not only do you gotta pay me, you gotta pay me time and a half! Finally, I'm 'bout to make real money! Oh, and if the boss gets smart with me, I'll just tell him to fuck off!

All of that is well and good for about three weeks to three months, depending on the individual. Within a short window of time, the partying gets old. Having a beard is more work than shaving. Hangovers hurt (you're not a young pup). You wish someone paid your fat ass to work out. You absolutely can still get put on bullshit details. You still don't get paid a ton of money, only now BAH and

Tricare ain't a thing. Oh, and turns out you can't tell your boss to fuck off after all; rent is due on the first, and as you like to eat, you do, in fact, still need this job.

Then, almost out of nowhere, it occurs to you that you're no longer part of the team. That gate that you used to be able to drive through at any time now doesn't let you in. You went from being a soldier to being a civilian, and you must now prove you have a valid reason to come on post. It's a necessary thing to happen, but that doesn't make it any less cold. The guys who were your brothers are now spread all over the United States. They all went back home or made a new home somewhere else.

They, like you, got a job. Started a family. Settled down and started to try to live the next phase of their lives. You thought you were just like everyone else, but almost anywhere you go serves as a daily reminder that you aren't, and that goes double if you ever deployed or saw combat. You stand a little taller. Speak a little more honestly. Work a little harder. Care a little more.

You don't understand all the bitching that people have about not getting "free" shit. You really are confused as to why other people are pissed that they are expected to work until the job is done, not just clock out at five. And for the love of God, why can't anyone enjoy your dark humor? You've been reported to HR three times this month.

For many, that starts to lead to a life that lacks excitement and is no longer fulfilling. You become the guy you swore you'd never be. You actually miss being in. The things you used to think were stupid, you now look back on and smile. They were making men out of us! You long for the sense of purpose and coworkers who were so much more than fellow worker bees—those who'd die for you.

All of this is then compounded because we've been at war for twenty years. As of this writing, we have seen our policy absolutely crumble. The withdrawal was done hastily, severely underestimating the capabilities of the Taliban while simultaneously overestimating the strength of the government in power. We watched this play out on social media as we saw the War on Terror that started with Americans choosing to jump to their deaths to avoid their fate end with local Afghans falling to their deaths as they tried to hold onto a plane leaving Kabul.

Even before the last couple of years, before COVID, before the loss of hard-earned ground in both Iraq and Afghanistan, our veterans needed transitional support; these events just forced that need to multiply, but it's always been there. That much is evident by the fact that the bulk of our veteran suicides belongs to the Vietnam generation.

That's why, as we started working in the space and dealing with veterans and advocates for them, we saw a common theme emerge: they were failing in transition. If we were to have any hope of putting a dent in the numbers we were losing, we had to get better about transitional support, an area where we fail miserably.

Basic and boot camps exist to take the civilian out of you, but we don't have a reverse program to help put the warrior back into civilian life. We absolutely have to find a way to fix this. We have to get these men and women help in transitioning. The evidence was compelling: veterans who were enrolled in the VA healthcare system were much, much less likely to commit suicide than those who were not. Furthermore, as published in a press release from TAPS, burn pits are rapidly becoming a major issue for those who served. They are being referred to as "the new Agent Orange."

> *"Many of these service members returned home from a combat zone seemingly healthy, but later died as a result of long-term effects from their deployment, including as a result of illnesses. Millions of service members are estimated to have been exposed to environmental toxins since 9/11. These exposures include, but are not limited to, exposure to emissions from open-*

air burn pits. In 2017, nearly a quarter of the new surviving military family members who came to TAPS for support did so after their loved one succumbed to an illness. Illness is second only to suicide as the manner of death for new surviving family members coming to TAPS for support, and now far exceeds the number of deaths due to hostile action."[8]

So, the key here was to aid in transition while simultaneously removing the stigma associated with utilizing the VA. The issue is that what drives the stigma of getting help from the VA is the root of why men and women joined the service in the first place. They joined to give aid, not accept handouts. I cannot tell you the number of times I have heard veterans say, "Oh, I am okay, give it to someone who needs it more than I do."

There is this belief that utilizing the VA, its services, or its funds somehow robs others of their ability to do the same. Nothing could be further from the truth. This really becomes an issue because, like anything bureaucratic, getting approved takes a long-ass time, even if you have all your paperwork. If the veteran waits until they need the services to apply, in many cases (especially rapid cancers associated with burn pits), they'll die before they or their family would get the benefits, and therein lies the problem: the word "benefits."

Words have meanings, and meanings matter. There is the meaning of the word according to Webster's and then there is also a meaning that can be applied, justly or not, based on the context in which it is used. So what does ol' Webster's say about benefits?

ben·e·fit /ˈbenəfit/ (noun)

1. an advantage or profit gained from something.
"enjoy the benefits of being a member"

2.. a payment or gift made by an employer, the state, or an insurance company.

The issue is, veterans don't want to profit or gain anything, and look at what Webster's uses as an example: "welfare benefits." Even Webster's implies it's a handout!

That is the root of what we are fighting. Yes, the VA absolutely has issues; some are undoubtedly better than others (Martinsburg has been awesome in my experience) but the biggest hindrance isn't in jumping through the hoops of the VA, it's getting the veterans to even consider jumping in the first place.

So how do we change this? In my opinion, one of the easiest ways to change behavior is to change perception. How can we do that with VA healthcare? Start calling it what it is: VA workers' compensation. Again, words matter, so let's take a look at the definition of workers' compensation.

variants: *or less commonly* **workers' comp** \ - ˈkämp \
Definition of *workers' compensation*
: a system of insurance that reimburses an employer for damages that must be paid to an employee for injury occurring in the course of employment

As a small business owner, I have to carry it. I have to provide it for anyone who gets injured on the job. And absolutely no one has any issue using it. Military life (even without a deployment) is rough on the body. The military and the nation's government are service member employers, and we absolutely should cover those injuries and ailments that are derived from that service. In order to do that, we must remove the silly notion that it is somehow bad for a veteran to enroll in the very system meant to support them for the selfless service they rendered.

Now, let me address the elephant in the room. "But what about some shitbag freeloader who takes advantage of the system?" Well, I'll simply ask it back: "What if they do?" Who cares? What matters more, a handful of scumbags who cheat the system at a nominal expense to us, the taxpayers, or ensuring that every veteran who needs help gets it? I cannot speak for you, but as for me, I'll tolerate the fact that every system gets gamed by some shithead in order to help the heroes who walk amongst us.

We believe in this so much, we worked to raise a million dollars and join forces with Goodwill to open the very first Platoon Veteran Services center at Goodwill in Frederick, Maryland. The center opened its doors in 2022 and routinely sees over 3,000 veterans per year come through its doors or utilize one of our partners' services. We exist to do two things:

1. Be best-in-class transitional support for our warfighters.
2. Replicate this facility all across America to ensure it's the standard nationwide.

This center has been years in the making. Just like everything else in life, it's come with lots of ups and lots of downs. Many closed doors and ideas that just didn't work. Changes in players and changes in directions and goals. But also, just like in life, it came about not because we were perfect, harder working, or even smarter. It came to life because we simply refused to quit.

No matter what we had to face. No matter how high the mountain or how scary the road was in front of us, we channeled the courage of our warfighters we serve and simply "Charlie miked." We continued the mission. We outlasted the last thing that held us back. Looking back on the long, strange ride to get here, I am reminded of a question that was posed at the very first event we ever held, a screening of the documentary, *Project 22*.

At the conclusion of this very powerful film that we amassed several hundred people in a dollar theater to watch, a hand shot up in the back of the room. When acknowledged, the gentleman asked a very simple, but very poignant question: "What next?"

The room fell silent, and I felt the eyes of the room shift back to me and the directors of the film. I was new to this and I didn't know much about suicide, the VA, transition issues, or anything else, to be honest. But my answer is the same to you today as it was to him back then, the same it will be forever, no matter the problem you face in life. "You take the next step forward."

You look around and you find your herd. You find the people willing to take the next right step and then the one after that, together. Some days you're gonna walk in the wrong direction and need to backtrack. Other days you're gonna feel like you're living the life, standing in the open planes with the sun on your back. And other days, still, you'll need to lower you head, raise your horns and walk together into the oncoming storm.

The key to survival and success remains the same: take the next step.

Chapter Sixteen

Sins of the Father

"Wanted to fill his boots but I got bigger feet."
—Struggle Jennings

I have always hated the excuses deadbeat parents (especially men) use. "I didn't have anyone to show me how to do it." Or, "My daddy was abusive and a drunk, so I didn't know how to be a dad." Those lines are absolute crocks of shit used by little boys who played a man's game and didn't know what to do when they won. I didn't make a mistake when I said "won." If you get the opportunity to be a daddy, you absolutely won in life. There are countless men out there who want to have children but can't, and here you sit not only squandering the blessing, but taking it one step further and abusing it.

Only the weak use "but it happened to me" to justify repeating that sin. You, the injured and the abused, may not know what a good father looks like, but you have an even more powerful teacher: you have felt the repercussions of a bad one. You have seen the playbook of what bad looks like. It is easy; simply don't do the same shit. But yet, every day, we watch these boys walk in the exact same footprints as their predecessors, scarring for the life of the generation that follows them. Nothing changes until something changes.

For me, I promised myself, if given the chance, I'd change it. Lying in my rack in Iraq, I sent up a prayer to God. "Dear Lord, if you let me make it out of here alive, the only thing I ask for is to let me have a family." God did grant me that prayer, and on July 24, 2015, my whole wide world changed with the birth of my pride and joy, River Farrar.

I had found myself married, and just one year later, we welcomed River into our tribe. It was the crowning moment of my life. I was now a father. Now, while I had an immense sense of pride (and if you touched her I'd have ripped your face off), I didn't experience this huge emotional flip everyone talks about. I can't speak for mothers since I ain't one, but the truth is, I think a lot (if not most) dudes are just saying they felt that way 'cause they are scared to say the truth. When the baby first comes out, there's not a huge amount of connection between them and Dad. Which makes sense—they didn't grow in us.

Like I said, don't get me wrong, I loved her, and I was thrilled to have her, but I didn't feel the way everyone else said I was supposed to feel. Go figure. Problem is, you start to overthink it and wonder if something is wrong with you. For anyone reading this thinking, "Yeah, I felt the same way!" don't worry; we aren't outliers. Almost every dude I've talked to said they felt the same way. It's just no one was honest about it 'cause they didn't want to look bad.

Listen, I love my girls, but the first year is an absolute clusterfuck. Anyone who tells you differently is either lying or gave birth to Jesus. This is doubly true for dads, especially the first few weeks and months after the little bundle of joy is born. Oftentimes you feel like you are worthless. Some days seem like you bring nothing to the table outside breast pump washing, regardless of how much effort put in. The baby doesn't even appear to like you. You don't look like Mom, smell like Mom, and based on your inability to produce milk, you damn sure don't taste like Mom. It can appear as if you serve literally no purpose in their eyes.

There were so many midnight feedings where I just held my little girl and tried to impart on her how much I loved her, and yet I couldn't tell if any of that was getting through. Speaking of feeding, God bless the women who breastfeed and bottle it. I understand that is liquid gold, but it has got to be, hands down, the most anticlimactic thing I have ever done. You pump and pump and pump and at the end of it, you get like one ounce of milk. It's mind-boggling to me. And you look like you are in so much pain. On top of that, if you develop mastitis, you now can't feed 'em and your breasts are killing you. Zero doubt about it: men got off easy on the baby game.

While you may not necessarily feel this huge connection, there comes a moment when that all changes for you. For me, that's when I started to spend mornings with my baby girl. I had been putting River to bed every night and then heading off to work in the morning while my wife was on maternity leave. Those six weeks blew by without me realizing they were gone. Then, just like that, it was my day to stay home until the nanny came.

Now, putting River down was a nightmare. She just screamed at the top of her lungs until she fell asleep. I just walked around the house with her, patting her back until she passed out. It was the craziest thing. I'll never forget how nervous I was trying to lay her down in her crib without waking her.

So, up until that moment, all I really knew of River and sleep was this pissing, shitting, screaming machine. I had never woken her up in the morning for over a month. That day, I went into her room and found this little giggling squirming mini-me that was having just the best time in the world. She looked up at me and our eyes met, and just like that, my whole world flipped upside down. I knew then that she was mine and I was hers. I had loved her before but now I was also smitten with her. I walked over to her crib and began what would become our daily daddy-daughter talks.

Every morning, I would walk into her room and talk to her as I filmed it on the camera. I would run through all these imaginary stories, acting out what I thought her facial expressions were trying to convey. I did this for her first two years of life, right up until she moved on to her big girl bed. We quickly became best buds. I lived to hear her giggles and get her belly. I was wrapped all the way around her little finger and I loved her with all my heart—Hell, still am, and I still do.

I learned a lot as we went through that first year of parenting, and most surprisingly was how well the Army had prepared me for fatherhood. I could operate on little sleep with a boss who could switch from yelling at you at the top of their lungs to giggling and expecting you to go on a "fun run" and like it in the next second. I was already trained in humping a million pounds of gear that I never used and only carried for some make-believe situation that never happened.

The Army had prepared me to use baby wipes and to do the dirty work. Changing shitty diapers is a breeze after you have used an Iraqi port-a-john. MREs had prepared me to not only like, but love eating any "puffs" that River hadn't consumed (and to be frank, I gained most of the weight from those things). Police call had prepared me for always having to pick up other people's shit, and most importantly, 1700 formations prepared me for finding out there was a ton more work to do before we could get released for the day.

While the first year of being a parent was one of the hardest things I have ever done in my life, it goes without saying that it was the most rewarding. So much so that we knew we wanted to have another. As River had taken us many attempts, we got right to work to try again. On April Fool's Day, I was sitting in the kitchen when she told me another young woman I knew of had gotten pregnant. My mouth dropped open. The girl in question wasn't even twenty-one yet. Then my wife yelled out "April Fool's!" and I picked my mouth up off the floor. But no sooner than I could shake off the whiplash, my wife said, "She's not, but I am." Baby number two was on the way.

We were extremely excited about having the second child, and as she became pregnant with little to no effort, we thought the hardest part of the process was over. Once again, life would show us that just when you think you got everything figured out, you don't know shit. Little did we know that we were about to get rocked.

Without warning, my wife started to have some issues that gave us concern for the baby. We had a few scares and were dealing with a lot of angst at the start of the pregnancy. However, as we started to near the end of the first trimester, everything seemed to level out and we thought we were in the clear. One night, we were up at the annual nationals party for Desert Knights Motorcycle Club when she said she wasn't feeling great and was just gonna head home. I told her I would head on home with her, but she insisted, as I was already a little buzzed and it was the yearly party, for me to stay. She said she was sure she was fine, and just wanted to sleep in her own bed. I said okay, kissed her, and she headed out with a friend. Not leaving that night is one of my biggest regrets ever.

Maybe an hour after she had gone, my phone rang. I picked it up to hear her sobbing on the other end of the phone. We often joked that she didn't have emotions and that she never wasted any tears. To say she wasn't a crier would be the understatement of the year, so to hear her like this, I knew right away what was wrong.

"I lost the baby!" she bellowed. My heart sank instantly. She hadn't been gone that long, so I knew she couldn't have made it home yet. She lost the baby on the side of the road. Writing this now still fucks with me. To know I wasn't there with her at that moment was arguably my biggest failing as a man, husband, and father. It is something I've never forgiven myself for. I should have left when she did.

I tried to console her, but understandably it was of little use. She kept saying she saw the baby on the road and that she had just left it there. I know it still eats at her to this day. But, what was she to do? Nothing. She had no other choice. Even so, it is a pain that still today, years later and after our divorce, I wish I could take away. No one deserves that. But sadly, life just doesn't really give a shit about what you deserve.

This put a far greater strain on our marriage. I gave my share of bullshit. We had many similarities. We were both driven, stubborn, and pigheaded. Both were used to getting our own way and I think that served us well and for a long time. With that said, we also had some major differences. She liked to travel and party. I preferred staying at home, working nonstop, and honestly being somewhat of a loner. Add that to our pigheaded natures and it made us fight like cats and dogs. This had started well before the miscarriage and postpartum, something I honestly had very little understanding of. Like pretty much all our mental health issues, we didn't talk about it, much to each other's detriment. She'd often joked she wasn't very emotional and as such people (myself included) didn't always give her credit for the fact that it was affecting her, which in turn caused it to affect her even more.

Once the miscarriage became public knowledge, instead of folks asking about her, they'd ask how I was doing. That undoubtedly wasn't fair to her and it only multiplied the pain of dealing with it. On top of that, I wasn't there like I should have been. I was processing it myself and working to keep my own headspace and timing working right. It was just a fucked up situation all the way around.

As a result, we started to drift further and further apart. We even separated for a time. I fought hard to save us, and it worked for a time. With all that was going on, I did my absolute best to have the spirit of the buffalo and take it all directly, to just absorb it, stoic. In that time, things got to be probably the best they ever were for us. And on January 2, 2019, we had our second child, Willow Wyn Farrar. This time, knowing what I knew about being a father, I was smitten from day one.

I thought things were going the right way this time. We were cognizant of the postpartum and we tackled the baby together. I noticed she grew much closer to Willow than she had with River at that age, and it warmed my heart. I thought I had finally figured life out, and most importantly, I had figured out family. Life was good. Then, as had happened in the past time and time again, the bottom fell out.

In the middle of having a beautiful and happy family and on pace for the best year in company history, another world-changing event took place, and again I found myself living through something you only thought would happen in a movie. COVID struck first in China, but with little fanfare, at least here within the United States. Once it hit Italy, it became a different story altogether. When it hit the United States, it flipped our world upside down.

Now, I am not gonna delve into the politics of it all in this book, but what started off as fourteen days to flatten the curve is still giving us fits as I write this. Matter of fact, it seems that variants and other concerns may have us headed towards further shutdowns. So while I can't speak intelligently about how this will end, I can tell you the start damn near broke us.

The fitness industry was devastated. At SOLDIERFIT alone, we got gutted, cut literally in half in just the first month of Coronavirus lockdowns. People called and froze or canceled their memberships in record numbers. Our revenue plummeted. We were trying to rob Peter to pay Paul. Dave and I decided to forego paychecks in order to pay our full-time staff. With no help forthcoming, we had to cut all of our part-time people, ultimately getting rid of certain positions in the company altogether. It was one of the worst times in my life.

I remember thinking to myself, *We know you guys are gonna shut us down, so why not fucking do it already?* Every moment the state and national governments waited only hurt us more because they were scaring people so badly that no one would come in. At that time, as places closed across the country, I had faith in what they said, "Just fourteen days to flatten the curve." I should have known better. When the governor finally gave the call to force us to close, it was a bit of relief for just four minutes.

That was the time it took me to get the news, take a deep breath or two, and go around and tell my staff to go home. As I walked through the empty gym, alone, I allowed myself to shed a tear. All the years of hard work, blood, sweat, and tears, stood empty in front of me. As I turned the lights off one by one, I felt like I was on the last episode of *Cheers*. And as I walked out the door and locked it behind me, I had to wonder if it were the last time I'd close up.

I allowed myself to feel sorry for myself only one more time over that period. Outside of that, it was straight hustle mode in order to pull through it. To this day, I am still surprised how many folks just sat back and took the wait-and-see approach. They simply closed their doors and sheltered in place. We closed our doors and were doing virtual workouts the next day. We set up streaming in a private Facebook group so that we could run workouts multiple times per day.

In the group and on other social media, I sought to do updates and status checks. I looked to provide value in any way that I could. I even was able to get Tim Kendy to do a video interview with me on tips for the average person to navigate the pandemic. We fought with every ounce of our being to provide hope and assistance so that we could make our company more than just a membership; we wanted it to be a relationship where they felt like they were family.

Every way that we could think of to improve our offerings, we did. We invested $30,000 and built out a film studio in the spare space we had in our Fredericks gym for remote workout routines. I put out weekly videos on Friday, doing my best to keep our members (and the general public) motivated and looking for the light at the end of the tunnel.

What started off as fourteen days to flatten the curve continued for several months. I watched and listened to the fears and concerns that were eating my fellow business owners alive. All of us were trying to "pivot" and find ways to sustain our dreams. Honestly, it felt like we pivoted so much that we ended up right back at square one. I knew plenty of good people who lost everything they had, and in truth, I was worried the same might happen to me.

The gym industry was hit extremely hard. Even though there was no scientific proof that gyms were more contagious than anywhere else, we were the first ones to have our doors shuttered and among the last allowed to reopen. Matter of fact, it would turn out that everything pointed to the opposite being true: that gyms were one of our best defenses against it.

In a study out of Colorado, out of over 44 million check-ins, there was a .0023% infection rate, or otherwise, statistically irrelevant. Furthermore, the CDC found about "78 percent of people who have been hospitalized, needed a ventilator or died from Covid-19 have been overweight or obese."[9] So, the government that was screaming, "Listen to the science!" has continued to fail to do just that (at the time of writing this), and as a result, many gyms have gone out of business permanently.

Thankfully, our hard work to keep our members engaged paid off. We were able to weather the storm, keep our employees paid, and put food on their tables. It remains one of my proudest accomplishments as a business owner. When we were given the green light to reopen our doors, we saw ourselves break a company record for new monthly signups. We were far from out of the woods, but we were headed on the right track. As 2020 came to a close, I thought I had come through the worst of it, and I was determined to make it 202WON. It was a great marketing slogan, but little did I know at the time I was about to the have the rug pulled right out from under my feet. Again.

I was sitting in a chair getting a pedicure with my oldest daughter for a daddy-daughter date when I got a text I didn't see coming. "I don't think I am in love with you anymore." I sat there, dumbfounded. I had thought that we had been doing the best we had ever done. I knew we just had a bad weekend, but I figured it was just the usual tiff that comes with being married. I guess I missed it by a mile.

Over the next few months, we went back and forth. A couple times I thought it was gonna work out. I thought I'd saved us again. I had thought that maybe this was the result of everyone but me getting COVID in December, which left us all quarantined for the entire month. Maybe it was a bit of leftover depression; Lord knows we'd all been put through the wringer. But in March, she came home and said it was over. She'd made her final decision, and as much it hurt her, she wanted to live her life on her own terms. Just like that, it was over.

I sat in the house, devastated. Honestly, I didn't do well for most of the year. All I'd ever wanted was a family and all I could see at the time was that it was lost. I wanted to make sure that my kids had an amazing life, one that I didn't, and I had failed to keep their mom happy enough to stay with me. All I could see was failure. My kids weren't going to be here anymore when I came home. I could only focus on the loss.

I wrestled with this daily while trying to put on a happy face at work and in front of my girls. Then, there came the first of two days I was dreading: the night we told River we were getting divorced. I have done a lot of awful things in my life, but this was by far the worst. It was gut-wrenching for both me and her mother. Seeing her little face red with tears was heartbreaking.

We did our best to console her and eventually we were able to get her to bed. The absolute worst day of my life came just a few days later. I knew it was happening, and I thought I had prepared myself for it, but when I came home from work to find everything moved out and my family gone, it crushed me.

I walked through the house, a shell of what it once was. I saw all of her stuff moved out. No more clothes in her closet, her side of the dresser emptied. In the bathroom, her sink was bare. No hair dryer or straightener. No shampoo or conditioner. No loofa. Her nightstand was cleared off and out. In the kids' rooms, half of their clothes were gone. Most heartbreaking of all: so, too, were they. I sat down at the foot of my bed, buried my head in my hands, and cried like a baby.

After about a half hour, I figured I hadn't felt enough self-loathing, so I jumped on my motorcycle and rode out to where we took our last family photos together. I had picked up a six-pack and I sat there drinking 'em one by one as I watched the sun set on the dream that was that family. As nightfall came, I got up and rode home, shivering against the chill of the night air, my tears feeling like they were freezing in their tracks on my cheeks.

While the pain was a heavy burden to carry, I had a job to do. We had agreed on 50/50 custody, which meant I got my baby girls every Monday and Wednesday, and every other weekend. I lived for those moments, and when they were gone, the house seemed to multiply the sound of silence. I couldn't stay there alone, so I spent much of my time without them going out. I did anything I could to occupy my time and my thoughts.

Bit by bit, it got easier. I read a book by Ryan Holiday called *The Obstacle is the Way* and it resonated with me so much that I even purchased a necklace that I wear every day with the title written on the front and the quote from Marcus Aurelius on the back. "The impediment to action advances action. What stands in the way becomes the way." I had always believed in that stoic mindset, but as happens to us all from time to time, I had lost my way.

I didn't think that there could be any good that would come from my wife leaving. I thought that without the family unit in place, without a mother and a father as one, I had failed as a parent. I wondered how I could possibly be a good dad if I didn't see them every day.

For far too long, I continued to focus on only the negative. I couldn't see the 99 great things I had going on and could only focus on the one bad thing. The truth was, yeah, the divorce sucked, but man, it could have been so much worse. This wasn't just a theory; I had seen many of my brothers suffer through much worse circumstances.

There are literally countless dads out there who longed to be a father to their children but who are hindered by the mother. Those women who use children as pawns to inflict great pain and anguish on their exes, whom they loathed. I was beyond blessed in this aspect. While my ex and I weren't going to stay together, she was respectful of my role as a father, and even gave me a great deal of credit for being a good one. Yes, it sucked that I wouldn't have my girls in my house every day, but I was so lucky that it wasn't just one weekend a month.

For me, the light at the end of the tunnel came on my first night going out with my two girls. We went and got pizza and made a grocery store run. I found myself laughing at my girls and having a good time. While it wasn't ideal to be getting divorced, I realized I had done all of this without a fight. The stress level was extremely low—matter of fact, it was non-existent. It dawned on me that perhaps my ex was braver than I was, to leave when things weren't 100 percent right between us.

I was so determined to have a family that I was willing to endure any hardship to keep it. I was willing to keep fighting every day so long as it meant that we stayed together. I didn't care so much what the public thought—I cared what I thought. I was determined to have a family, no matter how dysfunctional that family might be.

But here, with her living her life and me living mine, I started to notice something different. Well, that's not quite true. Other people noticed it and started pointing it out first. I started getting compliment after compliment about my smile. Over and over, people started pointing out that I was smiling at all. I hadn't realized it before, but I never smiled. I always had a scowl on my face. I wasn't attempting to look like an angry ass on purpose, it was just happening.

I wasn't alone. Looking at pictures of my ex with her new boyfriend told the same story. She was genuinely happy. She had found in him something she didn't find in me, and she appeared at peace. When I saw that, it sealed the deal for me. No matter how I felt about it ending, it ended in a way that provided peace for both of us, and who doesn't want that?

So, as I started out in this new world of mine, I began to realize that perhaps the divorce was a blessing in disguise. So many positive things happened because of it. I started my coaching business, which has taking off. I doubled down on my efforts with Platoon 22, resigning from the board of directors and stepping into the role of executive director. I began writing this book, something I had been afraid to do for years. Most importantly, I became a better dad. I understood I didn't have the next day with my girls anymore. From now until they grow up, my time will be cut in half. I have to share them with another household, so I better do my part to show them that I love them every minute I have them.

Chapter Seventeen

After Action Review

"By three methods we may learn wisdom: first, by reflection, which is noblest; second, by imitation, which is easiest; and third by experience, which is the bitterest."
—Confucius

At the time of this writing, I still have struggles. I haven't found love. Sometimes, I truly wonder if I ever will. I have decided to allow Jesus into my life and joined my local church. I plan to get baptized soon. Like everything else in life, religion is challenging at times, but that's what makes it a worthwhile journey.

If you made it this far, I want to take the time to say thank you for caring enough to read my story. It has been cathartic for me to, after forty-three years on the planet, get these stories out. I have so many wishes for you. I pray that my story lets you know that you are not alone. That there are many others out there who are struggling to figure it out, too.

You may be unsure of your next move, but with luck, reading this may have inspired to at least take a step. That you learned that no matter how bad things get, you can always do the next right thing. I wrote this book not in an attempt to tell you what to do, but in hopes to show you all the things I have done wrong, and the way I got a few things right. I cannot offer you relationship advice (clearly I ain't great at them), and even though I do my best, I wouldn't profess to tell you how to be a good parent. I am still trying to honor my promise not to repeat my father's sins myself.

This is what I know about life: the storms are never done. So many people struggle with this because they want the answer now and want it to be pleasant. They want it clearly defined and assured of success. They refuse to start if the GPS doesn't show a straight line to the win.

They fall victim to fear and second guesses. The inner critic raises its voice and uses anxiety to keep them paralyzed, but anxiety is just the worry of future pain. Pain that, more often than not, never comes in the dramatic manner imagined. It's a made-up nightmare that stops people in their tracks. And when the most important thing you can do is take the next step forward, that's a death sentence.

Instead of fearing the pain, the key is to accept that you will feel it over and over in life. Pain is a given; happiness, my friend, is not. In an odd twist of fate, those who accept the pain are the ones who spend more of their time being happy. They don't fear the storms because they always knew they were coming and that they, too, shall pass.

Those who run from them live a life in constant worry about when the next one comes. So much so that they can't even enjoy the sunny days. And with that much built-up terror, when that first storm cloud appears on the horizon, just like the cows, they run, and no matter how fast or how long, the storm always catches up to them. They are too tired to fight when it does, and the storm claims another victim.

Those who embrace the storms understand that they aren't bad or good, simply a cycle and season in the natural order of things. Storms serve their purpose; in every case, new life and opportunities arise in their wake, so why run from them? Why prolong your misery because you're just too big of a bitch to face the pain?

I promise you that there is no "making it." Until you die, there will never be a "last storm." You can't move anywhere where it is always sunny. The rain will come, even in a tropical paradise. You can't find a job that you will love every aspect of. Every job has its tedious bitch work, and great effort done behind the scenes with no applause or accolades. No matter which way you point your compass, it will eventually lead you to dark and foreboding clouds with a rumble of thunder and lightning on the horizon.

Now, I want to make sure that I am honest with you. I don't want you to believe that there are unafraid people. That's not the case. While some are more courageous than others, we all feel fear. All of us have a storm that scares us. That's the only way we even know what courage is. One cannot be brave in the absence of fear.

No, they must stand there in the breach with shaking knees and decide. That, my friends, is the moment that makes or breaks you. When your knees tremble, what do you do? Do you turn and run? Do you fall to the ground and crumble? Or do you step forward?

I made a personal pledge to myself years ago. No matter the storm in front of me, faith, family, business, or even war, I will face them all the same—the way of the buffalo.

Head down.

Horns up.

Into the storm.

SOURCES

[1] "Spotlight #3: Young People and Domestic Abuse." Safelives, 2020. https://safelives.org.uk/knowledge-hub/spotlights/spotlight-3-young-people-and-domestic-abuse.

[2] Scope of the problem: Statistics2020 (2020) RAINN. Available at: https://www.rainn.org/statistics/scope-problem

[3] Goldberg, A. et al. (2011) in Pentagon 9/11. Washington, D.C.: Historical Office, Office of the Secretary of Defense, pp. 23–24.

[4] Roos, D. (2019) How the Pentagon's design saved lives on September 11, History. A&E. Available at: https://www.history.com/news/pentagon-design-september-11-attacks

[5] Partnership, A.W. (2022) Landmark study finds that former service members take their lives at a rate 2.4 times higher than official VA reports, PR Newswire. Available at: https://www.prnewswire.com/news-releases/landmark-study-finds-that-former-service-members-take-their-lives-at-a-rate-2-4-times-higher-than-official-va-reports-301626650.html

[6] Kang, H.K. et al. (2015) "Suicide risk among 1.3 million veterans who were on active duty during the Iraq and Afghanistan wars," Annals of Epidemiology, 25(2). Available at: https://doi.org/10.1016/j.annepidem.2014.11.020.

[7] Price, J. (2018) Battling depression and suicide among female veterans, NPR. NPR. Available at: https://www.npr.org/2018/05/29/614011243/battling-depression-and-suicide-among-female-veterans

[8] "TAPS STATEMENT ON MILITARY BURN PIT COURT DECI-SION" (2018) taps.org [Preprint]. Available at: https://www.taps.org/press/2018/feb20b.

[9] Lovelace Jr., B. (2021) CDC study finds about 78% of people hospitalized for Covid were overweight or obese, CNBC. Available at: https://www.cnbc.com/2021/03/08/covid-cdc-study-finds-roughly-78percent-of-people-hospitalized-were-overweight-or-obese.html

ABOUT THE AUTHOR

Danny Farrar has lived the lows and highs common to many veterans following their tours of duty, and he founded Platoon 22 in 2014 to help stem the tragic lows that have overwhelmed too many of our military heroes. The nonprofit organization works to reduce incidents of veteran suicides by empowering them and our nation's first responders through a variety of programs and services, and it partnered in 2019 with Goodwill Industries of Monocacy Valley on a two million capital campaign for a Veterans Services Center in Frederick, Md.His work on the facility, which will best in class transitional support for our warfighters and their families throughout the Mid-Atlantic, is a natural fit for this U.S. Army veteran and former firefighter, who has dedicated his life to helping his brothers and sisters following their tours of duty. Farrar joined the Army as an infantryman shortly after graduating high school, and he served on the first unit that went into the Pentagon during the terrorist attacks of 9/11. He completed a combat tour in Iraq in 2005-06 as part of an eight-year career in the military, which took its toll upon returning home in the form of a period of homeless and, worse, an attempted suicide. Through a connection in the Mixed Martial Arts community, he started Soldierfit in 2007. As its CEO, he has expanded the workout facility franchise from its single home to 15 locations in several states that employ more than 100 people. Soldierfit trainers combine principles of Army boot camp with modern exercise best practices, and the U.S.

Chamber of Commerce named Soldierfit its 2016 Eastern Region Small Business of the Year. Farrar previously served on the VetFran Committee, which helps to connect franchise owners with military veterans, and captained Maryland's chapter of the International Franchise Association's Franchise Action Network. The Maryland Daily Record in 2013 named him to its Top 40 Under 40 VIP list for his professional accomplishments and commitment to inspiring change in his community, The Military Do-gooder award, named one of the top 50 CEO's in Frederick, MD, and was most recently awarded the Baltimore Raven's community quarterback award for his work with Platoon 22. Farrar resides in Frederick, Md. with his two daughters.

www.ingramcontent.com/pod-product-compliance
Lightning Source LLC
Chambersburg PA
CBHW030504100426
42813CB00002B/334

* 9 7 8 1 9 5 5 6 9 0 4 8 5 *